THE CHALLENGE OF BOLOGNA

THE CHALLENGE
OF BOLOGNA

What United States Higher Education
Has to Learn From Europe, and
Why It Matters That We Learn It

Paul L. Gaston

Foreword by Carol Geary Schneider

STERLING, VIRGINIA

COPYRIGHT © 2010 BY STYLUS PUBLISHING, LLC.

Published by Stylus Publishing, LLC
22883 Quicksilver Drive
Sterling, Virginia 20166-2102

Library of Congress Cataloging-in-Publication-Data
Gaston, Paul L.
    The challenge of Bologna : what United States higher education has to learn from Europe, and why it matters that we learn it / Paul L. Gaston.
        p.   cm.
    Includes bibliographical references and index.
    ISBN 978-1-57922-366-3 (cloth : alk. paper)
    1. Education, Higher—Europe.   2. Education, Higher—United States.   3. Bologna process (European higher education)   4. Comparative education—Europe.
5. Comparative education—United States.   6. Education and state—Europe.   7. Education and state—United States.   I. Title.
LA628.G37   2010
378.4—dc22   2009033538

13-digit ISBN: 978-1-57922-366-3 (cloth)

Printed in the United States of America

All first editions printed on acid free paper
that meets the American National Standards Institute
Z39-48 Standard.

Bulk Purchases

Quantity discounts are available for use in workshops and for staff development.
Call 1-800-232-0223

First Edition, 2010

10   9   8   7   6   5   4   3   2   1

For Tyler Lee Gaston
July 20, 1980–July 1, 2004

CONTENTS

ACKNOWLEDGMENTS

I want to thank my colleagues at Kent State University and to express my particular gratitude to the university's board of trustees and President Lester A. Lefton. By appointing me as Trustees Professor in 2007, the board enabled me to resume teaching and research after 25 years as a dean and provost—a long deferred aspiration. I thank also Carol Geary Schneider, who graciously contributed the foreword, and my other colleagues at the Association of American Colleges and Universities (AAC&U). Their work on defining liberal education as "America's promise" has helped me to clarify important distinctions between U.S. and European educational values. And my work since 2001 as a faculty member in the AAC&U Institute for General Education has offered on-the-ground experience that helps to inform this study. I thank especially my wife, Eileen, a skilled and creative teacher, for offering essential support and understanding.

For much of the last century, Americans took special pride in a higher education system that had become the envy of the world. And, as we move into this new global century, many of our top research universities remain highly ranked and highly admired around the globe.

Yet today, U.S. confidence in the strength of our higher education system is plainly under siege. Derek Bok, former president of Harvard University, helped fuel the angst with a widely read research synthesis on student learning in college. Bok's title—*Our Underachieving Colleges*—forthrightly signaled his verdict on where U.S. higher education stands and a call to vigorous action. Similarly, employers and pundits have pointed to the rise of rapidly expanding Asian economies and educational systems, warning that unless corrective actions are taken U.S. leadership in science, technology, mathematics, and engineering may soon become a distant memory.

There is also the steady drumbeat of data points from the Organization for Economic Cooperation and Development (OECD) showing that the United States has been falling fast from its perch as the nation with the highest proportion of college graduates. While older Americans still lead the world in the number of college degrees, many nations have moved ahead of the United States when it comes to the postsecondary attainment of younger adults.

To date, U.S. policy and philanthropic leaders have responded with a renewed emphasis on what the Obama administration describes as *access and completion* and what others term *double the numbers*. The new U.S. policy goal is a dramatic increase in the percentage of Americans who enroll in college and actually complete their studies, undergirded by a laserlike focus on those U.S. groups—racial and ethnic minorities, low-income learners, working adults—that historically have been least likely to achieve college degrees.

The Challenge of Bologna

As Paul Gaston's probing analysis of *The Challenge of Bologna* makes clear, however, expanding U.S. college completion rates is only a partial response to the competition American higher education now faces in this turbulent era of global interdependence. After all, many countries also are rapidly investing in expanded postsecondary enrollment. A nation that wants to secure its standing as an acknowledged leader in higher learning will need more than increased degree production to maintain its intellectual edge.

The real news from Europe, as Gaston painstakingly shows us, is not that more Europeans will achieve postsecondary credentials, but rather that the decade-long effort known as Bologna has resulted in a widespread reengagement with the question of what kinds of higher learning today's graduates actually need. To their credit, as Europeans undertook an epochal effort to harmonize dozens of very disparate university systems, they decided to make students' demonstrated levels of learning the touchstone for transfer protocols and for guiding student progress toward next-level degree programs. Today, European educators are winning kudos—and a growing following—for their high-profile, far-flung, and increasingly influential efforts to set standards for educational quality and to ensure the substantive quality of the postsecondary degrees they award.

The goal of the Bologna Process is what we might call High Numbers of High Achieving Graduates. There is a social dimension to the Bologna effort, fueled by the recognized need to make higher learning more inclusive and more successful as a catalyst for social mobility and cultural cohesion. But those involved in Bologna also want students' credentials to be valued and valuable across disparate educational contexts and especially in the context of a fast-paced and ever more demanding global economy.

Toward Global Dialogue and Engagement

Americans are just starting to take notice. Some are keenly interested, some are ambivalent, and some have already concluded that the Bologna move toward shared benchmarks for postsecondary qualifications flies directly in the face of that freedom from ministerial direction that U.S. higher education has long prized and fiercely protected.

Whatever their initial reaction to the Bologna developments, however, all U.S. educators will certainly need a fuller understanding of what is happening on other shores and of the motives that are propelling this high-profile international effort. Paul Gaston's fine study meets that need.

Seasoned by his own long history with U.S. educational change initiatives, campus based and national, Gaston provides in this volume a thoughtful and balanced analysis. He gives due weight to the significance of the Bologna accomplishments but also keeps firmly in view the distinctive features of U.S. higher education and the vitality of higher education reforms that already are in progress, albeit with less national fanfare and support, on our own shores.

This year, thanks to the interest of the Lumina Foundation in the Bologna Process and its potential implications for U.S. higher education, I've taken part in a series of stateside Bologna discussions—some with those leading the Bologna work in various European and Latin American countries and Canada, some with U.S. educational leaders of varying minds—on the question of whether any such effort could take root in the United States at all.

As head of the Association of American Colleges and Universities (AAC&U), the major U.S. higher education association committed to strengthening the quality of U.S. collegiate learning, I applaud these efforts to put U.S. educators in active dialogue with other nations about the future of higher learning and about the most productive direction for educational focus and renewal.

I also want to underscore Gaston's insight that such dialogue must and can be multilateral. European, Canadian, and Latin American leaders are bringing a record of significant progress and recent accomplishments in the Bologna Process to the dialogue. But U.S. educators also bring work on far-reaching reforms to the table as well.

Inattentive though U.S. educators may have been to the Bologna process, the Europeans themselves have in fact drawn extensively on U.S. precept and practice, both in designing their overarching qualifications framework and in their approach to establishing what students should achieve. The Dublin Descriptors—a broad template that establishes the Bologna parameters for what needs to be included in a degree framework—acknowledge their use of related work done within the AAC&U community on learning outcomes that all college students need to achieve. While the Dublin Descriptors are different in several ways from the essential learning outcomes that the AAC&U community has developed, both frameworks share a common concern with developing higher levels of intellectual and practical competencies, fostering what the Europeans call *judgment*, teaching students to apply their learning and laying a foundation for lifelong learning. The Bologna process is now translating these expectations into requirements and progressively higher levels of expected attainment for specific disciplines. But a comparable focus on intended learning outcomes also is emerging—with active faculty leadership—in numerous academic and professional fields in the United States.

Similarly, the Bologna shift in focus from what teachers teach toward students' own intended level of accomplishment resonates with some three decades of similar efforts on this side of the Atlantic. Arguably, Europe is poised to sprint ahead of the United States with its strong emphasis on making students' actual involvement in learning—their expected time on task—the baseline for establishing the number of credits students can earn through disparate courses of study. But Gaston is astute in his use of the relay race metaphor to show that Europeans and Americans are ultimately working on the same big educational question: how to move beyond the resources and reputation metrics that ruled the day in the last century toward a more contemporary focus on educational purposes, enabling practices and actual learning outcomes as the new standard for educational quality in the 21st century.

How Europeans and Americans Can Learn From One Another

Recognizing these intersecting concerns and the historic differences between European and U.S. designs for higher learning, where might a productive dialogue between U.S. educators and Bologna participants actually begin?

In his final chapter, Gaston explicitly calls for a transnational dialogue about the U.S. tradition of liberal or broad education at the collegiate level and its relevance for the new global context. Picking up on that invitation, I want to suggest five areas a multilateral dialogue about the relative advantages of field-specific versus liberal or broad education is needed and potentially illuminating.

Articulating and Achieving the Multiple Aims of Education

As *The Challenge of Bologna* makes clear, one of the drivers for the Bologna Process is also its limitation: the primary focus on preparing students for the economy and career success. There have been efforts over the past decade to enlarge the initial vision, but economic readiness still plays a dominant role in the Bologna dynamic.

U.S. leaders face comparable pressures to make jobs the index of educational effectiveness and success. But U.S. educators have countered forcefully if not yet decisively with the recognition that higher education also plays a central role in building civic capital. Over the past two decades, in national and regional U.S. institutions, there has been a major investment in building curricula, pedagogies, and cocurricular programs that engage students with the wider community and especially with societal and environmental dilemmas—equity, justice, hunger, and climate change, to name just a few—that pose fundamental challenges to the sustainability of any democracy. Evidence is emerging that there are real civic and intercultural gains for students who take part in such efforts.

Through the Council of Europe, there also has been a robust trans-Atlantic dialogue on the role of the university in democratic engagement and learning. Probing these issues, the United States and Europe have acknowledged that global diasporas now are making societal diversity a flashpoint and a testing ground for liberal democracies. With older concepts of civic identity and membership now under enormous pressure, the university can and should become an important catalyst for reexamining the meaning, application, and viability of democratic values and practices.

Gaston's text provides abundant evidence that European universities are far from willing to accept an educational framework that makes employability the primary metric for success. Bologna and U.S. educators would be well advised then to work together in persuasively articulating—and fulfilling—the case that everyone has a stake in producing graduates who are prepared and expected to take responsibility for the future of the democratic promise. The economy is important, but so too for self-governing societies are the sustainability and integrity of a vibrant civil society. The Bologna commitment to educational quality needs to address, as a central concern, the role of higher learning in fostering civic learning and engagement.

Facilitating Cross-Disciplinary Learning

To anyone anchored in U.S. higher education, the most arresting aspect of the Bologna process has been the decision to focus cross-national qualifications and degree expectations on a single field of study or, in U.S. jargon, on the major. "Are Europeans reifying the disciplines?" one U.S. historian inquired tartly after sitting through a thorough discussion of the Bologna Tuning Process (discussed in chapter 10) in the disciplines.

This was a telling first response. In AAC&U's work on learning outcomes, we know that one of the points of real convergence between educators and employers is their shared recognition that to deal with the complex problems that characterize our society, 21st-century learners need a strong grounding in multidisciplinary frameworks. Research shows, in fact, that 76% of responding employers would recommend a broad rather than a field-specific education to young people they were advising about college (Hart, AAC&U Outcomes, 2007).

"We want that 360 degree perspective," employers insist. "We need college graduates who are ready to work in cross-functional, cross-disciplinary work teams." U.S. colleges and universities increasingly tout their interdisciplinary programs and strengths, while U.S. students routinely choose double majors, majors and minors, and/or interdisciplinary majors. It is hard to argue, from the U.S. vantage point, that baccalaureate study in a single academic field is the best way to prepare for a global future.

Admittedly, the Bologna process emphasizes the integration of general competencies within any discipline, and practitioners of some fields themselves insist on cognate studies as complements to their disciplines. But an open question remains on whether intensive focus on a single academic discipline is now unduly limiting, either at the baccalaureate level or beyond. U.S. and European educators would benefit mightily from a far-reaching probe of the connections between disciplinary and cross-disciplinary study as they create 21st-century designs for higher learning and global preparation.

Teaching Students to Apply Their Learning in New Contexts

To its credit, the Bologna Process has made applying knowledge one of its five organizing principles for postsecondary excellence. U.S. educators have been moving in a similar direction, with many proposing that it is high time to erase the artificial distinctions that have long prevailed between studies deemed liberal, interpreted to mean they were not related to job training, and those considered practical because they intentionally prepare students for careers. There is now much more big picture thinking going on in U.S. professional fields such as engineering or health, and much more emphasis on real-world applications in the so-called traditional liberal arts and sciences.

These developments notwithstanding, however, many faculty in all nations still stand somewhat removed from the question of how well students are really learning to apply—and amend—their understandings in real-world contexts. Few would contend that higher education is fully successful in teaching students how to transfer their learning, reliably and generatively, from the academy to the community. As U.S. and European educators wrestle with the creation of productive connections between knowledge and practice, everyone has something to gain from a determined trans-Atlantic effort to develop robust evidence about what works in building graduates' capacities to work in real-world settings and to make effective judgments in contexts of uncertainty. This, one might argue, is the fundamental challenge that all higher education systems face as postsecondary learning becomes an expected destination for a large fraction of the population rather than a privilege reserved for the fortunate few.

Probing the Future of General Education

General education has been, for more than a century, one of the defining features of U.S. higher education. Some Bologna countries also have—or aspire to—a tradition of general studies beyond the major field, but most do not. Indeed, many Europeans and some Americans assume that the U.S. needs general education requirements mainly because so many U.S. college students haven't mastered the foundational arts and sciences knowledge that secondary schools already expect in Europe.

Viewed through this lens, general education can seem mainly compensatory, helping U.S. graduates catch up with more rigorously prepared international peers. And, using the same lens, some U.S. reformers assume that once precollegiate education is brought to a higher standard in the United States, Americans can then embrace the European design for a three-year baccalaureate degree, focused mainly on a particular field of study.

These widespread assumptions about the purpose and content of U.S. general education are, however, seriously out of date. They miss entirely what is actually happening in U.S. general education. Across all sectors, U.S. colleges and universities have been moving ever farther away from practices that once positioned general education mainly as a series of survey or distribution courses designed to impart foundational knowledge about science, culture, history, and society. In fact, a 2009 AAC&U study showed that only 15% of U.S. colleges and universities still cling exclusively to this old distribution-model design for general education.

Instead, general education is being redesigned stateside as a strategy for teaching students how to set their particular interests in larger contexts and how to integrate and apply their learning at progressively higher levels of effort and achievement. Proponents of integrative learning also see general education as a way to foster students' creativity and curiosity. Pushing students out of their comfort zone in specific disciplines, embracing topics that stretch beyond anyone's individual expertise, these problem-based designs for general education have in fact attracted international attention. Educators from around the globe are studying U.S. liberal arts practices to see what might be usefully applied in their own cultural contexts.

It remains true, of course, that general education also plays a remedial role throughout U.S. higher education. But even if U.S. schools actually solve pervasive problems of underpreparation, few U.S. educators believe that high school alone can build the facility in cross-disciplinary, integrative, and problem-based learning that employers now seek and civil society needs.

Bologna educators already are aiming for a certain level of integrative learning with their signature emphasis on embedding general (or generic) competencies in all fields of advanced study, whatever the subject matter. But Bologna educators are not yet leading the way on making integrative *topics and problems* a requisite focus for postsecondary learning.

Europeans have much to gain from a close look at where U.S. general education is heading, even as U.S. educators acknowledge they have a very long way to go in making integrative general education a demonstrable achievement and not just an ambitious goal.

Designing Assessments That Show What Students Can Actually Do

Self-consciously driving a far-reaching shift from teaching to learning, the Bologna Process has worked energetically to create frameworks for assessment that show what students can do with their knowledge. Absent any agreed-upon national framework for quality assurance, the United States is nonetheless moving in a similar direction. With general and specialized studies now increasingly involving students in research, extensive writing, problem-based projects, and significant experiences of community-based learning, U.S. educators also are setting in place a framework that potentially enables them to make students' actual work the primary source of evidence about students' learning gains in college.

In addition, the Bologna Process has creatively pioneered the concept of a diploma supplement, describing not just what courses a student completed for credit but rather what the program actually expected the student to know and learn how to do. As most would agree, the diploma supplement is still a work in progress, more focused on institutional expectations than on students' actual achievements. Nonetheless, it is a breakthrough idea that already is stirring warranted interest in some U.S. state systems.

Assessments and transcripts thus present themselves as another fruitful arena for international dialogue, experimentation, and mutual learning. And here, I would argue, is an arena in which the United States would have much to gain—politically as well as conceptually—from close study of the Bologna quality assurance models.

As Gaston's summary of U.S. developments in accountability points out, the United States is still struggling to create common reference points for assessing students' learning in college. For the most part, the accountability debate has focused on tests of general competencies, such as critical thinking and writing, addressed outside the context of students' actual field of concentration.

This is at best a limited set of indicators. Once the accountability issues are better understood in the United States—and freed from their tether to the existing state of standardized testing technology—one surely will want to know what students are learning above and beyond general skills.

The Bologna quality assurance process is intensely focused, by contrast, on what students actually are gaining from their primary area of concentration, the academic field, or discipline. As policy analyst Clifford Adelman has repeatedly pointed out, the Bologna approach to the assessment loop leaves comparable U.S. efforts far behind. Those concerned about the U.S. direction on accountability would do well to hold up the Bologna example to U.S. policy leaders.

AAC&U has taken the position that the most productive designs for learning and assessment focus on students' ability to locate their particular interests in a larger context and especially on their progress in developing the knowledge, skill, and dispositions to apply their knowledge to the complex, unscripted intellectual and practical tasks they will face in the economy as citizens and in their own lives (AAC&U, 2008) That said, if one had to choose between the dominant approaches to accountability in the United States versus the dominant approach in Europe, it would be far more illuminating to see what students can do with their majors than to know how well they do on tests that are intentionally designed to bypass the major field.

The real opportunity here, of course, is to recognize that new priorities for postsecondary study—that historic shift from teaching to learning—necessarily call for new designs for determining students' actual gains over time and program. And that's the opportunity educators on both sides of the Atlantic ought to seize.

The Bologna Process has already led to a reinvigoration of quality assurance strategies in Europe. Similarly, the new U.S. focus on learning outcomes has produced a set of widely tested rubrics keyed to the Essential Learning Outcomes presented through the AAC&U community and that also show what student progress ought to look like from the first to the final year of college (see http://www.aacu.org/leap/vision.cfm).

With these new assets in hand, the time is extremely ripe for a trans-Atlantic effort that translates the new focus on student learning outcomes into new social norms for expected assessment practice.

The long-term goal for Bologna and the United States is to give students and the public a reliable guide to the learning from higher education that matters the most, whether for work, citizenship, or a fulfilling life. Nothing makes the student mind concentrate more effectively, of course, than on knowing what will be on the test. To the extent that our tests of student accomplishment can focus on students' actual academic and field-based work, they—and society—will successfully meet the challenge of Bologna and the promise of democracy.

Carol Geary Schneider
President, AAC&U

I n 1999 a declaration formalizing the European process was signed at—
and informally named for—the oldest university on the Continent:
Bologna. The stated intent of the agreement was "to establish a more
complete and far-reaching Europe," "to consolidate and enrich the European citizenship," to build competences among Europeans in tandem with
"an awareness of shared values," to confirm within higher education "a common social and cultural space," and to promote "the necessary European
dimensions in higher Education" (Bologna, 1999).

Since the launch of what has come to be known as the Bologna Process,
Europe has observed the beginnings of a potentially profound transformation in higher education, most particularly with regard to the degrees that
are offered, an overarching understanding of what each degree signifies, areas
of consensus regarding what the different disciplines seek to accomplish, and
the means by which students document their educational attainments. The
three-year baccalaureate may be the most conspicuous of the reforms, but it
may not be the most significant.

Supporters and Skeptics

Bologna has attracted many admirers. By far the most diligent and influential, Clifford Adelman (2008) of the Institute for Higher Education Policy,
has described Bologna as a challenge to higher education in the United States
and a club well worth joining. Some initiatives under way in the United
States, such as a current effort in three states to define learning outcomes for
a few disciplines, may represent steps toward a membership application.

Yet there are concerns as well. Some observers, European students in
particular, have questioned whether the glittering reports of progress represent real change and have described the implementation efforts of some participating nations as à la carte: Such nations implement some priorities while
ignoring others. Even before the global recession that began in 2008, nations
were not making significant investments in the Bologna reforms, and the
influence of the recession appears to have prompted some higher education
initiatives (e.g., tuition and fee increases) unassociated with and perhaps contrary to the spirit of Bologna. Moreover, a lack of autonomy has impeded

some institutions from responding with greater alacrity to the reform initiatives, while a granting of greater authority to others has required them to budget for greater self-sufficiency. And it has also become clear that the ministers in 1999 underestimated the strength of cultural preferences informing idiosyncratic higher education traditions. For these and other reasons, implementation of the Bologna Process slowed during the latter half of the decade.

Concerns over principle have arisen also with regard to the overriding emphasis of Bologna's founding documents on the role of higher education in supporting economic development. While an emphasis on the expansion of knowledge and the fulfillment of human potential should pay significant economic dividends, a reductive view of higher education as primarily a means to promote prosperity may alienate important constituencies.

Perhaps the most persuasive expression of this concern appears in an introductory statement by Sjur Bergan (2009), cosecretary of the Intergovernmental Committee for the Council of Europe/UNESCO Higher Education and Research Division, to the April 2009 ministerial meeting in Leuven/Louvain-la-Neuve, Belgium. He observes that the supporters of Bologna "could easily be led to believe that the competences we need are those that help the economy in the short term." While economic growth must be an important consideration, he emphasizes that "we need so much more." Societies must be sustainable economically, but they must also be sustainable "politically, culturally, socially and environmentally." Such societies will feature "engaged citizens and . . . people who care about each other," encourage "intellectual curiosity and the pleasure of discovery," and foster "the ability to conduct intercultural dialogue."

The Nature of the Challenge

These concerns notwithstanding—and whatever the eventual fate of the Bologna Process may be—higher educators in the United States should regard as significant the challenges it poses and collaborate on a judicious and constructive response. The primary issue is not that Europe has created an agenda for reform that the United States must emulate to remain competitive—though that is a consideration. Rather, the aspirations that inform Bologna are for the most part ones we share and at least to some extent are pursuing already. With the exception of Bologna's stated determination to assert a new European ascendency, the action lines, or objectives, of the Process reflect issues that have been of concern in the United States for many years: consistency (how degrees are defined, how disciplines are structured), continuity (how one degree level should encourage students to attempt the next), quality assurance (accountability ideas), and mobility (issues of transferability and transcript transparency). But if the European priorities are familiar, they should also be compelling because Europe has embarked on a course of reform far better coordinated and comprehensive than any the United States can offer—and has done so with a far greater sense of urgency.

Approaching Bologna

This study offers two perspectives, the first chronological, the second thematic. After examining briefly the roots of the Bologna Process in the history of higher education, and more recently in that of modern Europe, we follow its development from one biennium to the next as educational reform and political phenomenon. We observe how the Process has developed through an expansion of its agenda, through the addition of new members, through the establishment of new benchmarks, and through its responses to periodic internal and external assessments. In the light of that chronology, we then focus on the three Bologna priorities most closely related to long-standing issues in the United States, those of access and mobility, structure, and effectiveness.

In the final chapter, these chronological and thematic threads come together as we consider what a comprehensive reform agenda in the United States—informed by but not governed by the Bologna Process—might look like. I suggest that we should aspire not to full membership in the Bologna club but to new international leadership in higher education. And that leadership should build on the lessons of Bologna while sustaining values important not only to higher education in the United States, but also to the character of the nation.

Tracking Bologna

Although the April 2009 conference in Leuven/Louvain-la-Neuve offers an appropriate vantage point for achieving a perspective on what has been and may be accomplished, the story of Bologna will continue to unfold, at least for another decade. And we will in time understand even more clearly the first decade of reform. The volume of the material that will be available to future historians of higher education is almost unimaginably abundant. And most of the millions of pages are online. I am grateful for the access provided by the Bologna Process, the European Union, and ancillary Web sites to a wide variety of studies, perspectives, summaries, and position papers. For the first time in my career, the great majority of the sources I have used are available on well-maintained Web sites. One such Web site, managed by the current Bologna secretariat, includes many of the most important documents referenced here and can serve as a convenient portal for readers interested in primary texts; the Web address leads the listing of references.

The work of two authors must inform any study of the Bologna Process. Laurel S. Terry (2008) has a particular interest in the implications of the Bologna Process for legal education, but her thorough chronological account of the Bologna decade offers a secure point of departure for further study. Clifford Adelman sounded through his May 2008 report, *The Bologna Club: What U.S. Higher Education Can Learn From a Decade of European Reconstruction*, what one headline described as a wake-up call for U.S. higher education. In April 2009 he published an expanded and updated overview, *The Bologna Process for U.S. Eyes: Re-learning Higher Education in the Age of Convergence*. Both are carefully documented and thoughtfully organized examinations of higher education reform in Europe. Both are also enthusiastic calls for the United States to break out of its "room of mirrors," where, as Adelman says, we operate under the delusion that we are "so unique that nothing occurring beyond that room matters" (2009, p. 189).

As will become apparent, my perspective may differ in some ways from those implicit in these important sources. As I have previously suggested, while the Bologna Process should offer helpful prompts for higher education reform in the United States, it is important also to acknowledge the considerable advances taking place in the United States and to clarify the values they rest on—values in some ways markedly different from those evident in Bologna. I will even suggest that Europe would do well to give more attention to good practices in the United States. We in fact have much to learn from one another.

In addition, guarded optimism with regard to the future of the Bologna Process must be tempered by an awareness of fault lines that have appeared over the years, by the identification of some internal contradictions apparent in the process of implementation and by an acknowledgment of the impact of a deep economic recession on international initiatives in general. With Terry and Adelman, I cheer the Europeans for what they have accomplished—but with two cheers, rather than three.

AN EXPEDITIOUS OVERVIEW

Understanding the Bologna Process and its challenge for U.S. higher education requires the two perspectives this book has sought to offer: One follows the process of Bologna and the other focuses on its primary emphases. Any brief summary of such a multifaceted undertaking will inevitably understate its complexity. However, because some readers may find an overview convenient, this preliminary chapter addresses frequently asked questions.

What Is the Bologna Process?

Meeting in Bologna, Italy, traditionally identified as the site of Europe's oldest university, ministers for education representing 29 European nations agreed in June 1999 to the creation of a European Higher Education Area (EHEA) by 2010. The Bologna Declaration they signed sets forth the initial priorities of the Process and records the ministers' support.

What Were the Precedents?

Economic recovery following World War II emphasized the need for closer cooperation among European nations. The 1957 Treaties of Rome established the European Economic Community. The 1965 Brussels Treaty (otherwise known—confusingly—as the Second Treaty of Rome) established the current European Community governance structure. In 1988 university rectors meeting to celebrate the 900th anniversary of the University of Bologna put their signatures on a Magna Charta Universitatum, which celebrates academic freedom as a source of creative thought and productive research. In 1992 the Maastricht Treaty on the European Union (EU) made more explicit the Continent's aspirations for a resurgent role in the world (Treaty, 1992). The Lisbon Convention of 1997 seeks to facilitate the evaluation of foreign educational credentials. And the 1998 Sorbonne Treaty, signed by the education ministers from the United Kingdom, France, Germany, and Italy, represents an immediate precursor.

Who Is Involved?

In addition to the member nations, the Bologna Process includes representation from the European Commission and eight consultative members: the Council of Europe (COE), the European Center for Higher Education (CEPES), the European University Association (EUA), the European Association of Institutions in Higher Education (EURASHE), the European Students' Union (ESU), the European Association for Quality Assurance in Higher Education (ENQA), the Education International Pan-European Structure, and Business Europe.

What Was the Primary Impetus Behind the Bologna Declaration?

The ministers who signed the declaration (Bologna, 1999) emphasized the role of higher education in supporting European economic growth and the international resurgence of the Continent.

What Does the EHEA Signify?

A single European system of higher education has never been the objective. Bologna (1999) envisions national systems of higher education presenting closely comparable structures, offering expanded opportunities for mobility across borders, maintaining academic records according to a shared protocol, and engaging in quality assurance measures according to shared overarching standards.

What Is the Structure of the Process?

European national education ministers meet biennially with the consultative members to review progress reports on the *action lines*, or goals of the Process, and to agree on the agenda for the next biennium. Between biennial meetings, primary responsibility rests with a Bologna follow-up group (BFUG) chaired by the country that has rotated into the presidency of the EU. The BFUG organizes conferences and seminars, calls for national reports, inventories action to date, and assists the ministers in framing the communiqués that summarize the results of their biennial meetings. Day-to-day operations are managed by a secretariat provided by the nation that will host the next biennial conference.

How Well Does This Structure Work?

There are trade-offs. The voluntary, cooperative nature of the Process has encouraged harmony among stakeholders with different interests and varying degrees of support for the EU. However, the lack of a central administration with authority to enforce compliance has allowed significant disparities from one nation to another in the funding, pace, extent, and depth of higher education reform.

What Has the Bologna Process Sought to Accomplish?

The 1999 meeting in Bologna identified six broad action lines: the creation of easily readable and comparable degrees documented through diploma supplements provided to every student, the organization of higher education into two main cycles (undergraduate and graduate), the management of educational credentials through a recognized system of credits, the encouragement of educational mobility through the expansion of cross-border opportunities for study and teaching, development of a stronger commitment to quality assurance based on comparable criteria and methodologies, and promotion of "the necessary European dimensions in higher education," particularly in terms of "curricular development, interinstitutional cooperation, mobility schemes and integrated programmes of study, training and research" (Bologna, 1999).

Have Other Action Lines Been Added?

Early in the Process the agenda was expanded to include doctoral programs, a *social dimension* to expand access to higher education and to encourage a more diversified student body, and lifelong learning.

Who Are the Participants?

The list of participating nations has grown considerably since the inception—from 29 in 1999 to 46 in 2009. Virtually all European nations are involved, from Shannon (Ireland) to Vladivostok (Russia). Table 1 on pp. 5–6 lists participants, indicates the year membership was granted, and distinguishes between EU and non-EU members.

Are There European Countries Not Participating in the Bologna Process?

The largest is Belarus. All nations participating in Bologna must subscribe to the European Cultural Convention of the Council of Europe (COE). Although Belarus has not accepted the convention, the nation has begun to model its higher education reform efforts after those of the Bologna Process. The only other European nonparticipants are Monaco and San Marino.

Are There Countries Outside Europe Formally Affiliated With the Bologna Process?

No. However, as Claire Morris, president of the Association of Universities and Colleges of Canada (AUCC), observed in January 2009, "the reform process in Europe is, in essence, an attempt to address many of the same challenges that we all are facing in the ever-changing world of higher education" (AUCC, 2009). Bologna invited a number of interested parties, including the United States and Canada, to a policy forum immediately following the April 2009 biennial ministerial meeting in Leuven/Louvain-la-Neuve, Belgium.

How Are the Bologna Process and the EU Related?

The EU has no authority over higher education in member states, the EU and the EHEA are not coterminous, and Bologna's supporters insist on its status as a voluntary undertaking of cooperating nations—an important assertion for countries that remain suspicious of centralization and standardization. Similarly, the EU describes Bologna as one of two educational reforms closely related to the 2000 Lisbon Strategy for Growth and Jobs (also known as the Lisbon Agenda). The other is the Copenhagen Process, which seeks greater international cooperation on vocational education.

But many of the initiatives undertaken by Bologna reflect activities supported by the EU. For instance, Bologna relies on the transfer of academic credit across national boundaries as facilitated by the European Credit Transfer and Accumulation System (ECTS), on the more effective documentation

TABLE 1
Nations Participating in the Bologna Process

Participating Country	Full Bologna Member Since	EU Member
Albania	2003	No
Andorra	2003	No
Armenia	2005	No
Austria	1999	Yes
Azerbaijan	2005	No
Belgium	1999	Yes
Bosnia-Herzegovina	2003	No
Bulgaria	1999	Yes
Croatia	2001	Candidate
Cyprus	2001	Yes
Czech Republic	1999	Yes
Denmark	1999	Yes
Estonia	1999	Yes
Finland	1999	Yes
France	1999	Yes
Georgia	2005	No
Germany	1999	Yes
Greece	1999	Yes
Holy See	2003	No
Hungary	1999	Yes
Iceland	1999	No
Ireland	1999	Yes
Italy	1999	Yes
Latvia	1999	Yes
Liechtenstein	1999	No

TABLE 1 (Continued)

Participating Country	Full Bologna Member Since	EU Member
Lithuania	1999	Yes
Luxembourg	1999	Yes
Malta	1999	Yes
Moldova	2005	No
Montenegro (2003–2007 as Serbia-Montenegro)	2003	No
Netherlands	1999	Yes
Norway	1999	No
Poland	1999	Yes
Portugal	1999	Yes
Romania	1999	Yes
Russian Federation	2003	No
Serbia (2003–2007 as Serbia-Montenegro)	2003	No
Slovak Republic	1999	Yes
Slovenia	1999	Yes
Spain	1999	Yes
Sweden	1999	Yes
Switzerland	1999	No
The Former Yugoslav Republic of Macedonia	2003	Candidate
Turkey	2001	Candidate
Ukraine	2005	No
United Kingdom	1999	Yes

of academic competencies presented for credit (Europass), and on the development of shared standards for improved accountability and quality assurance (ENQA). Programs dedicated to encouraging student mobility predated Bologna but now operate on behalf of Bologna under the auspices of the EU. These include Erasmus and, encompassing a broader international perspective, Erasmus Mundus (2009). And the EU has assisted Bologna in tracking its progress through the analyses conducted by Eurydice

(2008) and through commissioning polling that measured support for Bologna among faculty and staff members. In the priority it has assigned to productive research, in its commitment to competitiveness and innovation, and in its concern for maintaining a stable source of funding for investment in higher education reform, the EU has become an ever stronger and more influential partner in the Bologna Process.

Finally, the EU has supported development of the European Qualifications Framework (EQF) meant to bring greater comparability and coherence to lifelong learning throughout Europe. But the EQF also represents a *second* overarching qualifications framework, similar to but distinct from the EHEA framework—"at the very least," according to Bergan (2007), "hardly a brilliant communication strategy" (p. 175).

How Are the Lisbon Convention and the Lisbon Agenda Related to the Bologna Process?

The Lisbon Convention (1997) is an agreement on the recognition of educational qualifications adopted at a COE/UNESCO meeting in April 1997. The convention encourages consistent, convenient assessment throughout Europe of educational credentials earned in any European country. This agreement also encourages use of a diploma supplement as a means of enhancing such assessment. Bologna has made good use of complementary initiatives already under way at the time of the declaration (Bologna, 1999). The Lisbon Strategy (or Agenda), an initiative of the European Union, expresses a broad commitment to the resurgence of Europe as a leading knowledge-based economy. Because the Bologna Process and the Lisbon Agenda share a priority on higher education, there is the risk of confusion. For instance, an EC communication of May 10, 2006, without referring to the Bologna Process "urges Member States to press on with the modernisation of Europe's universities" so they may increase the contribution of the universities "to the Lisbon Agenda for more growth, and more and better jobs" (Lisbon, 2008).

How Are ENQA and the European Quality Assurance Register (EQAR) Related?

The ENQA is an organization made up of quality assurance agencies in Europe that have qualified for membership through their compliance with published standards and guidelines. The ENQA holds meetings, identifies and promotes good practice in the field, and qualifies its members for listing on the EQAR as a service to programs and institutions engaged in quality assurance.

- Although the ministers have defined pursuit of the social dimension as a vital element in the Bologna Process, they have largely delegated to the individual nations responsibility for the development of action plans.
- Priorities associated with the enhancement of employability include more effective communication with potential employers (especially with regard to the bachelor's degree), the enhancement of career guidance, and sustained attention to the role of higher education in ensuring and supporting lifelong learning.
- An increasing emphasis on lifelong learning should continue to emerge.
- An increasingly global perspective on the part of the EHEA should appear as the Bologna Process develops accessible and informative materials for distribution and as intercontinental consultations increase.

What Have Been the Impediments to Success—and What Are the Concerns for the Future?

Few of the participating nations have made a significant financial investment in the Bologna reforms. For instance, after six years, in 2005 fewer than half the universities involved had appointed an internal coordinator for the reform process. The economic recession late in the decade slowed progress, and the rate of recovery will affect momentum. A continuing lack of autonomy in many national higher education systems limits the alacrity institutions are able to demonstrate with regard to the reform agreements. And increasing resistance to Bologna, in the form of opposition to standardization, privatization, and globalization, has emerged on the streets of Italy, France, and Spain. Perhaps of greatest concern is the use of the Bologna umbrella by some governments to advance higher education pricing structures unrelated to and sometimes antithetical to Bologna.

Will the Emphasis of the Bologna Process Change?

According to one perspective expressed at a seminar on the Bologna Process at Ghent University in May 2008, it should. "In the last decade the Bologna Process has been focusing on structural reforms. In the next stage the focus will shift to the learning process itself." The approach must become more "student-centred" and the attention to discipline-specific outcomes should be accompanied by a "blurring [of] boundaries between disciples" (Bologna 2020, 2008).

The Ghent discussions also pointed to a possible shift in the values animating Bologna, from the early emphasis on increased competition to "solidarity and cooperation."

Why Does the Bologna Process Represent a Challenge to the United States?

The United States is—or should be—pursuing most of the same priorities but has been doing so in many cases for a long time and on a piecemeal basis. By creating an aggressive and comprehensive agenda, one braiding several reform strands into a coordinated effort, Bologna challenges the United States to consider the advantages of a more fully unified approach. At the same time, specific Bologna advances in the arenas of accountability may encourage U.S. policy makers to seek a similarly well-coordinated effort. Similarly, Bologna's commitment to increased mobility stands in contrast with the sharp increases by U.S. public universities in out-of-state tuitions, just as its (not entirely successful) promotion of the 3-year baccalaureate calls on U.S. higher education to explain and defend the convention of the 4-year degree. The European diploma supplement suggests a credential U.S. students would find useful, and efforts to make European higher education more transparent to the public may draw renewed attention to the welter of confusing degree and program designations in the United States.

WHY PAY ATTENTION
TO BOLOGNA?

The Bologna Process is all about a vision, a vision of breaking down educational borders and creating a European Higher Education Area where learning is encouraged, facilitated and enabled in a simplified, integrated way across the continent. The Process is about delivering this vision, translating the concept into a reality on the ground.

(ESU, 2009a).

This succinct definition of the most ambitious higher education reform in human history, framed by the European Students Union (ESU) in a February 2009 declaration, captures an ideal and points to a challenge. The ideal is that of the European Higher Education Area (EHEA), the encompassing goal of the Bologna Process; the challenge is that of turning that goal into a reality "on the ground," nation by nation, institution by institution.

(ESU, 2009a).

Already, much has been accomplished. Those involved in Bologna can claim substantial progress with regard to some major objectives and tangible results with respect to some others. The vision of a system of comparable degrees has largely been realized, at least on paper. And greater comparability in programs offering the degrees has developed. In part, as a result, another objective, increased mobility for faculty members and students, shows at least marginal gains. And awareness of the importance

of quality assurance has clearly grown, as well as recognition that broad cooperation in the interest of expanded accountability will be critical to securing
and maintaining the Bologna agenda.

Other, perhaps even more ambitious, objectives are still to be realized.
Achieving effective quality assurance in ways likely to promote more effective
learning remains a challenge. The frequently referenced *social dimension* of
the process, a commitment to encourage the higher education of those historically underrepresented in traditional student bodies, will continue to
inform Bologna's agenda but has largely been delegated to the participating
nations for action. And while the determination to restore Europe as the
world's most effective and influential higher educator remains a stated goal,
a broader vision in which Europe acts as a leading but cooperative global
colleague appears to be emerging.

In short, while Bologna "at age 10" had accomplished much, there was
much left to be accomplished. And so, acknowledging how much remained
to be done, the education ministers representing the Bologna countries met
in April 2009 in Leuven/Louvain-la-Neuve, Belgium, to initiate Bologna's
second decade. By renewing and reaffirming their voluntary agreement, they
were acknowledging the students' view that "A renewed and ambitious Bologna agenda is . . . essential to make the original vision of the EHEA an
unequivocal reality for all European students, regardless of origin, back-
ground, means or ability, by 2020" (ESU, 2009a).

Two Compelling Motives

The ideal as defined by the students and the reality as shown by the documentation of unfinished business have deep roots in the two compelling
motives that lie at the heart of the Bologna Process. The first is the strengthening of the European economy. The second is the restoration of Europe to
its rightful role as higher educator to the world. The action lines that define
the various activities within the Process are intended as important means to
these ends, but the image of a prosperous and once again prestigious Europe
has provided a primary source of the political will behind them. If the Bologna Process should in time achieve its now far more complex and nuanced
agenda for the reform of higher education, the vigor inherent in these two
primal motives will help to explain its success. Beginning with the discussions at the Sorbonne and through the successive reiterations of Bologna's
priorities, the education ministers of Europe have sustained an increasingly
complicated effort by drawing on its founding vision.

On the other hand, if the Bologna Process should in time join the long history of ambitious but incomplete reform efforts, the limitations in these motives may provide part of the explanation. From the earliest stages, the emphasis on economic development has created some disaffection, to the extent that the education ministers have over time allowed a more moderate and inclusive interpretation. And the commitment to recapturing European preeminence in higher education seems to have discouraged consideration of exemplary practices elsewhere, with the result that some reform efforts that might have drawn on the successful experience of others have advanced very slowly indeed.

The continuing effort to reconcile the ends of the Bologna Process, European prosperity, and ascendancy with its means, the various arenas of reform in higher education, provides the main line of the narrative that will take us through the first decade of the 21st century. And the story, though still far from complete, is already a compelling one, instructive as a study in political initiative, in organizational management, in social dynamics, and in the evolution of higher education.

Why Pay Attention?

A story once planned to end after one decade will continue into another. But however notable the story of Bologna may be in its own right, we read it also for two reasons closer to home. To the extent that Bologna is accomplishing goals that the United States has or should set for itself, we must see what we can learn. To the extent that Europe is becoming a more formidable competitor for the world's students, we must work to protect our interests and values. And because some measure of Bologna's success reflects its comprehensive approach to multifaceted reform according to an ambitious timeline, the Process calls into question the more leisurely and piecemeal approach in the United States.

The commitment within Europe to making higher education more accessible, to encouraging the mobility of students and faculty members, to rationalizing and making consistent the evaluation of credits, and to defining and measuring learning outcomes for all disciplines offers a convenient point of departure because these goals are ones we profess to share. If Europe should find it possible to increase the percentage of the population participating in higher education while college education is becoming affordable to fewer and fewer Americans, the United States may come to understand that its long-standing competitive advantage in this regard is increasingly at risk. Indeed, with respect to college graduation rates in many of the Bologna nations, the United States is already falling behind. And as cramped budgets lead states to throw up higher barriers to student mobility by further increasing tuition and fees for out-of-state students, the United States will stand in even sharper contrast to an EHEA that seeks to promote student and faculty mobility across increasingly permeable borders. In sum, to the extent that the commitment of U.S. higher education to becoming more effective should appear to suffer by comparison with the reform well under way in Europe, the conclusion should follow that the United States has work to do.

And though the United States has enjoyed an advantage for a long time as the higher education destination of choice for the world's students, with benefits to U.S. universities financially and in the increased diversity of their faculties and student bodies, there are signs that these trends may be changing as well. While more Europeans were studying in the United States than vice versa as the first decade drew to a close, the United States is already beginning to fall behind as Europe retains more of its students while attracting increased numbers internationally.

For all these reasons, it is important that the Bologna Process be well understood by U.S. educators and policy makers. Such understanding should illuminate a formidable challenge and point to an agenda for change as compelling as any other national priority. Indeed, there may be no priority more compelling in the long run.

Hence the United States should take on the challenge of Bologna—and do so with some alacrity. The issues testing the world's economies are emphasizing as never before the critical importance of higher education to political development, fiscal stability, and cultural understanding. Moreover, in part as a result of economic recession but also as an expression of a long-standing retreat from investment in the public interest, higher education in the United States in many respects appears to be moving backward, not forward. Accessibility is declining, barriers to interstate student mobility are rising, and information about the performance of higher educators is becoming in some ways more opaque. There is much to be learned from Bologna, and we should read, mark, inwardly digest—and act.

A Challenge—and a Timely Opportunity

Action should not be merely reaction, however. Paradoxically, if the Bologna Process offers a compelling example the United States would be foolish to ignore, it offers also an opportunity for the reassertion of U.S. leadership in higher education through reform that builds on and improves that example.

While those in the Bologna Process have deprived themselves of the advantages to be found in identifying and improving on a competitor's best practices, the United States need not make that same mistake. By giving careful attention to how and where Bologna has succeeded, and by observing where it has fallen short and why, we will be in a position to increase our own efforts at higher education reform from a position of strength.

Even though there is some catching up to do, the lesson is not that higher education in the United States should attempt simply to align itself with Europe's example. In many respects, values characteristic of U.S. higher education do not appear as priorities of the Bologna Process—or at least were not evident until recently. The principle of independent, nongovernmental peer assessment; the belief that all undergraduates should have the benefits of a liberal education; and the understanding that a learning environment characterized by cultural and ethnic diversity supports more effective education are important elements in U.S. higher education without clear analogues in the European movement, and they are well worth defending. Hence, rather than attempting to overtake Europe, as though the United States were its opponent in a sprint, the United States might instead envision a relay race in which it should prepare itself to accept the baton of educational reform from a tiring European runner in order to claim the next leg.

Making Sense of Bologna

Understanding the runner ahead is no easy task, however. For one thing, the Bologna Process is less a pan-European governmental initiative than a shared commitment of the many participating nations. Like the U.S. federal government, the European Union (EU) enjoys little direct authority over education. Hence the support of the EU for the Bologna Process has carefully acknowledged the higher education "sovereignty" of the participating nations. For another, Bologna has worked with and through many other agencies and initiatives to further its objectives. The welter of acronyms, associations, and bureaucratic relationships has created an intimidating thicket of reports, analyses, and declarations not easily penetrated.

It would be possible to become so attentive to every report, every conference, every agency, and every survey that the thousands of Bologna trees would soon overwhelm an effort to observe the forest. But if higher education in the United States is to find in the Bologna Process useful examples for its own development and a summons to increase its own commitment and effort, it is the forest—the overall thrust of Bologna, its remarkable vision, its accomplishments, its considerable oversights, and the impediments to its full realization—that require our closest attention.

This overview seeks not only to inform discussion, then, but to prompt it. As noted in the preface, scholars such as Laurel Terry and Clifford Adelman have already published detailed studies of the development and accomplishments of Bologna. Adelman's April 2009 report for the Institute for Higher Education Policy, especially, offers many instructive particulars and provides helpful prescriptions for strengthening U.S. higher education. His work illustrates the principle that consideration of the Bologna Process has the advantage of providing a focused framework for a commitment to more thoroughgoing reform in the United States.

But as my image of the relay runner suggests, there may lie in present circumstances not only an opportunity for the United States to learn from Bologna's priorities and accomplishments but to use what can be learned to good advantage. By seizing that opportunity, we could indeed realize for ourselves the driving ambitions of the Bologna Process: economic growth and a revived ascendancy in higher education worldwide. But we will do something else that is far more important. By enhancing U.S. higher education, we will expand knowledge, educate more students more efficiently and effectively, and tell the most important story educators can tell in language people will understand.

Samuel Johnson memorably said that the prospect of being hanged "concentrates a man's mind wonderfully." The same might be said of the Bologna Process. The recognition that higher education in the United States is falling behind, at least in some important areas, with respect to an increasingly determined and committed Europe provides not only a summons but also a to-do list of urgent priorities. Having learned to appreciate the considerable promise that the Bologna Process offers and the lessons it has to teach, positive and negative, we may find our minds sufficiently concentrated for the formidable tasks we face and for the remarkable opportunity we have.

2

THE ROAD TO BOLOGNA

Universities, defined as multidisciplinary degree-granting academic institutions, were educating students long before there was a political entity known as Europe. As early as the ninth century, students in Morocco, Egypt, and Iraq, for instance, were convening in specific locations to study with scholars residing there. But because higher education as the world has come to know it bears most clearly the stamp of European universities founded in the second millennium, it may not be presumptuous for European education ministers to claim that "universities were born in Europe" (Sorbonne, 1998). As one historian of higher education observes, "Three springs—Salerno, Bologna, and Paris—form the headwaters of the European university" (Driver, 1971, p. 102). Of these, the University of Bologna, with a traditional founding date of 1088, is considered the oldest (Bergan, 2007, p. 19). With a particular emphasis on jurisprudence, Bologna drew students to study law with masters with whom they contracted.

From these early stages, while higher education has brought opportunities for instruction and research to nearly all parts of the world, European universities have exercised a singular authority. Many of the conventions with regard to curricular structure, scheduling, the accommodation of students, the encouragement of scholarship, the provisioning of libraries, and the funding of instruction that continue to guide systems and institutions of higher education from China to Nebraska reflect European models. Most especially, as Sjur Bergan (2007) has observed, the European university introduced a qualifications framework: "A formal course of study led to a formal and certified qualification" (pp. 19–20). While the competing intellectual claims made by universities throughout the world may be formidable, such practical precedents established in Europe have remained influential.

Given their long ascendancy in influence and prestige, European universities for many centuries represented the heart of higher education. They were broadly accessible for the most part, with few formal requirements for admission and a relaxed approach to scheduling. Unlike the highly organized institutions they were to become, universities were "dominated rather by those forms of communal corporate organization which were characteristic of collective life in guilds, confraternities, colleges, and families" (Schwinges, 2003, p. 172). If we now think of a university as a place, a campus, or complex of buildings, medieval scholars would instead have pictured small gatherings of individuals, scholars and masters, intent on study. But in another sense, given the difficulties of travel and the expenses of student life, universities were then accessible primarily to those with considerable wealth or patronage. Regarded as enclaves for the protected pursuit of knowledge and devotion, they ordinarily functioned as halcyon retreats where the sons of privilege, having dedicated their lives to imparting and furthering knowledge, sought to educate the next privileged generation.

Of course, from one country to another, there were periods of hiatus when universities were closed, suppressed, or even persecuted. But to a considerable extent, the history of Europe in intellectual, political, and religious terms tracks closely the history of its institutions of higher education. In giving the name Bologna to higher education reform, Europeans recall a proud history.

A Turning Point

The 20th century represented a turning point for higher education in Europe.

First, European universities suffered from unprecedented social disruptions arising from military and ideological conflict. Two devastating wars, economic catastrophes, social crises, and political stalemates raised national and ethnic borders, reduced funding available for higher education, compromised the scholarly and human values of many universities, and exacerbated issues of access. Universities in Russia were closed by the czar at the beginning of the century then required, after reopening under Marxism, to emphasize productivity for the state within explicit restrictions. In the 1930s in Germany and Italy and in the territories they occupied, Fascists compromised, marginalized, and exploited universities. Throughout the Reich, universities expelled Jewish professors, burned books regarded as subversive, and countenanced the execution of students judged to be seditious.

Second, the catastrophic loss of life in the world wars and in other conflicts created critical gaps in Europe in leadership and in the workforce. Broader access to higher education represented one means of addressing the problem, just as an increasing sense of entitlement emerged among those formerly not invited to higher education. In short, there developed a growing demand for access to universities ill prepared to welcome increased numbers.

The third point was the influence of the United States. From the far more expansive view of higher education implicit in the Morrill Act of 1862 to the even greater extension of access through the GI Bill of 1944, the United States offered an example of an unprecedented commitment to the education of the public. Moreover, through remarkable growth in the number and size of its higher education institutions, its appeal to international students, and its demonstrated leadership in important areas of research, the United States in many ways surpassed Europe as the recognized standard for how higher education should be organized and delivered.

European Developments

To be sure, even as Europe was finding its preeminence in higher education threatened, it witnessed in the course of the 20th century a number of events that suggested an increasing public responsiveness toward meeting growing educational demands. To the extent that such developments may foreshadow the Bologna Process, they deserve attention.

For instance, in 1903 the Sorbonne awarded a doctorate to Marie Curie, a graduate of Poland's so-called flying university, an informal assembly of residential cells that had opened higher education to women through small private classes in Warsaw and eastern Poland. The success of this grassroots effort became evident not only in the accomplishments of its graduates but also in its eventual acknowledgment by the government. In Poland and throughout Europe, the interests of women would have to be considered as a matter of course in efforts to improve higher education.

And European higher education would in time no longer be regarded as an enclave primarily of the privileged. In 1908 a report by a joint committee comprising workers and Oxford University officials affirmed an expanding interest in higher education and offered recommendations for addressing it (Workers' Educational Association, 1908). Most notably, the report acknowledged that improvements in the quality and accessibility of "elementary" education had given impetus to "the intellectual momentum of the whole nation." Schools were for the first time providing "the basis of intelligence which makes a future training possible." In turn, better basic education had prompted in workers "a keen desire for advanced study under competent guidance" (p. 43). The report concludes with a commitment to access that anticipates a principle of the Bologna Process: "A modern university must be accessible to every class, not merely in the formal sense that it admits every applicant of good character who satisfies its educational requirements, but in the practical sense of making it certain that no one will be excluded merely on the ground of poverty" (p. 49).

Increasing Access

That this impetus had wide European roots appears in the influence Scandinavian "folk high schools" exerted on the 1909 creation by chocolatier George Cadbury of Fircroft College in Birmingham, England. Created to provide laborers, clerks, and farmers with a general rather than vocational education, Fircroft still today offers "a unique experience where students live and learn in an attractive and supportive environment" (Fircroft, 2009).

In Germany, the Hohenrodter Bund, an association of advocates for adult education, would seek similarly to respond to the growing popular demand for higher education, but also, as the Oxford report (Workers' Educational Association, 1908) suggested, to channel it appropriately. Just as the Oxford report and the creation of Fircroft College assumed that broader access to higher education would preserve rather than threaten the prevailing class structure, nowhere in the European expansion of adult education does there appear an explicit interest in the growth of social mobility. Such education would enrich the lives of adult students *within* their respective classes, not encourage overweening aspirations.

Just as a Danish model had inspired a British prototype in Fircroft, in the early 1920s an English example, that of the Woodbrooke Quaker Study Centre, inspired the opening of the International People's College (IPC) in Elsinore, Denmark. The objective of the college was to bring together people from countries that had faced off as enemies during World War I that they might learn from one another—a genuinely international undertaking. Appropriately, in 1949 UNESCO chose the IPC as the site for its first international conference on adult education. Like Fircroft, the IPC has continued to adapt to changing circumstances and remains an active presence.

Collaboration and Cooperation

Another step toward broader international understanding was taken when educators convened in Calais, France, to form the Ligue Internationale Pour l'Education Nouvelle. Thus initiated in 1921, the league spread to more than 20 countries and claimed within its membership such notables as Jean Piaget, Maria Montessori, John Dewey, and Carl Jung. Conferences subsequently sponsored by the league took up issues such as multicultural education and lifelong learning that would later form part of the Bologna agenda.

An even more explicit move toward international academic cooperation within Europe that intended to offer "a coordinating centre for institutions and societies concerned with education" arose in Geneva in 1925 with the founding of the International Bureau of Education (IBE, 2009). At first focused on the support of educational research and the creation of a clearing-house for documents related to higher education, the IBE in 1929 invited governments to become members. As the current online history maintained by the IBE indicates, "It thus became the first intergovernmental organiza-tion in the field of education" (IBE). The IBE would in time join UNESCO as a specialized institute.

World War II, though for the duration highly disruptive to international cooperation, also proved a kind of catalyst for postwar efforts. Even in the midst of the conflict, education ministers from countries opposed to the Axis powers met in England to plan a coordinated approach to the restoration of higher education following the war. Then, once the war ended, the confer-ence they had planned convened, and the delegates agreed to form a new organization that would establish the "intellectual and moral solidarity of mankind and, in so doing, prevent the outbreak of another world war" (UNESCO, 2009). Of the 44 countries that attended, 37 signed on as UNESCO founders. In 1967, breaking down a long-standing division between East and West, UNESCO convened in Vienna a Continent-wide ministerial-level conference on access to higher education. Today, UNESCO has 193 member states, including the Russian Federation, 12 nations from the former Soviet Union, China, and 19 African countries.

Despite these promising beginnings, the integration of higher education in Europe slowed somewhat during the early years of rebuilding following the war. Economic development had to take precedence. Yet through such development important structures emerged that would support increasing educational cooperation and coordination. The Council of Europe (COE), founded in 1949, provided a platform for early discussions among its mem-bers with regard to higher education. And the Treaties of Rome (1957) that created the European Economic Community expressed a determination "to lay the foundations of an ever closer union among the peoples of Europe," to eliminate barriers dividing Europe, and to remove existing obstacles in the interest of "steady expansion, balanced trade and fair competition." Though at first focused on the tariff-free exchange of goods across boundaries, the treaty would in time support also the recognition that a more effective part-nership in higher education could be built on a similar continental commitment.

The International Baccalaureate and Erasmus

In the second half of the 20th century, impetus in Europe toward cross-border cooperation and coordination in higher education continued to grow. The 1967 UNESCO conference offers one example. The introduction the following year of the international baccalaureate (IB) represents another. Developed in Geneva in 1968 to offer broader access to higher education internationally, the IB diploma program prescribes for secondary school students a demanding curriculum and comprehensive testing. The mission of the program suggests how well aligned it is with the move toward lower borders and broader mobility. According to its Web site, the IB seeks nothing less than the education of young people who will "help to create a better and more peaceful world through intercultural understanding and respect" (Baccalaureate, n.d.).

A dramatic advance in European cooperation in higher education appeared in 1987 with the introduction of the European Region Action Scheme for the Mobility of University Students. A bold idea for promoting the advantages of study abroad, the initiative also arrived with one of the most clever and appropriate of acronyms: ERASMUS. Not only was Erasmus of Rotterdam highly mobile as a scholar and as a teacher, having affiliations with universities throughout Europe, but he was as well a great benefactor of higher education. Indeed, as the program's official overview indicates, Erasmus willed his estate to the University of Basel, there becoming "a pioneer of the mobility grants which now bear his name" (Erasmus, 2008).

The Erasmus program facilitates college students' mobility across national boundaries by endeavoring to ensure that credits students earn at approved institutions in other countries will transfer at full value to their home institutions. But Erasmus also *encourages* such movement by excusing students from the payment of additional tuition and fees to the institutions they visit. Even the additional costs of living in another country for as long as an academic year may be borne in part by Erasmus through a competitive grants program. As a result, today roughly 90% of universities in Europe participate in the program and nearly 2 million students have taken part since its inception. It is not too much to say, with the European Commission (EC), that Erasmus "inspired the establishment of the Bologna Process" (EC Education, 2009). Now a constituent program in the EU's Lifelong Learning Programme, Erasmus aspires to enroll 3 million students by 2012 (Erasmus, 2008).

An important offshoot, Erasmus Mundus (2009), offers encouragement of global educational mobility as a means toward greater understanding among nations and cultures. The program provides scholarships for individual students as well as support for participating institutions. And the program directly serves the priorities of Bologna through its support of European joint degrees at the graduate level and through projects "to promote European higher education systems worldwide" (Erasmus Mundus, 2009).

The Magna Charta Universitatum

The idea for an academic "great charter" was advanced in 1986 by the University of Bologna. The obvious precursor is of course the Magna Carta Libertatum, the English charter of liberties forced on King John in 1215. A draft of the academic charter completed in January 1988 was signed in the main square of Bologna in September by the rectors of 430 universities—both as a celebration of the university's 900th anniversary and as a ringing declaration of principle by higher educators. Advancing an expansive vision of the university, this statement has served throughout the Bologna Process as a contrast to more narrowly focused views of higher education. It defines the university as "an autonomous institution at the heart of societies differently organized because of geography and historical heritage" (Magna Charta, 1988). It further emphasizes the role of the university in maintaining and transmitting culture and in balancing teaching and research productively. And it insists that in order to fulfill its role, the university must support research and teaching "morally and intellectually independent of all political authority and economic power" (Magna Charta).

The issue of autonomy has arisen frequently in discussions concerning Bologna and in recent national debates on the proper roles of universities. The Magna Charta Universitatum, a declaration not of education ministers but of university rectors, helps to define one side of what may be a growing divide. While the priorities of ministers and rectors have often coincided through the course of the Bologna Process, the tensions between them have become apparent also. And the charter signed in Bologna more than a decade before the ministers convened to frame a process of higher education reform remains an important reference.

Approaching Bologna

New collaborative efforts at the governmental level appear less frequently in the 1960s and 1970s. It had become evident that for the many European cultures divided by years of competition, antagonism, and realignment, the road to cooperation based on shared interests at first could be neither easy nor direct. But that road in the 1980s widened considerably. The remarkable accomplishments of that decade, which express a new interest in the advantages of substantive partnership, emerged relatively quickly.

Among the steps that might be seen as leading toward the Bologna Process (and to its bureaucratic lookalike, the 2002 Copenhagen Process) was the Community Programme in Education and Training for Technology (COMETT). Initiated by the EU in 1986 to improve technology training through increased cooperation among providers, COMETT sought more robust partnerships among institutions, firms, and educators, the expansion of access to technical training, and improvements in the sophistication of such training.

Response was vigorous. In its first four years, the program became a platform for 125 university-enterprise partnerships, for more than 4,000 individual student "traineeships," and for nearly 250 staff exchanges between universities and their corporate partners. Most of these fell within production and manufacturing, as was the intent, but representatives from disciplines such as management, biology, chemistry, and computer technology also participated. In the second phase of the program, these initiatives expanded in scope and influence. In turn, the Action Program for the Vocational Training of Young People (PETRA) was authorized in 1993 and again in 1998. Though not all of these programs are still extant, the creation of collaborative alliances with regard to vocational education contributed to the platform for the broader aims of Bologna (and, later, Copenhagen).

Other programs, such as Youth for Europe, Lingua, and Eurotecnet followed. While this is not the place for a report on the motives, accomplishments, and evolution of each, what they have in common is instructive. None of these programs won easy approval at the governmental level. The processes leading to adoption reveal familiar arguments and underestimates with regard to likely demand and use. Not surprising. What has been surprising, however, is the alacrity with which such programs have been welcomed by those able to benefit from them. Through this period, administrators of one program after another reported that participation far outstripped expectations. Perhaps the least ambiguous indicator of growing support for such partnerships lies in budgets. Between 1980 and 1984, total allocations for such cooperative initiatives were approximately 14 million. Ten years later, support had risen to 1 billion!

A New Europe

A political platform essential for the development of Bologna was set in place in 1992 through the epochal treaty signed at Maastricht, the Netherlands, that became effective on November 1, 1993. This Treaty on European Union (TEU, 1992), designed to promote political integration on the Continent, defined European citizenship, clarified and strengthened the authority of the European Parliament, and laid the groundwork for the introduction of the euro currency. The treaty provided also for the assignment of responsibility for education to the European Parliament and Council. In fact, Article 126 of the treaty specifically calls on the European community to "contribute to the development of quality education by encouraging cooperation between Member States and, if necessary, by supporting and supplementing their action." On the other hand, any actions taken would respect "the responsibility of the Member States for the content of teaching and the organization of education systems and their cultural and linguistic diversity" (TEU).

This was of course the third important treaty in the coalescence of the European community. Earlier actions had created a European Economic Community and more formally established its superstructure: a commission, parliament, council, and court. But as important as these earlier steps were, it was the TEU that made Bologna possible. Indeed, the goals of that treaty offer an interesting preview of many of the themes that would reappear in Paris and Bologna. Among the priorities set forth by the treaty are developing "the European dimension" in education, fostering greater mobility for students and teachers, supporting greater cooperation between "educational establishments," providing for "exchanges of information and experience," and building distance education. To achieve these ends, the council was charged to invite recommendations and to "adopt incentive measures" (TEU, 1992). A further move toward a platform for Bologna was the creation in 1995 of an EU directorate-general for education and culture charged with support for lifelong learning and student mobility.

Lisbon

There are two even more direct precursors.

The first emerged in the form of a treaty signed at a 1997 meeting in Lisbon, Portugal. That document, officially titled *Convention on the Recognition of Qualifications Concerning Higher Education in the European Region*, sought to smooth the process through which educational credentials earned in one European country are evaluated and assigned credit in another (Lisbon Convention, 1997). Because the convention represents a primary means for the Bologna Process to pursue its emphasis on student mobility, adoption of the Lisbon Convention by Bologna members remains a performance standard for the Process.

This was not the first such agreement on this issue, but it was the first one intended to be comprehensive. Agreements still in effect in 1997 dated for the most part from the 1950s or early 1960s, and a lot had happened in the meantime. For one thing, higher education had become more diverse. Institutions other than traditional universities, including many new private institutions especially in central and eastern Europe, in 1997 accounted for a majority of enrolled students. And there had been an increase in the mobility of students. By replacing the several conventions that had developed to address different circumstances with the Lisbon Convention, the joint effort of the Council of Europe and UNESCO offered an opportunity for a shared vision.

There was also clarity in the principles of the convention, which held above all that students who had earned academic credentials should enjoy "adequate access . . . to an assessment of these qualifications" (Lisbon Convention, 1997, III.1). While the applicant accepts primary responsibility for providing adequate information "in good faith," responsibility for demonstrating that an applicant does *not* meet "the relevant requirements" is assigned to "the body undertaking the assessment" (Lisbon Convention, III.3.2, 5).

The Sorbonne Declaration

An even more direct precursor of the Bologna Process lies in the 1998 Joint Declaration on Harmonisation of the Architecture of the European Higher Education System (Sorbonne, 1998). Only three pages long, the document sets forth many of the values that would inform Bologna. Indeed, Bologna may be seen in some respects as a more detailed rewriting of Sorbonne in the interest of greater clarity and inclusivity.

Meeting in May 1998 at the University of Paris on its 800th anniversary, the education ministers of France, Germany, Italy, and the United Kingdom envisioned "a Europe of knowledge" with "intellectual, cultural, social and technical" strengths grounded in the continent's universities (Sorbonne, 1998, ¶ 1). Looking back to a time when students moved freely among European universities, the four ministers proposed "an open European area for higher learning" (¶ 4) that would rely on closer cooperation and encourage greater mobility. Moreover, through the proposed reforms, the "international recognition" of European higher education would be enhanced and its "attractive potential" would be more fully realized (¶ 5).

The practical heart of the declaration lies in a differentiation between undergraduate and graduate education according to a consistent standard and in its proposal for documenting student performance according to a shared understanding of academic credits and the learning outcomes they signify. The objective is that students should be able to undertake, interrupt, and reenter higher education more or less at will, regardless of their age or their location.

The first cycle (or undergraduate) degree would merit "international recognition," while the graduate cycle, emphasizing research and independent discovery, would offer a shorter master's degree and "a longer doctor's degree" bridged by opportunities for transfer from one to the next. Both cycles would encourage greater mobility within Europe for students and teachers alike (Sorbonne, 1998, ¶ 8, ¶ 9). Acknowledging the conventions on student mobility approved in Lisbon, the Sorbonne Declaration sought to "build on them and go further" by engaging European governments directly in the "progressive harmonisation" of study cycles. The semester would become the standard academic term. Moreover, knowledge and competencies gained through comparably defined degrees would be validated through the European Credit Transfer and Accumulation System (ECTS) or a similar protocol (¶ 13).

In sum, the commitment to "improving external recognition and facilitating student mobility as well as employability" directly anticipates action lines that would be confirmed at Bologna. The Sorbonne signatories sought nothing less than "a European area of higher education, where national identities and common interests can interact and strengthen each other for the benefit of Europe, of its students, and more generally of its citizens" (Sorbonne, 1998, ¶ 14).

At the close of their declaration, the four ministers invited not only other EU members, but all other European countries as well, to join them in their pursuit of "a European area of higher education, where national identities and common interests can interact and strengthen each other for the benefit of Europe, of its students, and more generally of its citizens" (Sorbonne, 1998, ¶ 14). The benefits of this focus on higher education would emerge finally as the means to an even larger end: "to consolidate Europe's standing in the world" (Sorbonne, ¶ 14).

To further this vision of an expanded forum, the Italian minister present at the Sorbonne invited his colleagues to reconvene the following year in Bologna, where ministers representing other European nations as well as university representatives and observers might join the discussion. But when a skeptical reaction to some elements of the Sorbonne Declaration began to emerge, it became apparent that a meeting envisioned initially as a follow-up should stand on its own. Hence Bologna convened less as a sequel to the

Sorbonne meeting than as a fresh point of departure. By bringing together a broader set of stakeholders to address both more clearly envisioned opportunities and emerging concerns, Bologna provided a platform for the development and implementation of an ambitious reform agenda. That agenda in turn directed higher education in Europe through the course of the new century's first decade (Bologna, 1999).

Concerns

Concerns that prompted the rethinking evident at the Bologna conference are worth acknowledging because they have continued to shadow the process of reform.

The first was triggered by the use of the word *harmonisation* in the Sorbonne Declaration. There were misgivings that the reform effort, giving too little regard to the diversity of strengths, means, and ends among Europe's academic programs, would seek to reduce them to a common standard. The clarification offered in response, that the word as used in the Sorbonne Declaration was meant to refer only to the *architecture* of higher education systems, was helpful. But concerns that Bologna might require increasing conformity with detailed expectations have persisted. In fact, a continuing challenge for Bologna in its second decade will be a resulting structural discontinuity: The responsibility for implementing a program seeking greater comparability and commonality, if not uniformity, rests with nations that hold at high value the specificity and singularity of their systems of higher education.

Second, the declaration's call for greater uniformity in the length of academic programs and for easily recognizable degree cycles recalled for many observers a *3-5-8 scheme* (cumulative years required for bachelor's, master's, and doctoral degrees) then under discussion in France. But advocates for Bologna argued that their structural proposals should be seen as very different. The first Trends report written prior to Bologna insisted, in fact, that the Sorbonne discussions had shown "no significant convergence towards a 3-5-8 model" (EUA Trends I, 1999). Others responded negatively to the similarity between the structure proposed by the Sorbonne Declaration and the Anglo-Saxon structure of higher education in the United Kingdom and the United States. By ignoring such resemblances, the Sorbonne and Bologna statements prompted the suspicion that the "Anglo Saxon structure of higher education was accepted in Bologna as the general European model without much discussion" simply because of "the exceptional English 'success' on a global scale," particularly in the recruitment of international students (Lorenz, 2006, p. 127).

Finally, the signing of the Sorbonne Declaration by the ministers of the four largest EU countries had prompted the apprehension that the proposed reforms would have as their point of departure only a limited discussion among a few ministers. The call to the meeting in Bologna allayed this concern by promising far broader consultation. And the promise has been kept. Indeed, at its conclusion, 29 nations, 15 of them EU members, signed the resulting Bologna Declaration. The project would no longer belong to a "big four." Its base would spread to envelop all of Europe. But it would of course remain an initiative with its source in governments rather than in higher education.

An Analytical Platform

The 60-page Trends study commissioned by what was shortly to become the European University Association (EUA) proved to be the first in a series of biennial reports on European higher education reform related to the Bologna Process. Far more than an analysis of Sorbonne, it exerted a signal influence on the Bologna Declaration by offering a thorough analysis of existing structures and a detailed justification for the necessity of reform (EUA Trends I, 1999).

There are three sections in the study, one describing structural "trends and issues" in European higher education, another offering "information on learning structures" in the EU, and an appendix summarizing the Sorbonne Declaration and pointing out gaps and inconsistencies. The shared priorities of these sections are the mapping of areas of "convergence and divergence" in Europe's higher education systems, the identification of developments likely to influence these structures, and the proposal of opportunities for "greater convergences and effectiveness in the future" (EUA Trends I, 1999).

The complexity of the task Bologna would undertake is apparent in the study's identification of "more systems than countries" (EUA Trends I, 1999). Accordingly, the study documents a wide breadth of program standards, sharp contrasts in assumptions regarding student access, marked differences in fees, "huge differences" in the organization and duration of programs of study, a wide variation in practices of examination and attestation, and a strikingly broad range of degrees available. Despite the already considerable discussion around the emergence of a three-year first degree, the study found little evidence that a pattern was as yet emerging. Noting many different program lengths and student enrollment patterns, the authors observe that required credits might serve as a better comparative measure than years or semesters. But a clearer picture emerges with regard to graduate study, at least at the master's level, where the authors find, with some exceptions, "a significant level of convergence" among opportunities to complete both the undergraduate and master's degrees in about five years (EUA Trends I).

Interestingly, the study pauses at this point to acknowledge fears that the European discussions might lead to the adoption of a mainly American model. But that need not be a concern, the authors say. While there may be a clearer distinction in U.S. higher education between undergraduate and graduate study, the wide variety of institutions, curricula, degrees, and program lengths should allay European anxieties. In sum, "the US system has its own structure, logic, history and also its own weaknesses and difficulties," while Europe "needs to develop its own system(s) to suit its own needs" (EUA Trends I, 1999).

That system (or systems) should reflect current European trends, the report suggests. One of the most prominent, favoring programs shorter in duration, could address a number of concerns, including high dropout rates, high costs of attendance, deferred entry to the labor force, and inherent disincentives for international students and students with limited means. But new bachelor's and master's programs with shorter time to completion would require that employer acceptance of the new credentials keep pace with the innovations of universities. Surveying one country after another, the authors locate only two, Greece and the Netherlands, that are not "experimenting with two-tier curricula" (EUA Trends I, 1999).

Other trends identified by the study include the following:

- The progressive "unification" of higher education, meaning the authorization of different kinds of institutions, public and private, to offer full degrees, to describe themselves as universities, and to join in mergers intended to create more highly visible and competitive institutions.
- Coalescence around two related issues, the award of credits based on course-based study and the organization of the academic calendar according to semesters.
- Increased autonomy for universities, "even though university autonomy still means very different things in different countries."
- Increased competition from "foreign universities" intruding on European soil and from "transnational" distance education providers such as the University of Phoenix. (EUA Trends I, 1999)

As a response to such trends, the study proposes steps toward greater convergence, one of which would have to be broad agreement on regulations governing "meaningful bachelor's degrees." Such degrees, accredited where possible by European disciplinary bodies, would represent substantive gains in efficiency, encourage employer acceptance, and reduce confusion and complexity. While disavowing interest in "a rigid, uniform model," the study calls for a four-step model, leading from the subdegree level (about two years), through the bachelor's degree (three or four years), to the master's (a total of about five years in higher education), and the doctoral degree (about eight years total). Such a structure, described by a shared nomenclature, would allow for variations while providing far greater comparability and transparency.

Closely germane to greater convergence among disparate programs are two additional reforms, acceptance of a common system for the recognition and transfer of academic credits, on the one hand, and a deeply shared commitment to assessment and quality assurance on the other. To this end, wide adoption of the ECTS system, which documents different systems of grading and translates among them to create (ideally) a common academic currency, would offer a means of sustaining an easily understood standard, of facilitating transfer of students within Europe, and of recruiting international students more effectively.

But the credibility of such an approach would depend on a commitment to quality assurance based on peer reviewed outputs standards developed for higher education systems and within the disciplines. Moreover, national agencies charged with quality assurance should work increasingly in tandem with one another to create "European networks" of shared understanding and practice. And there should be a "second pillar" of quality assurance, namely, independent subject-based evaluation capable of awarding "quality labels"—but not providing rankings (EUA Trends I, 1999).

These reforms should provide a point of departure for new learning opportunities, the study concludes. Programs to provide greater encouragement for student and faculty mobility should emerge. Accelerated master's programs could stimulate vertical mobility. Recruitment of international students should prosper. Much might be possible.

For those attending the Bologna forum, the study concludes, the "key words" should be "quality," "mobility," "diversity," and "openness." The authors of Trends I would not be disappointed as the road to Bologna finally arrived at its destination.

3

POINT OF DEPARTURE

The 1999 Bologna Declaration provided the 29 education ministers who signed it with an unprecedented opportunity: to articulate a historic consensus on higher education reform, to identify a limited set of priorities to guide action, and to set into motion a pragmatic process of implementation. Their efforts would prove momentous. Well before the target date of 2010, significant reforms were in place, and the European Higher Education Area (EHEA) was realized in many important respects. The confidence of the ministers has proved to be well intended and well grounded—if somewhat overoptimistic with regard to the pace of the reforms and the depth of their penetration within nations and institutions.

At the outset of many ambitious reform efforts, there can be a tendency to underestimate the complexity of the task ahead and to overestimate the support the reform will enjoy at all levels of implementation. From the perspective of a decade, it now seems clear that the ministers' meeting at Bologna demonstrated that tendency—but perhaps to a lesser extent than is usual. For the vision and determination evident in the Bologna Declaration has shaped the processes of implementation, interpretation, and modification from one biennium to the next. As the Bologna Process approached its initial deadline of 2010, the ministers would not be able to claim that their mission had been accomplished in full or that its influence was uniform throughout Europe. However, they would be able to affirm a significant advance. Some major objectives appeared substantially complete. And the promise of continued success would justify the investment of an additional decade.

From a base of 29 charter signers, Bologna would expand through the first decade of the new century to encompass 46 European countries, from Ireland and Iceland in the west to the easternmost reaches of the Russian Federation. Not unexpectedly, different rates of progress toward full implementation would become evident, traditional barriers to mobility would prove more substantial than had been anticipated, and durable restrictions on institutional autonomy would stand in the way of more aggressive advancement. The technical definition of inertia does not mean there cannot be movement, but that movement will require the application of an external force to a body at rest. That force in Europe has been the Bologna Process.

Building on Sorbonne

As we have seen, many of the most important aspirations associated with the Bologna Process were voiced about a year earlier, when the four signers of the Sorbonne Declaration (France, Germany, Italy, and the United Kingdom) found themselves in agreement. But if the 29 ministers assembled at Bologna took as a point of departure the principles of Sorbonne, their own accomplishments were substantial. Drawing in part on the findings evident in the EUA Trends I (1999) study prepared prior to their meeting, the signatories of the Bologna Declaration were able to create in the course of a relatively brief assembly the primary impetus for a dynamic and broad-ranging reform movement. And they did so in a cogent, compact document of fewer than 1,000 words. Though there have been many useful summaries and analyses, we should begin with the document itself (Bologna, 1999).

A More Complete Europe

The most conspicuous incentive for the Bologna Declaration appears in a shared determination to create "a more complete and far-reaching Europe," one grounded in the continent's "intellectual, cultural, social and scientific dimensions" (Bologna, 1999, ¶ 1). The statement offers an important reminder that the process of higher education reform in Europe has never been only about education. There has been evident throughout a profound aspiration to restore Europe to primacy—in part through higher education. "A Europe of Knowledge" thus represents an "indispensable" element in a broader goal "to consolidate and enrich the European citizenship" (¶ 2).

By this view, the critical role of education is to provide Europeans with "the necessary competences to face the challenges of a new millennium, together with an awareness of shared values and belonging to a common social and cultural space" (Bologna, 1999, ¶ 2). Further, higher education has an important political value in its capacity for the "strengthening of stable, peaceful and democratic societies" (¶ 3). As fascinating for what it does not say—there are no references to the pleasures of learning, to the importance of acquaintance with different cultures, or to the value of education beyond the curriculum, for instance—as for what it does, the declaration, like the process itself, pursues a tight focus on workforce development, the consolidation of societies and cultures, and political stability.

Glancing back at the Sorbonne (1998) Declaration, the framers of Bologna (1999) cite its general emphasis on the promotion of "citizens' mobility and employability and the Continent's overall development" (¶ 4). But the concerns of the ministers at Bologna were more specific and more urgent. Their interest in achieving increased momentum toward "greater compatibility and comparability" among European systems of higher education prompts an emphasis on "concrete measures to achieve tangible forward steps" (¶ 7). And because "the vitality and efficiency of any civilisation can be measured by the appeal that its culture has for other countries" (a revealing and perhaps questionable assumption), such steps must increase "the international competitiveness of the European system of higher education" to the extent that it "acquires a world-wide degree of attraction equal to our extraordinary cultural and scientific traditions" (¶ 8).

There are many worthy motives apparent in Bologna, and the aspiration among the education ministers to recruit a larger share for Europe of the world's well-qualified (and well-heeled) students is among them. In fact, some observers believe that is the foremost motive (Lorenz, 2006). But clearly there is a larger sense of framing, in educational terms, a Europe greater than the sum of its parts. And that aspiration merits particular attention from the United States where the competing interests of 50 states may result in a higher education system *less* than the sum of its parts.

Actions to Be Taken

To set forth an aggressive agenda as its point of departure, the declaration defines six objectives intended "to promote the European system of higher education world-wide" (Bologna, 1999, ¶ 9). They are as follows:

- Create "easily readable and comparable degrees," made more fully transparent through broad adoption of a "diploma supplement," to promote employability of European students and "the international competitiveness of the European higher education system."
- Organize higher education according to "two main cycles," undergraduate and graduate. The first would be intended to qualify the degree recipient for entry to the labor market. The second would lead students to master's degrees. (Attention to doctoral programs would come later.)

- Manage educational credentials according to a recognized system of credits.
- Encourage mobility by expanding student access to cross-border opportunities for study and training and by protecting the "statutory rights" of faculty members and administrators who chose to work "in a European context."
- Promote a stronger commitment to quality assurance by supporting the development of "comparable criteria and methodologies."
- Advance "the necessary European dimensions in higher education," particularly in terms of "curricular development, inter-institutional cooperation, mobility schemes and integrated programmes of study, training and research." (¶¶ 10–15)

While expressing due recognition of "the diversity of cultures, languages, national education systems and of University autonomy," the signers commit, in sum, "to consolidate the European area of higher education" and to reconvene every two years "in order to assess the progress achieved and the new steps to be taken" (¶¶ 16–17).

Emerging Concerns

Work in preparation for the follow-up meeting in Prague two years later documented an immediate, positive response to the Bologna Declaration and pointed to some new steps required to sustain the momentum. But some misgivings emerged as well. An example may be found in a meeting of Bologna principals in Lisbon in June 2000, after which Gerhard M. Schuwey (2000), then director of the Federal Office for Education and Science in Switzerland, cited two reservations. The first, which he attributed to humanities faculty, was that the proposed two-tier system based on an efficient three-year baccalaureate might not "meet the purpose of a broad general education." The second issue Schuwey reported is closely related: the fear of Swiss academic leadership "that a first degree too narrowly focused on the vocational training would endanger the scientific [i.e., 'scholarly'] level of the academic education."

While this is but one constituency heard from, many of the concerns that have surfaced during the Bologna Process similarly have their source in the declaration—in its prominent Eurocentrism, the straightforward pragmatism of its economic priorities, and its lack of attention to what would come to be defined as the social dimension of reform. On the other hand, by expressing a shared resolve in a brief, substantive statement that included the means for its progressive revision and realization, the framers of Bologna were clearly intent on getting something done. In that sense, the "Bologna 29" accomplished exemplary committee work. Despite shifting political and economic influences within Europe, the efforts they set in motion continue a decade later along lines drawn in 1999.

Organizing Bologna

A comprehensive history of the Bologna Process would describe in detail the structures, communications, Web sites, documents, and organizational alliances that have developed in this most complex and ambitious of higher education reforms. And the studies of Laurel Terry (2008) and Clifford Adelman (2008, 2009) offer a strong beginning. Yet even this succinct overview should point out three principles that have guided the process and contributed to its success and to the challenges it faces.

The first is that of distributed authority. Rather than create an enduring bureaucracy, the education ministers decided on a rota through which different countries and their respective ministers would exercise provisional authority in preparing for the next biennial meeting. As a result, concerns about a possible higher education autocracy have been muted, and supporters of the process have found it possible to make progress in many cases without exacerbating concerns over national autonomy and institutional distinctiveness.

Second, the decision to manage implementation according to a series of biennial conferences has supported the momentum of the process and provided opportunities for regular refreshment of its sense of urgency. Each biennial meeting, supported by thorough reports on progress from the perspectives of the universities and the students and by "stocktaking" reports commissioned by the ministers, has offered as well the opportunity to invite and accept additional nations as participants.

Finally, the commitment almost from the beginning of the process to an unprecedented level of transparency has created a record both staggering in its volume and impressive in its depth. As a means of organizing the record, in each biennium the country appointed to convene the next ministerial meeting has assumed responsibility for creating a dedicated Web site.

In brief, administration of the process and its proceedings (many studies, task force reports, and other targeted ad hoc efforts, some of which will be described in later chapters) has resided since 2003 in a rotating secretariat, maintained by the host of the next meeting. The secretariat provides support for the work of the Bologna Follow-Up Group (BFUG), which includes

Bologna signatory representatives, envoys from organizations with a recognized interest in the process, appointees from the European Commission (EC), and for a BFUG executive board that provides active oversight for actions taken on behalf of the Bologna Process.

Working With Other Programs

As a further consequence of its determination to avoid (and of its lack of resources to establish) its own standing bureaucratic structure, the rotating authority has found it imperative to adopt the work of supportive organizations where appropriate and to share or offload priorities when possible. A thorough review of all the alliances developed through the Bologna Process also must await a definitive history, but Laurel Terry (2008) has made a good start in dividing such alliances between those made with organizations existing prior to the Bologna Process and those "created in the wake of the Bologna Process to help implement its initiatives" (p. 120).

The relationship between the Bologna Process and the European Union (EU) is clearly the most noteworthy of these alliances—and occasionally the most perplexing. While the process was not formed under the auspices of the EU, its first signatories were ministers representing EU countries, and even now many Bologna member states are also EU members (see pp. 5–6 in "An Expeditious Overview" for a list of Bologna participants indicating their EU affiliation.) Moreover, as Terry (2008) observes, an EU commissioner represents the sole voting member of the BFUG that is not a member state.

The complexity of the relationship between the EU and Bologna arises in part from the EU's original lack of authority for higher education. While an important guarantee of national autonomy, the limitation can lead to poor communication and misalignment between otherwise closely related educational initiatives. But if the interest of the EU in the priorities of Bologna cannot be expressed in regulatory language, it appears in a variety of sponsored initiatives, many of which have provided Bologna with guidance, support, and invigoration.

The Erasmus (2008) program, described in the preceding chapter, has been one of the most productive of these initiatives. From one perspective, with more than 200,000 European students studying and working abroad every year (Erasmus), Erasmus represents one of Bologna's successes, even though a participation rate of about 4% falls far short of its aspiration. More recently, Erasmus has added to its mobility agenda by encouraging the development of university courses with "a European dimension" and supporting

collaborative, transnational degree programs and program components (Erasmus Overview, n.d.).

There was growth in the scope of the ECTS as well. Developed initially as a means for facilitating the transfer of credits earned abroad and thereby encouraging mobility, the acronym now stands for the European Credit Transfer *and Accumulation* System. And higher education throughout Europe is now making increasing use of this system to track student progress toward degrees regardless of where the credits are earned. Adelman's (2009) analogy between the euro and the "common currency" provided by ECTS credits is helpful. Both are abstract indicators of value that participating parties agree to accept at face value. And just as a wallet of euros can make travel easier than one stocked with many different national currencies, so, too, can a transcript vouched for by ECTS encourage travel across educational borders (Adelman).

ECTS relates also to the issue of accountability in that the credits it registers are supposed to reflect comparable estimates of student workload, which are in turn meant to embody an understanding of the learning objectives of a course and the time required to achieve them. Even more recently, the mission of ECTS has expanded further. It now "informs curriculum design and quality assurance" (ECTS, 2008).

Other initiatives associated with (but not formally within) Bologna include the Lisbon Convention of 1997, described in chapter 2, p. 26, as a Bologna precursor, which sets forth principles for the evaluation of educational qualifications; the diploma supplement, a convention for documenting educational accomplishments to ensure their ready interpretation and acceptance; Eurydice, a program for the collection and dissemination of data concerning higher education; and the EU's 2000 Lisbon Strategy, a more sweeping and in some ways duplicative agenda for the acceleration of economic growth. All will be discussed later, though it is worth noting at once that Bologna is now more and more often described as aligned with the Lisbon Strategy.

Working With Other Organizations

In addition to working with other programs, those engaged in the Bologna Process have managed complex relationships involving other organizations and agencies that share a stake in higher education. We have glanced at the efforts of UNESCO with regard to higher education as long ago as the 1950s, but we have not yet acknowledged the more direct role of a particular UNESCO agency, the European Center for Higher Education (CEPES).

Envisioned in 1970 by the executive board of UNESCO and soon thereafter authorized by the UNESCO General Conference, the centre opened its headquarters two years later in Bucharest, Romania, where it remains. Anticipating many of the priorities of Bologna, the center took as its particular province promotion of the cooperative study of higher education and the encouragement of student and faculty exchanges (CEPES, 2008).

Unlike the sponsors of some more self-determining initiatives, CEPES has conceived of its recent mission as one directly complementing the main concerns of Bologna. In fact, embedded in its statement of mission is its role as "a consultative member of a Follow-up Group of the Bologna Process (BFUG), which is tasked with the implementation of the Bologna Process goals" (Mission, 2008). Hence its current activities include tracking higher education legislation, encouraging new approaches to governance, defining such issues as institutional autonomy and academic freedom, promoting advances in quality assurance and accreditation, and improving relations between higher education and industry.

The level of supportive activity CEPES maintains with regard to Bologna may be inferred from updates prepared for the BFUG. For instance, a report delivered prior to a March 2007 meeting offers detailed information on 10 projects that embody a shared interest. These include a seminar on "the Cultural Heritage and Academic Values of the European University," collaboration on the development of "ranking methodologies" in higher education, the publication of papers on contractual regulations governing academic staff, continued attention to the credentialing issues addressed by the Lisbon Convention, participation in an EU project on "benchmarking," and a study of demographic trends likely to affect the functioning of institutions of higher education (Mission, 2008).

Another organization with a strong interest in the Bologna Process, the Council of Europe (COE), includes 47 countries as members and invites representatives of four nations and one state—the United States, Canada, Japan, Mexico, and Vatican City—as observers. Distinct from the European Council, which convenes EU heads of state twice a year, the COE was established in 1949 to promote human rights and the rule of law, to support greater cultural consciousness within the Continent, to seek political stability through reform, and to convene collaborative initiatives to solve widely shared problems, such as discrimination against minorities, terrorism, bioethics, and cybercrime (COE, 2008).

One prescient expression of the COE mission from the perspective of Bologna appears in a pact signed in Paris in 1954 promoting the protection of the European cultural heritage. Under the terms of the European Cultural

Convention, participating governments agreed to encourage their citizens to become more fully acquainted with one another's languages and cultures. To this end, the signers pledged to expand the mobility of scholars while "promoting cultural activities of European interest" (Cultural Convention, 1954). As Terry (2008) notes, nations seeking to participate in the Bologna Process must first subscribe to the convention—which may help to explain why only Belarus, the only one of all major European countries not subscribing to the convention, has not joined Bologna.

Interested and Influential Parties

The Sorbonne and Bologna declarations as well as the early stages of the Process prompted concerns that those guiding the reform of higher education in Europe were not taking advantage of consultation with those most directly concerned: institutions of higher education and their faculty members and students. The education ministers corrected course, and consultations with university and student representatives have become steadily more influential. Two groups in particular, the European University Association (EUA) and the European Students' Union (ESU) have taken especially prominent roles.

Formed by the fusion in 2001 between the Association of European Universities and the Confederation of European Union Rectors' Conferences, the EUA now represents institutions in 46 countries. By its own description, "The Association's mandate in the Bologna process, contribution to EU research policy-making and relations with intergovernmental organisations, European institutions and international associations, ensure its capacity to debate issues which are crucial for universities in relation to higher education, research and innovation" (EUA, 2008).

As a "consultative member" of the Bologna Process, the EUA has exerted considerable influence through its sponsorship of the Trends reports prior to the biennial conferences and through publications and Web pages explaining the Process to the public. The EUA is now one of four members of the E4 group that includes the ESU, the European Association for Quality Assurance in Higher Education (ENQA), and the European Association of Institutions in Higher Education (EURASHE).

The ESU has emerged through the decade as a strong supporter of the Process in principle and as a vocal critic with regard to its pace and the scope of its implementation. With a mission "to represent and promote the educational, social, economic and cultural interests of students at a European level," the ESU (until May 2007 the National Unions of Students in Europe,

or ESIB), represents and coordinates the work of 49 national student organizations in 38 countries. Before 1999, by its own acknowledgment, the ESU pursued only a limited range of student-centered concerns. But approval of the Bologna Process changed that by necessitating "a greater presence by student representatives on a European level" (ESU, 2008). Subsequently the ESU has become a recognized observer in the Bologna Process and a member of the E4.

In its role as supportive skeptic, endorsing the Process in general but scrutinizing closely its claims of accomplishment, particularly at the national and institutional levels, the ESU has weighed in on a number of issues. Through its biennial commentaries, titled *Bologna With Student Eyes* (ESU 2003, 2005a, 2007, 2009b), and its *Bologna Black Book* (ESU, 2005b), the ESU has expressed concerns about impediments to access, financial and otherwise; questioned the depth of consultation taking place on issues of accountability; drawn attention to lapses in progress camouflaged by upbeat national reports; and kept the social dimension of the process steadily in the forefront.

The ESU has also sounded alarms about possible distortions of the Process. For instance, the ESU argues that a strong emphasis on the contributions of higher education to the economy must be offset by the reaffirmation of higher education as a public good. Similarly, the determination to increase the competitiveness of Europe must not promote a "privatisation agenda" that the ESU believes would lead to a "brain drain" out of Europe (ESU, 2009b, pp. 14, 105). And countries must not misappropriate the Bologna Process by using it as cover for controversial national reform agendas unrelated to or even inconsistent with the priorities of Bologna.

The list of E4 members was completed by the addition of European Association of Institutions in Higher Education (EURASHE, 2009), which includes institutional and association members as well as doctoral institutions represented by the EUA, and of ENQA (2009), which brings together quality assurance agencies in Bologna member states and provides a clearinghouse for information concerning assessment and evaluation.

Two other participating organizations are the Education International Pan-European Structure, speaking for powerful labor organizations that represent teachers (Education International and the European Trade Union Committee for Education), and Business Europe: The Confederation of European Business. Both have contributed reports to the BFUG.

Birthing Lessons From Bologna

As the next chapter indicates, Bologna did not emerge in 1999 with all its priorities in place, with all its participants on board, or with all its processes

and ancillary activities firmly fixed. But in comparison with many higher education reform initiatives in the United States through the past few decades, the Bologna Process was carefully conceived, judiciously and pragmatically framed, and well organized for success—at least, from an international perspective.

One vantage point from which to appreciate the lessons of Bologna is offered by an undertaking of potentially similar breadth in the United States, the U.S. secretary of education's 2005–2006 Commission on the Future of Higher Education. Instead of working from a determinedly partisan standpoint, as was the case with the so-called Spellings Commission, those engaged with the Bologna Process have by and large sought to separate the agenda of higher education reform from other European issues, such as the ratification of a European constitution, that might have proved distracting or divisive. Given that the ratification process was not complete until November 2009, with the signing on of the Czech Republic, Bologna's relative detachment from broader political issues appears remarkably prudent.

And rather than frame a forceful and judgmental mandate in terms likely to alienate many interested parties, as was the case with the charge to the U.S. commission, the Bologna Process issued a brief declaration of principle and began the work of drawing in concerned constituencies. Further, instead of presuming to "chart the future," as the 2006 report of the U.S. commission sought to do (Commission, 2006), the Bologna Declaration identified a handful of action lines for immediate attention and regular monitoring. And, finally, unlike the U.S. commission, which responded reproachfully to expressions of concern regarding its report, the ministers engaged with Bologna have demonstrated a readiness to track and respond to emerging misgivings. As already noted, when the results of their well-intended collaboration at the Sorbonne gave the impression of an exclusive and bureaucratic process, the ministers made certain that their agenda for the following meeting at Bologna would emphasize inclusiveness, transparency, and respect for the diversity of European higher education.

There are important lessons for the United States in the early stages of the Bologna Process. They will continue to arise as we review what Bologna has accomplished, and they will be further expressed in the proposals offered by Adelman (2009) and in the largely complementary suggestions that conclude this book. Of course, Bologna still has another decade to go, but, even now, compared with the limited half-life of most recent programs for higher education reform in the United States, Bologna offers useful procedural pointers, such as the following:

- *Acknowledge and build on reforms already evolving.* By contrast with the Spellings Commission, which showed little acquaintance with reforms under way relative to its priorities, the Bologna Process has sought as allies a number of initiatives consistent with its goals (Lederman, 2007).
- *Recognize and celebrate areas within the academy that are emerging as exemplary.* At the beginning of the Bologna Process and at each biennial stage, those responsible for taking stock have expressed concerns only after recognizing and commending progress. By contrast, though the U.S. approach to disciplinary accreditation through peer review has become for many around the world a standard for comparison and emulation, the Spellings Commission appeared to regard accreditation only as a problem to be fixed.
- *Bring other, similarly interested organizations into the tent.* Those engaged with the Bologna Process have invited the support of interested groups, listened to what they have had to say, and made use of their work where appropriate. Members of the Spellings Commission summoned witnesses, which is not at all the same thing, and otherwise remained well insulated behind staff members who had been assigned the lion's share of the work.
- *Avoid counterproductive assertions of bureaucratic authority.* Through its reliance on a rotating secretariat and an avoidance of a discrete bureaucratic structure, the Bologna Process has maintained an agility and responsiveness not usually associated with undertakings of its scope. By contrast, what goodwill the Spellings Commission enjoyed following the release of its recommendations was undermined by the U.S. Department of Education's proceeding to initiate the formal process of rules making even in the absence of legislation—a move that proved offensive even to Republican leaders. Those objecting found it difficult to accept the Education Department's claim that increased federal control of higher education was not the object.
- *Set achievable goals and regularly monitor their accomplishment in ways that build accountability and support.* As suggested earlier, the Bologna Declaration, while an important statement of well-conceived objectives, has been less important in day-to-day terms than the activities, reports, and concerns associated with an evolving process. In one sense, the commitment to developing biennial objectives manageable over a two-year period has allayed anxieties that the Process might move too far, too fast. Bologna has not overwhelmed its supporters. But in another sense, the biennial conferences, with their protocols

emphasizing accountability and visibility, have made it clear just how seriously the objectives are meant be taken.

Such suggestions are hardly remarkable, but those committed to genuine and enduring reform in the United States might do well to attend to them—and to other lessons, salutary and cautionary, apparent in the implementation of the Bologna Process through the course of a remarkable decade.

4

WORDS TO ACTIONS
Bologna, Prague, Berlin

T he most constructive and pragmatic decision taken by the ministers' meeting at Bologna was their commitment to a series of biennial conferences beginning in 2001 in Prague. These conferences would invite new nations to the table, monitor the growth of the Bologna community, assess the rate of progress with regard to the action lines, consider expansion of the project's scope, address emerging problems and concerns, and develop assignments for the succeeding biennium. More than any other single indicator, the continued vitality of these conferences has attested to the momentum of the Process and to the resilience of the understanding that created it. While not all positive developments with respect to the Bologna accords can be attributed directly to these conferences, it is difficult to imagine comparable progress without them. By following them, we follow Bologna's evolution during its first decade.

Yet the brief conferences held every two years, while convenient mileposts, have been significant principally because of the work done in preparation for and in response to them. As the participating nations have endeavored to respond following each conference to the priorities clarified through the consensus of their education ministers, other interested parties, including the Bologna Follow-Up Group (BFUG) and the consultative members, have scheduled seminars on various issues, entertained emerging points of view, encouraged further actions, recorded accomplishments, and offered recommendations through biennial reviews and advisories.

The most substantive of these biennial accounts have been the Stocktaking (2005, 2007, 2009) reports commissioned by the ministers themselves, the European University Association Trends reports (EUA Trends I, 1999; EUA Trends II, 2001; EUA Trends III, 2003; EUA Trends IV, 2005; EUA Trends V, 2007), and the *Bologna With Student Eyes* reports developed by the ESU (2003, 2005a, 2007, 2009b). Together, these go a long way toward documenting and explaining the course of the Bologna Process, but they have also had an important role in influencing and furthering that course.

After Bologna

The ministers who signed the Bologna Declaration in June 1999 voiced a determination that it stand for "not just a political statement, but a binding commitment to an action programme" (Bologna Explanation, 2000). Because the Bologna Process was not to have the authority to enforce compliance with its objectives, this assertion of a shared obligation was particularly important. Making good on their word, the ministers met three months later to create the two groups responsible for implementation. As noted in chapter 3, the BFUG included representatives from all of the signatory countries, envoys from European higher education associations, and a number of observers. A smaller working group, chaired by the European Union (EU) presidency (a biannual rotation among the EU states), included the EU troika (the foreign affairs minister in service to the acting presidency, the EU secretary-general for foreign policy, and the EU commissioner in charge of external relations), a representative of a Bologna participating nation, and representatives of higher education.

Not all activities relevant to Bologna were encompassed by the Process. For instance, prompted in part by the opportunity to play a more influential role, a convention of European higher education institutions in March 2001 resulted in the consolidation into the EUA of two formerly discrete organizations, the European Universities Rectors' Conferences and the Association of European Universities. Similarly, the European Students' Union (ESU, formerly the National Unions of Students in Europe [ESIB]) met to determine how student perspective on Bologna might most effectively be advanced. The result was the series of reports expressing a perspective "from student eyes." And at many other meetings as well the Bologna Process made its way onto the agenda. The number of events and meetings scheduled with reference to the Bologna Process between 1999 and 2001 alone suggests the strength of its initial impact on European higher education.

The record of the earliest stages of the Process is most effectively summarized in the May 2001 precursor to the later Stocktaking reports, *Furthering the Bologna Process*, developed for the BFUG by Pedro Lourtie (2001). Among the first initiatives were international seminars focused on the documentation and transfer of academic credits, on the bachelor's degree within the plan for a two-cycle (later three-cycle) structure, and on transnational education. And there was progress to report with regard to each of the action lines. The commitment of the ministers to creating "easily readable and comparable degrees" was supporting continued movement toward "a 'bachelor'/'master' structure" even though some lengthy professional programs leading directly to the master's remained intact. Backing for important improvements in the transfer and evaluation of credits, namely, adoption of the principles of the Lisbon Recognition Convention, use of the European Credit Transfer and Accumulation System (ECTS), and offering the diploma supplement, appeared unanimous. And interest in quality assurance and accreditation was seen as widespread "at least as a topic for discussion." Hence the ministers convening in Prague would be able to point to progress on all of the early goals of the Bologna Process—greater international competitiveness for the European higher education, greater mobility within Europe and among degree levels, and heightened employability of graduates (Lourtie, 2001, p. 2).

But Lourtie (2001) does not confine himself to documenting progress. He also "dwells on scenarios for the future" (p. 1) and anticipates points of stress. He offers a caution, for instance, against an overemphasis on the economic priorities of the process. "The fact that employability is one of the main goals of the Bologna Declaration does not mean that it is the only aim of higher education," he says, referring to "broader objectives in terms of personal and social development" (p. 18). He notes in particular the adverse reaction of student observers to the designation of students as clients, customers, and consumers. And he encourages greater attention to significant differences among institutions and national higher education cultures. "There are many different types of providers," he observes (p. 18). For instance, research represents a critical priority in some institutions, while instruction is the main concern for many transnational providers. Moreover, efforts to balance an overriding emphasis on employability with "the objectives of social, cultural and human development in general" are likely to reveal "differences in understanding" among countries and among institutions within countries (p. 19). Given such differences, Lourtie suggests attention be given "to what extent we all share the same values concerning higher education" so that values "common to the whole European Higher Education Area" may be more clearly defined (p. 19).

Lourtie (2001) calls also for a more concerted effort to define learning outcomes. Development of a European credit system should build on the existing ECTS, he acknowledges, but a system based on workload rather than on competencies would not represent genuine reform; that is, the creation of a common degree structure will be of value only to the extent that "convergence at the level of programme duration" corresponds to "convergence in terms of learning outcomes" (p. 20). And progress toward improved quality assurance and accreditation will require agreement on a common reference standard, though issues as to responsibility for the creation of such a standard are "delicate and controversial" (p. 21). In short, "It is necessary to reach some agreement on what are the objectives and learning outcomes, in terms of knowledge, competencies and skills, that are relevant to be sanctioned by a degree in a given subject area" (p. 20).

Finally, while acknowledging the gathering momentum of the process, Lourtie (2001) expresses some misgivings about the "rather informal basis" on which it is operating, "with no clearly specified mandate for the steering and enlarged follow-up groups, but to push the process forward" (p. 25). The Process should make its mandates specific, establish guidelines for the participation of new countries and organizations, and create an organizational structure that would "ensure that the process is efficiently run and the goals arc fulfilled" (p. 25).

The actions that followed at the Prague and Berlin conferences make it clear that the ministers, with the benefit of many reports and commentaries, including the April 2001 EUA Trends II report and the perspective expressed by the students, gave very close attention to the one they had asked Pedro Lourtie (2001) to prepare.

Prague

The 2001 Prague Summit on Higher Education convened May 18–19 with a cast of characters considerably larger than that present at Bologna. Participating countries at the time numbered 32 because of the addition of EU member Cyprus and non-EU members Turkey and Croatia. And the summit welcomed for the first time official representatives of the EUA, the ESIB (now the ESU), the European Association of Institutions in Higher Education (EURASHE), and the European Commission. Expansion from one perspective might appear to represent an important step toward many of Bologna's aspirations, but it would create far greater variation in the pace and scope of implementation nation by nation.

A considerably more ambitious agenda emerged from the Prague summit. After reaffirming the six broad goals set forth at Bologna, the ministers in their statement acknowledge documented progress as they encourage a sustained, more robust effort. First, while maintaining respect for "the underlying diversity of qualifications" (Prague Communiqué, 2001, p. 1) from one university to another, the ministers urge that higher education systems and institutions with the help of the European Network of Information Centres (ENIC) and the National Academic Recognition Information Centres (NARIC) continue working toward a "simple, efficient and fair recognition" (p. 1) of academic credentials. Second, while noting "with satisfaction" progress toward "a system essentially based on two main cycles" (p. 1), undergraduate and graduate, they call for redoubled effort. Third, the ministers affirm that the Bologna call for "a system of credits" (p. 2) should remain a prominent priority. Progress toward the adoption of a common and coherent credits system should continue, use of the diploma supplement should increase, and efforts to increase mobility, as framed in a 2000 Mobility Action Plan, should be expanded.

In addition to reaffirming the six initiatives agreed to in Bologna, the ministers agreed to add to the agenda three additional priorities:

1. Renewed attention to providing access to lifelong learning, "necessary to face the challenges of competitiveness" and to promote "social cohesion, equal opportunities and the quality of life" (p. 2).
2. Efforts to enhance the "attractiveness of European higher education to students from Europe and other parts of the world" (p. 2). This priority recalls the Sorbonne determination that Europe should regain its stature as the world's most inviting and prestigious provider of higher education.
3. Endorsement of the social dimension in the Bologna process, in this instance expressed by a commitment to make the process more inclusive of faculty members, students, and teachers at the institutional level (p. 2).

The Prague summit gave its attention to these new priorities and to the continuing six action lines. But one overriding emphasis emerged, namely, the means of documenting and attesting to educational quality. This original element in the Bologna recommendations would require the full cooperation of universities, faculty members, and students in the creation of "close European cooperation and mutual trust in and acceptance of national quality assurance systems" (Prague Communiqué, 2001, p. 3). In tandem with the development of "accreditation/certification mechanisms," such systems would not only promote high standards, but also support the comparability of credentials throughout Europe. Indeed, a shared commitment to quality would provide "the basic underlying condition for trust, relevance, mobility, compatibility and attractiveness in the European Higher Education Area" (pp. 2–3). A one-page statement by the EUA (2003) immediately following notes "with satisfaction" that efforts to develop effective approaches to assessment could facilitate both the "comparability of qualifications" across Europe and the integration of teaching and research.

Looking ahead, the ministers asked the BFUG to schedule seminars on five issues: "cooperation concerning accreditation and quality assurance, recognition issues and the use of credits in the Bologna process, the development of joint degrees, the social dimension, with specific attention to obstacles to mobility, and the enlargement of the Bologna process" (Prague Communiqué, 2001, p. 3). The ministers also scheduled a new follow-up meeting for 2003 in Berlin.

From Prague to Berlin

In preparing for their 2003 meeting in the German capital, the ministers faced a formidable array of documents intended to inform, guide, and influence their deliberations: reports from the issues-based seminars requested by the Prague Communiqué (2001), the ESU's 2003 *Bologna With Student Eyes* and the 2003 EUA Trends III commissioned from Pavel Zgaga (2003), *Bologna Process Between Prague and Berlin*. In addition, they would have the benefit of a Web site that provided all the submitted papers, a record of higher education legislation in European countries, and a glossary elucidating the higher education vocabulary. When the ministers convened in Berlin, as Laurel Terry (2008) observes, "significant preparatory work had been done" (p. 163).

And significant preparatory work was needed given the expansion of the Bologna agenda from six action lines (readable and comparable degrees, the two-cycle system, a system for the registration of academic credit, promotion of mobility, quality assurance, and promotion of the European dimension in higher education) to nine (adding lifelong learning, the social dimension, and promoting the attractiveness of the European Higher Education Area [EHEA]).

Commendations and Concerns

All the major reports prepared in advance of the meeting in Berlin offer favorable views of progress made during the biennium, but for the first time they advance also recommendations for modification of the process. The most prominent of these recommendations concern the character of the discussions taking place, the pace of implementation, and the depth to which reform is penetrating at an institutional level from one nation to another.

Through its Trends III (2003) report, the EUA urges that Bologna deliberations become more inclusive. "If the EHEA is to become a reality, it has to evolve from governmental intentions and legislation to institutional structures and processes, able to provide for the intense exchange and mutual cooperation necessary for such a cohesive area" (p. 7). Although the EUA survey of faculty members, student leaders, and university administrators had revealed strong support for the principles of Bologna, its results suggested also that reforms imposed from the outside are unlikely to become "embedded" in institutional cultures. Bologna must therefore reach out more resolutely to the "essential actors" at the institutional level, those responsible for implementation of reform initiatives (p. 7). Moreover, reform initiatives must be integrated with university functions and operations to take their appropriate place among other priorities. In short, universities must be given the time "to transform legislative changes into meaningful academic aims and institutional realities" (p. 2).

The EUA also recommends that certain concepts characteristic of Bologna be given concrete meaning (EUA Trends III, 2003). For instance, how should employability be defined with regard to bachelor's programs? How, exactly, should the two tiers of the curriculum be aligned with one another to encourage easy passage from one to the other? How should workload-based credits be related to competency expectations within academic programs? How might higher education more effectively accommodate an increasingly diverse student body? What should be the relation between higher education and lifelong learning? What conditions should prevail so that access to mobility might be enhanced? And how might meaningful quality assurance procedures be developed?

Issues of pace arise from two other perspectives. The author of the BFUG report (Zgaga, 2003) acknowledges the considerable goodwill evident in the Process but expresses the concern that a greater sense of urgency may be needed to produce substantive results. For instance, "while dissemination of good practice [in curricular reform] is extremely valuable, it doesn't suffice to achieve the stated objectives" (p. 45). What is needed instead is "intensive work on an EHEA qualifications framework" as a stimulus to countries "only just starting to plan" national frameworks (p. 46). And while programmatic "particularities" and curricular idiosyncrasies may deserve some recognition in the construction of such frameworks, no program should be exempt from review solely on grounds of "diversity" (p. 45). Similarly, while interest in the development of joint doctoral programs across national boundaries is commendable, a widely shared commitment to "more structured Doctoral studies in Europe" leading to "a transparent, readable and

Convening in Berlin

By the time the expanded group of ministers gathered in Berlin, the Bologna Process had been under way for nearly four years. Welcoming seven additional members, including Russia, the ministers sought to guide a process encompassing 40 countries. As many of the preparatory reports had suggested, it was time to take stock, to reaffirm the most important goals of Bologna, to place particular stress on some priorities, and to consider adding others. But because the ministers appeared persuaded that the process was still not moving forward quickly enough, much of the discussion focused on accelerating the reform. Accordingly, a headline summarizing the Berlin Communiqué would describe it as "a substantial document with concrete priorities for 2005" (Berlin News, 2003). And the priorities would prove not only more substantive, but also, because of a more systematic process requiring measurements against a firm intermediate deadline, more compelling.

Only one new action line emerged, that concerning doctoral studies, and it was defined as an extension of an existing action line, a further stage in creating a uniform structure. The two-cycle system, aligning undergraduate studies with studies at the graduate level, would henceforth be regarded as three cycles: undergraduate, master's, doctoral. Issues of transparency, quality assurance, common vocabulary, and the like, already prompting reforms to bachelor's and master's programs, would now inform the third cycle also. The move also had the advantage of aligning the priorities of Bologna more closely with those of the European Research Area (ERA) created by the EU in 2000 as an element in the Lisbon Strategy.

Of all the issues discussed, quality assurance, which had emerged as an emphasis in the Prague discussions, was again the most prominent. As Pedro Lourtie (2003) observes, there is good reason for such prominence, as the mutual trust that relies on reliable and credible assessment is vital to the success of all of the action lines. Hence, in their Berlin Communiqué (2003), the ministers place concerns with quality "at the heart of the setting up of a European Higher Education Area" and commit themselves to the further development of "mutually shared" means and standards for quality assurance at the institutional, national, and European levels (Berlin Communiqué, p. 3). Noting an EUA pilot involving annual studies focused on particular themes (research management, teaching and learning, etc.), the ministers instructed the European Association for Quality Assurance in Higher Education (ENQA) to work with other sources of quality assurance expertise to foster a consensus on institution-based quality assurance standards and procedures based on a system of peer review.

The ambitious timetable set forth for this process calls for participating nations to move toward national quality assurance systems that would define the responsibilities of concerned institutions and agencies, provide for the evaluation of programs and institutions according to internal and external assessment, and offer a system of accreditation or certification. Moreover, the member states would work together toward specifying the "workload, level, learning outcomes, competencies, and profile" (Berlin Communiqué, 2003, p. 4) for the cycles being implemented while collaborating with other members on an overarching framework of standards and expectations. Critical to this initiative would be the Tuning Project, discussed in detail in chapter 10, through which professors collaborate on the development of specifications within their disciplines. And a further complement would lie in the creation of a European Qualifications Framework (EQF) for lifelong learning.

The characteristic reluctance in the Bologna Process to draw on relevant experience elsewhere, particularly that of the United States, again is evident. For instance, while the ENQA must implement peer review as a critical element in accreditation, there is no mention of the world's longest tradition of quality assurance peer review, that of the United States. The extensive experience of regional and professional accreditors in the United States could offer those engaged in the Bologna Process some best practices and some warning flags. But the Bologna vision at the midpoint of the decade did not extend to the West. And that might be one reason why the ministers so greatly underestimated the time required for the development of national accountability standards. By the time of the 2009 Leuven/Louvain-la-Neuve conference, most Bologna participants had yet to affirm such standards and many were not close to doing so.

With its charge considerably expanded, the ENQA indicated that it would henceforth include members from all Bologna states, that it would reconsider its own organizational structure with regard to its triple task (providing services to members, sustaining a policy forum, facilitating transnational evaluations), and that it would move toward the qualitative registration of European quality assurance agencies: public, private, and professional.

Accounting for Credits

Another major thrust of the Berlin discussions was an interest in upgrading the ECTS from its important role as a clearinghouse for the transfer of academic credits into a site documenting also the accumulation of credits—a kind of pan-European registrar. And consistent with that interest, the ministers also made a commitment to providing the degree supplement to every graduate no later than 2005—as a matter of routine and at no cost to the student. Both initiatives were closely related to one of the original Bologna goals, the promotion of increased mobility for students and teachers within Europe. And neither would be fully realized in Bologna's first decade.

The ministers in Berlin noted with satisfaction an increase in mobility but declared their intent to reduce still further any remaining impediments. To this end, they expressed a particular interest in assuring the portability of national loans and grants. And they urged that the goal of increased mobility be extended more explicitly to doctoral and postdoctoral study, where the goal of joint (or European) doctorates might be pursued through a 2004–05 pilot study (Berlin Communiqué, 2003).

In a broader sense, this more explicit commitment to a European identity for higher education could inform the development of joint degrees built on integrated curricula at all levels. A consolidated curriculum development project would, it was hoped, lead first to the offering of joint master's programs as early as 2004 (Berlin Communiqué, 2003). And a Europe offering joint degrees on a continent without educational borders would align well with the Bologna vision of attractive, open European higher education. The ministers agreed to accelerate this process by extending scholarships to as many as 8,000 students from Europe and other continents through the Erasmus Mundus program. And to enhance Europe's capacity to attract students from other continents, the ministers pledged support for a marketing strategy (Berlin Communiqué).

In sum, while affirming all the Bologna priorities, the ministers at Berlin identified three intermediate priorities destined for particular emphasis in the ensuing biennium:

- The development of comparable (if not uniform) commitments to, methods for, and documentation of assessing the quality of educational programs.
- Broad adoption of the two-cycle system (with the third, doctoral, cycle now included) and of a widely accepted EQF.
- A shared commitment to framing—and validating—comparable, clearly defined degrees and their equivalent associated periods of study. (Berlin Communiqué, 2003, pp. 3–5)

But as the ministers sought especially to increase the pace of reform under the Bologna umbrella, they also wanted to make certain that Bologna would continue to serve European economic aspirations. Seemingly turning a deaf ear to student concerns about the perceived commodification of higher education, the ministers urged instead that Bologna be regarded as integral to the Lisbon Strategy, an aggressive statement of the EU's determination to make the continent by 2010 "the most competitive and dynamic knowledge-based economy in the world, capable of sustainable economic growth with more and better jobs and greater social cohesion" (Lisbon Statement, 2000, p. 2). The political appeal in an alignment of Bologna and Lisbon is not difficult to understand. The problematical consequences of that alignment would emerge over time.

The news summary approved for release following the Berlin Communiqué effectively captures the urgency of the Berlin discussions (Berlin News, 2003). The communiqué should not be regarded as "just more of what we saw in the past." In their priorities and their mandate for stocktaking, ministers emphasized above all "speeding up the realisation of the European Higher Education Area" (Berlin Communiqué, 2003, p. 1) With the countdown to the next meeting in Bergen under way, "Governments, institutions, quality assurance bodies and everyone else will have to work hard to meet the obligations decided upon in Berlin" (Berlin News, 2003).

And they would, to be sure. But hard enough?

frameworks for the degree cycles. *A Framework for Qualifications of the European Higher Education Area* (Framework, 2005) would provide a broad standard against which national frameworks could be developed and measured. By defining "goals, priorities and assumptions of higher education" in the light of Bologna Process objectives, the framework would define "what a learner knows, understands and is able to do on the basis of a given qualification—that is, it shows the expected learning outcomes for a given qualification." Application of the framework standards should reveal further the extent to which a particular degree provides "a broad, advanced knowledge base" as "preparation for the labour market." But the framework speaks also of "personal development" and "preparation for life as active citizens in a democratic society" (Framework, p. 7).

As a context for its recommendations, the working group had considered existing national frameworks and developed three broad observations. In its report, *A Framework for Qualifications of the European Higher Education Area,* the group observes that, first, degree-level expectations should reflect the advice of "all relevant stakeholders" (Framework, 2005, p. 54). Second, they should define widely agreed-upon purposes. Finally, they should support public confidence in higher education credentials by linking cycle-specific qualifications to academic standards and quality assurance programs.

Consistent with these principles, the group recommended a framework broad enough to accommodate significant variations at the national level. One source lay in the "Dublin descriptors" (n.d.)—so called because they were developed at meetings in Dublin in 2002 and 2004 of a Joint Quality Initiative informal group. But the overarching EHEA framework reflected a broader and more ambitious aim, "to serve as a reference point for those creating national frameworks" (Bergan, 2007, p. 163). This framework was intended to be not so specific as to force uniformity on the nations, but "to make sense of diversity—or rather to ensure a balance between diversity and unity" (Bergan, p. 163).

Through rubrics associated with the three cycles (corresponding with the bachelor's, master's, and doctoral degrees), the EHEA framework is meant to provide "generic statements of typical expectations of achievements and abilities associated with awards that represent the end of each of a [*sic*] Bologna cycle" (Framework, 2005, p. 9).

For example, students who complete the first cycle (bachelor's degree) would be expected to present "knowledge and understanding . . . that includes some aspects that will be informed by knowledge of the forefront of their field of study," to "have the ability to gather and interpret relevant . . . to inform judgments that include reflection on relevant social, scientific or ethical issues," and to "have developed those learning skills that are

5

URGENCY AND UNDERSTANDING

Bergen and London

The Bologna Follow-Up Group (BFUG) responded to the priorities set forth in Berlin by committing itself to an ambitious work plan for 2003–2005. Objectives to be accomplished prior to the 2005 Bergen Ministerial Conference would include developing overarching cycle-specific qualifications (i.e., degree-level rubrics) for the European Higher Education Area (EHEA) as a whole, providing oversight for the quality assurance project assigned to the European Association for Quality Assurance in Higher Education (ENQA), scheduling seminars on topics ranging from distance education to accreditation, and carrying out the stocktaking exercise the ministers requested. The process would no longer rely exclusively on goodwill. Participants would be expected to work hard to meet the obligations.

Because the Berlin meeting in 2003 had emphasized accelerating implementation of the Bologna Process—but had failed to address many of the concerns identified in studies developed prior to the meeting—it was likely that the meeting in Bergen, fully six years into the implementation of Bologna, would be especially pivotal. Accomplishments documented through the perspectives of the big three reports—the European University Association's (EUA) Trends IV (2005), the European Student Union (ESU) *Bologna With Student Eyes* (2005a), and the BFUG's own report (2005)—would offer the ministers convening in Bergen considerable grounds for optimism. But the impressive gains on several fronts would be viewed in the context of some noteworthy misgivings.

Qualifications and Expectations

As the meeting in Bergen approached, it became clear that much progress had been made in the development of pan-European

URGENCY AND UNDERSTANDING

Bergen and London

The Bologna Follow-Up Group (BFUG) responded to the priorities set forth in Berlin by committing itself to an ambitious work plan for 2003–2005. Objectives to be accomplished prior to the 2005 Bergen Ministerial Conference would include developing overarching cycle-specific qualifications (i.e., degree-level rubrics) for the European Higher Education Area (EHEA) as a whole, providing oversight for the quality assurance project assigned to the European Association for Quality Assurance in Higher Education (ENQA), scheduling seminars on topics ranging from distance education to accreditation, and carrying out the stocktaking exercise the ministers had requested. The process would no longer rely exclusively on goodwill. Participants would be expected to work hard to meet the obligations.

Because the Berlin meeting in 2003 had emphasized accelerating the implementation of the Bologna Process—but had failed to address many of the concerns identified in studies developed prior to the meeting—it seemed likely that the meeting in Bergen, fully six years into the implementation of Bologna, would be especially pivotal. Accomplishments documented through the perspectives of the big three reports—the European University Association's (EUA) Trends IV (2005), the European Students' Union's (ESU) *Bologna With Student Eyes* (2005a), and the BFUG's Stocktaking (2005)—would offer the ministers convening in Bergen considerable ground for optimism. But the impressive gains on several fronts would have to be viewed in the context of some noteworthy misgivings.

Qualifications and Expectations

As the meeting in Bergen approached, it became clear that significant progress had been made in the development of pan-European qualifications frameworks for the degree cycles. *A Framework for Qualifications of the European Higher Education Area* (Framework, 2005) would provide a broad standard against which national frameworks could be developed and measured. By defining "goals, priorities and assumptions of higher education" in the light of Bologna Process objectives, the framework would define "what a learner knows, understands and is able to do on the basis of a given qualification—that is, it shows the expected learning outcomes for a given qualification." Application of the framework standards should reveal further the extent to which a particular degree provides "a broad, advanced knowledge base" as "preparation for the labour market." But the framework speaks also of "personal development" and "preparation for life as active citizens in a democratic society" (Framework, p. 7).

As a context for its recommendations, the working group had considered existing national frameworks and developed three broad observations. In its report, *A Framework for Qualifications of the European Higher Education Area,* the group observes that, first, degree-level expectations should reflect the advice of "all relevant stakeholders" (Framework, 2005, p. 54). Second, they should define widely agreed-upon purposes. Finally, they should support public confidence in higher education credentials by linking cycle-specific qualifications to academic standards and quality assurance programs.

Consistent with these principles, the group recommended a framework broad enough to accommodate significant variations at the national level. One source lay in the "Dublin descriptors" (n.d.)—so called because they were developed at meetings in Dublin in 2002 and 2004 of a Joint Quality Initiative informal group. But the overarching EHEA framework reflected a broader and more ambitious aim, "to serve as a reference point for those creating national frameworks" (Bergan, 2007, p. 163). This framework was intended to be not so specific as to force uniformity on the nations, but "to make sense of diversity—or rather to ensure a balance between diversity and unity" (Bergan, p. 163).

Through rubrics associated with the three cycles (corresponding with the bachelor's, master's, and doctoral degrees), the EHEA framework is meant to provide "generic statements of typical expectations of achievements and abilities associated with awards that represent the end of each of a [*sic*] Bologna cycle" (Framework, 2005, p. 9).

For example, students who complete the first cycle (bachelor's degree) would be expected to present "knowledge and understanding . . . that includes some aspects that will be informed by knowledge of the forefront of their field of study," to "have the ability to gather and interpret relevant data . . . to inform judgments that include reflection on relevant social, scientific or ethical issues," and to "have developed those learning skills that are

The EUA chose a different method and developed a different perspective. Unlike the earlier Trends reports, the 2005 version (EUA Trends IV) relied less on statistical inputs than on field research based on visits to 62 participating universities. The idea was to offer a picture of Bologna on the ground, to document the penetration of the action lines within the academy.

Again, much of the news was encouraging. In contrast with concerns that the EUA had reported just two years earlier, its researchers found on the campuses they visited a "general acceptance of the need for reforms" and a recognition that the proposed changes represent "an opportunity to address problems which have long been known to exist" (EUA Trends IV, 2005, p. 2). But issues remained: a lack of sufficient financial support for the reforms, restraints on institutional autonomy, particularly in some nations, and a perceived lack of continuity in the leadership of the Process. For further reform to continue, strong, sensitive leadership, "allowing enough space for internal deliberation," would be necessary (p. 4).

The most forceful expressions of concern are to be found in the student perspective, *Bologna With Student Eyes* (ESU, 2005a). There is skepticism to begin with about institutional progress reports: "Not all that glitters is gold" (p. 3). The authors suggest that an appearance of progress may have been achieved in some instances simply through the relabeling of existing programs—a suspicion corroborated by at least one other observer at the time, Chris Lorenz (2006). In many cases, the authors assert, the hard work involved in rethinking and revising processes, structure, and curricula has not taken place. Symptoms include the following:

- The first-cycle credential intended to provide entry to the labor market has not been widely accepted either by employers or by national agencies, and additional barriers between the first and second cycles have appeared.
- Many countries cannot credibly report any progress toward improved quality assurance.
- The diploma supplement is not yet being widely offered, and formal acceptance of the Lisbon Recognition Convention does not always translate into improved recognition procedures in the ratifying nations.
- Implementation of the European Council Transfer and Accumulation System (ECTS) has been superficial and its usefulness limited.
- Promises that students would be invited to deeper participation in the Bologna Process—especially in the development of quality assurance measures—have not been kept.

- "In almost none of the countries" is the social dimension of Bologna understood and showing results. A "change in mentality" is required. (ESU, 2005a, p. 6)

In addition to these various reports and perspectives there was also the documentation by UNESCO and the Council of Europe (COE) on progress toward expanding the availability of joint degrees. While never intended to invite massive enrollments, the initiative has gained symbolic value because of its potential for demonstrating substantive academic collaboration across the boundaries of nations, languages, and distinct educational cultures. Work accomplished at a joint June 2004 meeting of the European Network of Information Centres (ENIC) and National Academic Recognition Information Centers (NARIC) networks emphasized "building bridges between education systems and qualifications . . . in the European Region as well as between this region and other parts of the world" (Strasbourg, 2004, p. 2). Following Berlin, these bodies had crafted a recommendation regarding the recognition of such degrees and a corresponding operational memorandum as a supplement to the Lisbon Convention.

The Ministers at Bergen

The title of the ministers' Bergen Communiqué (2005), "The European Higher Education Area: Achieving the Goal," affirms substantive progress on the three priorities identified in Berlin for detailed follow-up: movement toward a consistent degree structure, greater regularity in the evaluation and recognition of educational credentials, and improvements in accountability. Yet if the 2005 Stocktaking, Trends, and ESU reports and the Bergen Communiqué (2005) all express a sense of optimism, reading them comparatively creates a somewhat more complex and nuanced impression.

By all accounts, progress toward the creation of a unified degree system throughout Europe was evident in the widespread implementation of the two cycles, undergraduate and graduate. Yet there remained "legislative obstacles to structural reform in a few countries" (EUA Trends IV, 2005, p. 4). And while some institutions had made the requisite investment in the pursuit of a highly complex process, it was clear that others had not undertaken substantive discussion at the curricular level or were picking and choosing among the Bologna priorities—what the ESU (2005a) report again described as an "à la carte" approach.

As one might expect from its reflection of institutional perspectives, the EUA Trends IV (2005) study places particular emphasis on the challenges involved in genuine structural reform. In the view of the authors, the impacts of the required "cultural and social transformation" require "much greater and more sophisticated analysis" (p. 4). Will society in time attach sufficient value to the new first-cycle academic credentials? Will those credentials serve the needs of the market and support the advancement of graduates beyond entry-level appointments? And will the required shift to a focus on learning outcomes find a reflection in pedagogical change? EUA Trends IV concludes that "more public debate on the reforms is needed" (p. 4).

The recommendations with regard to the overarching qualifications frameworks and the standards for quality assurance agencies had signified an important step forward to more clearly defined educational credentials, nation by nation, and to a broader understanding of the essentials of quality assurance. What remained was the work, nation by nation, to create compatible degree-level frameworks by 2010 and to commit to quality assurance structures and organizations for certification and registration.

Increased educational mobility, to be supported through "automatic recognition of qualifications across Europe" (EUA Trends IV, 2005, p. 5) was clearly gaining some ground, but, as the ESU (2005a) report had observed, there was still a long way to go toward making effective use of ECTS and the diploma supplement. And while 36 of the 45 Bologna members had ratified the Lisbon Recognition Convention and reconfirmed their commitment to full implementation of its principles (Bergen Communiqué, 2005), the practical realization of these principles over time would require a growth in understanding and a broad acceptance of clearly defined learning outcomes.

Accomplishing that? Still a challenge. Similarly, while ECTS might be gaining ground as a mechanism for student transfer, its role in guiding institutional curricula toward a credible convergence on the definition of academic credits was difficult to document. And the development of national action plans for recognition of foreign credentials, while an urgent need, would by itself offer little assurance on the curricular reforms necessary for real improvement in recognition protocols.

Looking Beyond Bergen

The ministers express justifiable satisfaction in the work done prior to Bergen on a range of fronts. But each of the areas of progress prompted a corresponding range of concerns. Steps toward a unified degree system were dogged by persistent doubts with regard to the employability of bachelor's degree recipients. Structural, cultural, and financial impediments to movement from one degree cycle to the next were evident. And it was not entirely clear how an emerging focus on lifelong learning and improved vocational education, given particular emphasis within the broader Lisbon Strategy, might be more effectively aligned with the other Bologna action lines.

A broader systemic issue in the Bologna approach to accountability became evident in a lack of clear distinctions among the various priorities of assessment. Broadly speaking, the means of assessment are conventionally divided into those focused on the measurement of institutional performance for reasons of quality assurance and comparative evaluation and those whose focus is on enabling institutions, programs, and teachers to become stronger and more effective. Although both forms of assessment have value, if they are not kept discrete they may conflict. For instance, it is one thing to ask a faculty member to submit to the measurement of student outcomes with respect to explicit learning objectives so that the instructor's course may become more effective. It is quite another to adjust the compensation of that faculty member according to assessment results. Either incentive can offer powerful motivation, but appealing simultaneously to professional values and to immediate self-interest can result in confusion and frustration. The same issues can apply to departments and institutions. So far as Bologna is concerned, is accountability, that is, quality assurance, the first priority of assessment? Or should assessment work primarily to strengthen courses and institutions? The response in the Bologna Process has been "both."

Having acknowledged the concerns raised in the various reports from stakeholders, the ministers themselves saw fit to identify certain "further challenges and priorities" (Bergen Communiqué, 2005, p. 3). For one thing, they expressed a determination that the commitment to improved consistency among academic structures, enhanced accountability, and more effective teaching should not undermine research and innovation. At the same time, while expressing wariness of overregulation, the ministers also "urge universities to ensure that their doctoral programmes promote interdisciplinary training and the development of transferable skills, thus meeting the needs of the wider employment market" (p. 4).

In addition, they reiterate, albeit with little detail, their recognition of the social dimension. Quality higher education should become "equally accessible to all" through the creation of "appropriate conditions" (Bergen Communiqué, 2005, p. 4) for students challenged by their social and economic backgrounds. And as the ministers urge institutions and students to take advantage of emerging incentives to mobility across national borders, they pledge to work within their respective systems to remove or reduce remaining obstacles by facilitating the issuance of visas and work permits.

The ministers also for the first time explicitly link their long-standing interest in improving the attractiveness of the EHEA with a commitment to broader cooperation "with other parts of the world" (Bergen Communiqué, 2005, p. 4). Asking the BFUG to develop "a strategy for the external dimension," the ministers appear to broaden their horizons somewhat—at least so far as "neighboring regions" (p. 5). They express an interest in spreading the Bologna gospel to other continents, look forward to international dialogue on issues of shared concern, and seek to create a broader exchange of ideas and experiences with appropriate partners.

Engaging Constituencies

In addition to acknowledging what had been accomplished and to issuing assignments, the ministers gave some attention also to concerns regarding consultation and inclusivity that had been voiced prior to and following the conference in Berlin two years earlier. Indeed, the opening section of the 2005 Bergen Communiqué responds directly to assertions by the EUA and the ESU that the Bologna Process should engage more directly those most specifically responsible for its implementation, that is, teachers, academic administrators, and students. Under the heading of "Partnership," the ministers offer an overture recognizing "the central role" of higher education institutions, faculty members, and students as partners in the Bologna process. The role of such partners was becoming increasingly important, in fact, "now that the necessary legislative reforms are largely in place" (Bergen Communiqué, p. 1). At the outset of their communiqué, the ministers encourage their partners "to continue and intensify their efforts to establish the EHEA" (p. 1). And a similar concern that employers were not as fully involved in the Bologna Process as they should be prompts an interest in "intensified cooperation" with "organisations representing business and the social partners" (p. 1).

Many of these issues arise from the Stocktaking (2005) report's proposal of priorities to be pursued during the ensuing biennium. These include a more deliberate approach to including employers in the Bologna conversations, a working group to address issues of access that had been raised most conspicuously by students, nation-by-nation reports on improvements in the recognition of foreign credentials, greater attention to the resources required for implementation of the Bologna Process, and continuation of the stocktaking process itself.

Hence, with a stirring assurance of their commitment to "quality and transparency," to "cultural diversity," to "public responsibility for higher education," to increased European competitiveness, to improved funding for institutions, and to enhanced autonomy, the ministers agreed to meet again in London in 2007 (Bergen Communiqué, 2005, p. 5). But they did one thing more. For the first time, they agreed that the formal establishment of the EHEA in 2010 would not be the end of the story. The ministers would begin to look beyond 2010 to the continuing development of the Bologna Process.

London 2007: Reaffirmation, Reconsideration

Following their meeting in London in May 2007, the Bologna education ministers would affirm considerable forward movement: "We are developing an EHEA based on institutional autonomy, academic freedom, equal opportunities and democratic principles that will facilitate mobility, increase employability and strengthen Europe's attractiveness and competitiveness" (London Communiqué, 2007, p. 1).

A shift in tone? Compared to earlier calls for the acceleration of the action lines through the strong leadership of national educational administrators, this recognition of the centrality of higher education institutions to the Bologna Process is striking. Also notable is the understanding that a changing world will require sustained adaptability from those engaged in furthering the priorities of the Process. Less evident is the earlier enthusiasm for convergence among different national systems of higher education. In its place appears a heightened respect for the diversity of institutions and systems. To be sure, the ministers reaffirm a commitment to greater "compatibility and comparability," but they do so while recognizing institutions not only as centers of "learning, research, creativity and knowledge transfer," but also as a vital means through which "the values on which our societies are built" are defined and transferred (London Communiqué, 2007, p. 1).

The London Communiqué (2007) thus represents a reaffirmation of Bologna's priorities and a recognition of important lessons learned: the complexity of higher education reform, the importance of distributed authority to effective and sustainable implementation, and the need for closer alignment between the Bologna agenda and other forces of change and reform.

The View Eight Years Out

Each of the biennial meetings offers an opportunity to take stock and refine assumptions, but the 2007 meeting in London emerged as an occasion for a candid assessment of progress to date and for acknowledgment of the job that lay ahead far into the future. The EUA view is representative: "that the cultural impact of the Bologna process has often been under-estimated, that there remains much work to be done throughout society, and that the European Higher Education Area will continue to be 'work in progress' well beyond 2010" (EUA Trends V, 2007, p. 5).

That perception appears also in the Berlin Declaration issued on March 18, 2007, by the ESU. While commending the Bologna Process as one path toward "a better Europe for all," the students express two concerns. The first is that implementation appears to be under way "at two different speeds," more slowly in the newer Bologna members than in the charter group. The second is that throughout Bologna some action lines were receiving too little emphasis (ESU Berlin, 2007, p. 1). For instance, the students contend that the European priority regarding expansion of access through a commitment to equal opportunity has not taken hold at the national level. Moreover, given an "upsurge of xenophobia all around Europe," they express skepticism regarding an increase in mobility on the part of students and faculty members. This must become a "core focus," they contend. The students charge also that the Bologna commitment to the recognition of prior learning has not prompted concrete actions at the national or institutional levels, and they urge, not for the first time, that students be regarded as partners, not merely as clients, in the development of programs of quality assurance (ESU Berlin, 2007).

The Berlin declaration anticipated a far more comprehensive overview provided in the subsequent edition of *Bologna With Student Eyes* (ESU, 2007). There, action line by action line, the students assert that accomplishments have been overstated in the official reports, that momentum has slowed, that awareness of Bologna remains for the most part limited to government and the academy, and that some elements of the Bologna commitment, most notably the social dimension, have been neglected. The indictment includes articles such as the following:

- Few countries (other than Nordic ones) "can claim satisfactory overall progress in the action lines" (p. 5).
- The social dimension is "the most neglected action line at national level" (p. 5).
- "In many countries reforms are only implemented superficially" (p. 5).
- Financial obstacles continue to inhibit mobility, and foreign students "are rarely treated equally to domestic students" (p. 6).
- "Since 2005 there has hardly been any improvement on the involvement of students" in quality assurance efforts (p. 6).

- "There is a substantial lack of real curricular reform throughout the EHEA." For example, there is an "alarming number" of reports that suggest implementation of the three-cycle system has been accomplished simply by dividing existing five-year programs into two parts. (pp. 5–8)

The students hence call for renewed emphasis on the social dimension of the process, they urge that stocktaking prior to the 2009 summit pay close attention to diversity within higher education and to the elimination of discrimination, and they call for a commitment to reducing economic barriers to higher education that are in some instances growing rather than receding (ESU, 2007).

These concerns are largely corroborated by the stocktaking commissioned by the ministers. As was the case two years earlier, the heart of the report from the BFUG (Stocktaking, 2007) lies in a scorecard with multiple indicators measuring progress nation by nation toward full implementation of the degree cycles, quality assurance programs, recognition reforms (Lisbon, ECTS, diploma supplement), evaluation of prior learning, and joint degrees. For instance, the report uses green to designate nations in which at least 90% of university students are participating in programs that reflect Bologna principles, while red identifies those with no legislation furthering Bologna (Stocktaking).

With its many colorful scorecards, the 88-page report for the most part substantiates the impressions set forth in the other reports but reaches a somewhat more benign interpretation of them. In sum, while there has been good progress toward achieving the Bologna goals by 2010, "there are still some challenges to be faced" (Stocktaking, 2007, p. 7). There had been broad implementation of the three-cycle degree system, of some national frameworks for qualifications compatible with the EHEA overarching framework, of the *Standards and Guidelines for Quality Assurance* approved at Bergen, of some joint degree programs, and of policies for recognition of prior learning. But like the external reports, the stocktaking exercise points to a lack of uniformity across Europe in the pace of implementation and concedes that different action lines have received greater or lesser attention. Hence it calls on the ministers to set "clear policy goals and specific targets," particularly with regard to "the third cycle, employability, recognition, lifelong learning, flexible learning paths and the social dimension" (Stocktaking, p. 10).

While urging the ministers to reaffirm their commitment to further progress across *all* the action lines—nations should no longer have the privilege of à la carte selections—the Stocktaking (2007) report defines an overriding priority, full implementation by 2010 of national qualifications frameworks based on learning outcomes. An important objective in itself, such frameworks are essential also to related Bologna action lines: quality assurance, credit transfer and accumulation systems, lifelong learning, flexible learning paths, and the social dimension.

The Glass Half Full

In light of all of these various concerns and recommendations, perhaps the most striking finding in EUA Trends V (2007) is the expanding ownership of the Bologna Process. Earlier Trends reports and ministerial communiqués had expressed the concern that Bologna was being perceived as a governmental, top-down initiative. But this report acknowledges a commendable shift in focus, from legislation and other governmental actions "to implementation of reforms within institutions." Correspondingly, EUA Trends V reports also an increasing sense of urgency at the institutional level, "with the vast majority of the 908 institutions involved stating that they consider it vital to move rapidly towards a European Higher Education Area" (p. 7). While questions and concerns remain, the glass appears more than half full.

- More than 80% of reporting institutions indicate that a three-cycle academic structure has been accomplished—at least in institutional eyes. But would "national interpretations of the nature and purposes of the three cycles" (p. 7) prove compatible? Would differences between types of bachelor's and master's degrees be clarified? Would the continued presence in some countries of idiosyncratic pre-Bologna structures prove problematical? And would those taking degrees within the new structure find employment?
- There is a good story about Bologna well worth the telling, but better communication among governmental leaders, higher educators, and public stakeholders is needed to achieve broader appreciation for "why the reforms are taking place" (p. 6). Two audiences in particular are critical: employers, who must understand and trust the new degrees, and parents, who assist their children in making decisions about higher education.
- "A change of educational paradigm across the continent" could be observed, from a focus on what is *taught* to one on what is *learned*. But the understanding and integration essential to effective translation of that shift to the curricular level was seen as "a key medium-term challenge" (p. 8).

continuing focused attention. First, the London Communiqué (2007) calls for a 2009 report on progress toward achieving increased mobility for students and faculty. Second, the ministers invite for 2009 national reports on efforts addressing the social dimension of Bologna. Further, the ministers charge the BFUG to "consider in more detail" how employability with regard to each of the three degree cycles might better be assured. To this end, the ministers pledge to work with their respective governments to create a closer alignment between the new degree structure and entry expectations for careers in public service. Finally, with an eye on Bologna's global context, the ministers ask for a 2009 report from the BFUG regarding two other issues, progress in achieving "open-minded" assessment by European institutions of educational credentials earned "abroad" and improvements in the public information effort with regard to the EHEA (London Communiqué, p. 7).

Consolidation and Reflection

It is not atypical that such an ambitious and comprehensive program of reform would require a period of reflection and consolidation. But in comparison with the recommendations and commitments of the earlier communiqués, those developed by the ministers meeting in London in 2007 appear to lack the sense of urgency evident earlier. There are fewer references to the European community, a far greater emphasis on the responsibilities of the member nations, and an inclination to seek reports rather than to mandate actions.

Only two years earlier, in 2005, a broad consensus had developed in Berlin that much remained to be done and that a sense of urgency was required. And prior to the meeting in London, the 2007 EUA Trends V and ESU reports confirmed that significant shortfalls and obstacles remained. Perhaps the comparatively laconic tone of the 2007 London Communiqué reflects the acknowledgment that much has been accomplished. Perhaps there are also some signs of fatigue. What does seem clear above all is that as the ministers found themselves "looking forward to 2010 and beyond," they found it important, or at least prudent, to frame a strategy that looked to the long as well as the near term. Hence, on the now widely accepted assumption that implementation of the Bologna Process would continue beyond 2010, "as the EHEA continues to develop and respond to the challenges of globalisation," the ministers added a new section to the communiqué in which they shared a vision for the future (London Communiqué, 2007, p. 6).

By this vision, 2010, initially the deadline for the completion of the Bologna Process, should be viewed as an opportunity not only to emphasize once again the role of higher education in securing sustainable societies but to recalibrate and reinvigorate the principles of the Process for the long haul.

> We will take 2010 as an opportunity to reformulate the vision that motivated us in setting the Bologna Process in motion in 1999 and to make the case for an EHEA underpinned by values and visions that go beyond issues of structures and tools. We undertake to make 2010 an opportunity to reset our higher education systems on a course that looks beyond the immediate issues and makes them fit to take up the challenges that will determine our future. (London Communiqué, 2007, p. 7).

To further this end, the ministers instruct the BFUG to frame proposals to their 2009 meeting concerning "appropriate support structures," to consider commissioning an independent evaluation of the Bologna Process 1999–2009, and to make decisions "on the nature, content and place of a Ministerial meeting in 2010" (London Communiqué, 2007, p. 7).

To the End of the Beginning

By the time of the 2009 meeting in Belgium, it was clear that a formal designation of the EHEA in 2010 would offer ample reason for celebration. Even if the Bologna Process were to accomplish nothing more following its first decade, its sponsorship of comparable curricular structures at institutions throughout Europe, its promotion of a shared vocabulary for higher education, its emphasis on external and internal quality assurance, and its determined (if not entirely successful) encouragement of greater mobility would qualify the undertaking for consideration as a uniquely effective educational reform.

But if the record of accomplishment would become clearer in Leuven/Louvain-la-Neuve, no less clear would be the fault lines continuing to widen into impediments to further progress or even into threats to progress already achieved. Working from the gestation of the Bologna idea, the birth of Bologna in 1999, and the growth of the reform through the course of a decade, the ministers gathering in Leuven/Louvain-la-Neuve would be prepared to enlist themselves and their nations in a campaign planned for a second decade.

6

BEGINNING A NEW DECADE

Leuven/Louvain-la-Neuve

On April 28 and 29, 2009, "Ministers responsible for higher education in the 46 countries of the Bologna Process convened in Leuven/Louvain-la-Neuve, Belgium, to take stock of the achievements of the Bologna Process and to establish the priorities for the European Higher Education Area (EHEA) for the next decade" (Leuven/Louvain-la-Neuve Communiqué, 2009). Thus begins the statement concluding what may now be seen as the first stage of the Bologna Process. Projected in 1999 as a 10-year project, the Process entered its second decade with much accomplished—and with much remaining to be accomplished.

This communiqué is remarkable in three respects. First, it succinctly documents an impressive record of accomplishment. Giving only very selective attention to deep concerns expressed most directly in the student perspective described on pp. 79–82, they resolutely declare Bologna a success. Second, without lamenting the many obvious shortfalls relative to their early aspirations and commitments, the ministers renew the Process for a second decade and identify in broad terms the priorities that will guide it. Third, explicitly and between the lines, the Leuven/Louvain-la-Neuve Communiqué (2009) attests to an evolutionary growth in the complexity of the Process and in its sensitivity to values broader than those communicated in its early years.

But to appreciate the determined optimism and resilience expressed by the ministers, we should consider 3 of the 24 reports and position papers prepared to provide contexts for their deliberations. Many of these reports offer valuable information and distinctive perspectives, and together they add considerably to an already formidable record. But for present purposes, as in previous biennia, the most important are those from the European University Association (EUA), the European Students' Union (ESU), and the

Bologna Follow-Up Group (BFUG) stocktaking group authorized by the European Commission (EC).

The EUA Prague Declaration and Its Presidential Statement

Anticipating the Leuven/Louvain-la-Neuve conference, the EUA president, Jean-Marc Rapp, issued a four-page statement outlining the contributions the EUA had made to the Bologna Process since 2007 and setting forth its priorities "for the next decade" (Rapp, 2009). The statement also indicated that the biennial EUA Trends report, ordinarily published in advance of the ministerial conferences, was under development and would be published in early 2010. But in lieu of that report, Rapp pointed to the declaration that the EUA had just issued from Prague, a summons to the nations of Europe to forestall a deepening economic crisis through investment in higher education (EUA Prague, 2009).

Granted, the EUA Prague (2009) declaration at no point mentions the Bologna Process. But by virtue of its timing, its content, and its emphases, it might well have been directed explicitly to the imminent ministerial conference. Perhaps it was. But whether by intent or not, one of the most remarkable characteristics of the declaration is the extent to which it tracks closely the priorities that would concern the ministers. If the intent of the declaration was to send a message to Leuven about the importance of public funding, institutional autonomy, and the diversity of university missions, the Leuven/Louvain-la-Neuve Communiqué (2009) suggests that the ministers were willing to listen.

Prompted by the financial and economic crisis that had emerged in 2008, the Prague declaration begins with a straightforward message to political leaders: Invest in higher education and research. In language evocative of the objective and subjective aspirations of Bologna, the declaration argues that providing adequate support for Europe's universities will help to ameliorate the effects of global recession and speed recovery. Higher education creates knowledge, promotes innovation, develops skills, and offers a sustained approach to solving current problems and anticipating new ones. But higher education also creates citizens with open minds, tolerant individuals capable of continued "individual development and personal growth." Universities are thus "motors for economic recovery" and reservoirs of "highly trained and flexible citizens" capable of responding quickly to demands for research and labor market needs (EUA Prague, 2009).

For these reasons, the Prague declaration calls for public investment in higher education in the form of a European stimulus package that would ensure continuity during a period of declining private and business support. Governmental funding, following the model of the stimulus program then being offered in the United States, could diminish the risks of Europe's "losing a generation of talented people" and incurring "a serious decrease in research and innovation activity." And beyond its economic goals, such investment also "will underpin European solidarity and will work against the present increased risk of nationalism and protectionism" (EUA Prague, pp. 1–2).

The declaration (EUA Prague, 2009) recommends particular investments—in the funding of "young researchers," in a new emphasis on retraining and "up-skilling" (p. 2) workers, and in the improvement of university facilities—before setting forth its vision of higher education and a listing of 10 factors germane to higher education's success. Its visionary preamble, without specific reference to concerns that the EUA had offered in earlier reports with regard to the Bologna Process, emphasizes values that invoke just those concerns. Specifically, it speaks of *autonomous* universities "responsive to the changing and sometimes exceptional needs of our societies and economies" through their educating "increasingly diverse student bodies." Such universities will necessarily offer "different traditions, mission mixes, and strengths." The values placed by the Bologna Process on "enhanced cooperation, social cohesion and solidarity" are important, to be sure, but in a context of "esteem for diverse missions."

The list of "success factors" needed for higher education to fulfill its mission is remarkable as well. These factors include the extension of opportunities for lifelong learning, the recruitment and support of postdoctoral researchers, curricular and pedagogical reform, and the development of distinctive institutional research emphases in networks of regional and European collaboration. To accomplish these ends, universities "pursuing excellence in their different missions" will require "strengthened autonomy," more stable and diversified funding, greater accountability with respect to qualitative growth, global alliances expressive of "a more international outlook," regional partnerships based on "the various missions of universities," and enhanced mobility across national boundaries for students, faculty, and administrators (EUA Prague, 2009, pp. 3–4).

By comparison with the EUA's resonant Prague declaration, the statement from the EUA president (Rapp, 2009) directed specifically to the Bologna ministers advances the EUA's "priorities for the next decade" (pp. 3–4). While none of these priorities is startling in itself, taken together they add up to a systematic recommitment to the fundamentals of Bologna. And, in language that echoes closely that of the ESU (2009b) report described in the next section, the EUA calls for real reforms as opposed to superficial structural changes and the rhetoric of change. In fact, many of the specific priorities articulated by the EUA correspond to those suggested by the students, by the authors of the 2009 Stocktaking report, and by the ministers themselves in the Leuven/Louvain-la-Neuve Communiqué (2009). But there are a few distinctive emphases worth attention.

Sharing the concern expressed by others with the sometimes piecemeal approach to the implementation of the Bologna action lines, the EUA president asks in effect for a kind of master inventory: Determine what has and has not actually been achieved, go after the "unfinished business" in "the whole package of reforms," and mount a cooperative effort to communicate more effectively to society what has been accomplished and why (Rapp, 2009, p. 3). Clearly among the items of unfinished business is lifelong learning, but the distinctive perspective of the EUA is that broadening access for new and returning learners will require unprecedented collaboration among universities, governments, and "a range of local partners" (p. 3). Also distinctive to the EUA Statement is a close link between institutional accountability expressive of an "internal quality culture" and the elucidation throughout Europe of "the growing diversity of missions, profiles and activities of higher education institutions" (p. 3). But the EUA president has a broader point to make, namely, that institutional commitments remain for the most part under the control of national policies that "differ considerably from country to country." Hence discussion of this issue, and by extension of many others, "still has a long way to go" (p. 4).

In the final two priority statements, the EUA president calls for more cooperation in the interest of "a truly European Higher Education Area" but urges that such cooperation include "the entire academic community." If implementation with regard to all action lines is to be achieved, it must appear at "deeper and deeper" levels within institutions, and that can only be accomplished through their wide acceptance—a perspective shared by the students (Rapp, 2009, p. 4).

"Bologna With Student Eyes"

"Enjoy the reading and welcome to reality!" (ESU, 2009b, p. 16). So the authors of *Bologna With Student Eyes* introduce their 176-page scrutiny of the Process—its priorities, its progress, and above all its pace. In sum, the report indicates that students in Europe support the principles of Bologna but are moving beyond impatience with its pace to dissatisfaction with its direction and sense of priorities. From the report's perspective, "a cooling down of the implementation engine" has become "alarming." To the dismay of its authors, the fourth of their biennial reports can document only "patchy progress" (p. 7). Having expressed concern in its 2007 report that the Process was becoming fragmented, with member countries pursuing only those action lines they found amenable, the ESU in 2009 declared that it has found the situation "much the same, with the most commonly overlooked action line relating to the social dimension, the one element preventing the whole Process from being revealed as little more than a hollow skeleton of structural reforms" (p. 7).

Behind this criticism lie efforts to document the realities students are experiencing relative to the formal objectives of the Process and beneath the documentation of progress on paper: "While it is easy to claim that certain reforms are technically in place and to provide supporting evidence for this, listening to the student voice can reveal that these reforms are only in place at a rather superficial level, and that the situation on the ground is far less glossy than the paper on which such statements are made" (ESU, 2009b, p. 7).

Examples in the ESU (2009b) report of the divide between official documentation and the student perspective include the following:

- Student participation in the Process has increased in only one third of the Bologna countries, and even there many of the changes appear more "tokenistic" than "meaningful." Students are therefore complaining "widely" about their exclusion from meaningful roles in institutional governance (p. 8).
- Mobility has not increased to the extent that official pronouncements suggest, largely because the commitment has not been met by a coordinated effort among the participating countries. Hence, "the goal of making mobility the rule rather than the exception seems almost as elusive as ever" (p. 8).
- Students in only one third of the Bologna countries believe that the social dimension of the Bologna Process represents a priority for their governments. And on the ground there is evidence of discrimination against students with limited means, students with families, and students who must work.
- While the students acknowledge progress in the development of standards for quality assurance and continue to support the development of qualifications frameworks, they criticize the snail's pace at which such efforts appear to be moving.
- The students regard the diploma supplement as "a clear added benefit for a relatively small amount of effort." But they note that six years

after the Berlin Communiqué (2003) mandating this service for all students, the promise has not been kept. "Issuing practices vary considerably across EHEA countries, and worryingly, awareness of [the diploma supplement] among employers and the general public remains persistently low" (p. 11).

- The students endorse designation of the European Credit Transfer and Accumulation System (ECTS) as the designated system for validating and recording academic credits but are skeptical with regard to its capacity to record student workload and to encourage student-centered learning. Because of "poor implementation," there remains little understanding of the learning outcomes associated with academic credentials (p. 11).
- The paradigm shift from teaching to learning that informs the Bologna Process? "More of an aspiration than a reality" (p. 11).
- The strongest criticism in the student report is reserved for claims of progress regarding implementation of the three-cycle curricular structure. Student eyes see little change. And even in those countries claiming to have completed this process, students have serious questions about "the extent to which it is operational and delivering on its original purpose." Indeed, inadequate implementation of these reforms may even be working to the disadvantage of students: "There are few cases in which students get a job after the first cycle—which was the purpose of the reform—whilst there has also been insufficient promotion of the first cycle on a continent generally accustomed to longer degrees" (p. 10).

These are not the only issues taken up in *Bologna With Student Eyes* (ESU, 2009b), but they are representative of a continuing concern on the part of students that the Bologna Process is moving too slowly, that it lacks sufficient coordination among the participating countries, and that countries vary in which action lines they are pursuing and in the energy they are devoting to them. As we have seen, the students voiced the same concerns as early as 2003. In 2009 they have not gone away. In possible contrast to the Prague Declaration (EUA Prague, 2009), with its emphasis on institutional autonomy and on the diversity of higher education missions, this edition of *Bologna With Student Eyes* (ESU, 2009b) decries the promotion of national systems of higher education "ahead of the EHEA as a whole." The result is likely to be increased competitiveness, and that would undermine "the balance and sustainability of the EHEA" (p. 11).

These observations prompt the students to offer an exhortation to the ministers and recommendations for their action. The exhortation? "Commitments need to be matched by actions" (p. 11). To this end, the ministers should ask students and higher education institutions to join them in a candid appraisal of what has and has not been accomplished so that national action plans can be developed to ensure further progress. The ministers should reject the à la carte approach "much in evidence" in favor of "an express commitment to implement all Bologna action lines equally" (ESU, 2009b, p. 12).

Priorities requiring particular attention include efforts to achieve "real progress" on mobility, concerted actions to further the social dimension, and greater student participation in higher education governance and in quality assurance. Moreover, the learning process should become more "student centered," a National Qualifications Framework (NQF) should be completed by every Bologna country, and the move to a single widely understood three-cycle degree program standard should be completed. Finally, there should be full and universal use of the ECTS, an expansion in access to lifetime learning, the offering of comparable support for all doctoral students, the development of "a relationship with the rest of the world based on cooperation and sustainable development" and, most notably, "a commitment to education for all that is free of fees and charges and therefore genuinely accessible to all socio-economic groups" (ESU, 2009b, p. 12).

In sum, from the student perspective, words must become "concrete realities" (ESU, 2009b). How seriously would the education ministers take this advice? In fact, their Communiqué (2009) would appear to imply precisely an à la carte response to the students' insistence that all Bologna action lines be implemented equally. And how seriously would the participating nations take the students' call for free higher education? Many appear to be moving in the opposite direction.

2009 Stocktaking

Of the reports prepared prior to the ministerial conference, the most influential and carefully observed was the detailed BFUG Stocktaking (2009) commissioned by the EC. Like the Leuven/Louvain-la-Neuve Communiqué (2009) it was developed to support, this overview of the Bologna Process at its 10th anniversary, action line by action line, emphasizes all that is positive in the record. But the report also documents candidly many of the challenges posed by the EUA Prague (2009) declaration and many of the shortfalls, delays, and misdirections cited in the student perspective (ESU, 2009b). On the basis of its status check, the Stocktaking report offers specific recommendations—only some of which make their way into the Communiqué.

The 2009 Stocktaking is finally less positive than its predecessors, not necessarily because performance had lagged but because of a more rigorous standard applied to the evaluation of results. In 2005, "it was sufficient to show that work had been started," and in 2007, "it was often enough that some work towards achieving the goals could be demonstrated or that legislation was in place." But in 2009 the expectations applied were "substantially more demanding" (Stocktaking, 2009, p. 6). And these more demanding criteria lead to a mixed evaluation:

- While implementation of the common academic program cycles appears to be "only a question of time," the proportion of students whose programs are aligned with these cycles remains low. And as the ESU (2009b) report complained, those who complete the first cycle often must complete additional requirements (examinations, additional course work, practical experience) to gain access to the second (p. 6).
- The development of NQFs had not met expectations—by a wide margin. As of 2009, only six countries had completed the self-certification process, and some of them had had frameworks in place to begin with. Because many countries were seen as "just beginning," the report concludes that full implementation "will take some time" (pp. 13, 38).
- The commitment to a bachelor's degree that would serve throughout Europe as an entry-level credential appeared to have run afoul of "the established custom and practice of different countries." As a result, in some of these countries, "the labour market seems to completely reject bachelor graduates" (p. 8).
- Quality assurance was showing progress where success comes most easily—at the national level, with the acceptance in all Bologna countries of external assessment approaches of some kind. But where it matters most, at the institutional level, with the definition of learning outcomes and the use of appropriate assessment methods to measure them, there has been much less progress. Indeed, "learning outcomes are often confused with overall programme goals which are not measurable and therefore cannot be used in student assessment" (p. 8).
- Adoption of one of the most widely acknowledged accomplishments of the Bologna Process, namely, the diploma supplement, also is seen to be disappointing. As the students noted, early in the Process participants agreed that the supplement would be provided to all graduates

in all participating countries by 2005. But as of 2009, graduates in only half of the Bologna countries were receiving the supplement.

- Similarly, ambitious projections regarding implementation of the 1997 Lisbon Recognition Convention governing the evaluation and crediting of academic credentials had proved overoptimistic. The stocktaking process concluded that there is "a long way to go before there is a coherent approach to recognition of qualifications within the EHEA" (p. 9).

- A closely related initiative, implementation of the ECTS, also had showed mixed results. Ten years after its introduction in 1999, the ECTS was seen to depend most heavily for its eventual wide useful-ness on the alignment of academic credits with measures of student workload and learning outcomes, "two main challenges" yet to be met (p. 10).

- A more recent goal, the development from one country to another of comparable standards for the recognition of prior learning, also had prompted little progress. Some countries have policies in place but not much to offer in the way of recognition activity; in others recog-nition is taking place "without any national procedures or guidelines" (p. 10).

- The social dimension remains a construction zone. While "virtually all" Bologna countries express a commitment to expanding access and equity, only a few can point to an "integrated strategy" linking legis-lation, social policy, and institutions of higher education. Hence, "there is still a long way to go before the student body entering, par-ticipating in and completing higher education at all levels will reflect the diversity of populations in the EHEA" (p. 11).

Priorities for a New Decade

On the basis of these conclusions, the Stocktaking (2009) report offers three brief sets of recommendations: one directed to all stakeholders, another to countries, and a third pointing to a future stocktaking process. Because these recommendations suggest how the BFUG may interpret the few directives of the ensuing ministerial Leuven/Louvain-la-Neuve Communiqué (2009), they may offer a glimpse of how the Bologna Process will continue to evolve as it enters its second decade.

As in *Bologna With Student Eyes* (ESU, 2009b), an exhortation precedes the recommendations themselves. "All stakeholders must re-affirm their full commitment to the goals of the EHEA and play an active part in the process of achieving them." By way of support, "it is essential to adopt a more systematic approach to collecting and analysing data, to monitor progress on the agreed actions and to facilitate evidence-based policy-making and planning for the future" (Stocktaking, 2009, p. 16).

Again, the congruity between the student (ESU, 2009b) and Stocktaking (2009) reports is striking in tone and in detail. Even many of the recommendations—though not all—suggest a shared understanding of what should be done. Like the student perspective, the Stocktaking report urges that implementation of the three-cycle degree structure be brought to a successful conclusion, that NQFs be implemented throughout Europe, that the commitment to providing the diploma supplement to all graduates be met, and that the priority on quality assurance be achieved in ways that are comparable and relatively transparent. Similarly, the report calls for student-centered learning, for the expansion of access to lifetime learning, and for the promotion of student mobility among the degree cycles and across national boundaries. Conspicuous by its absence, however, is the students' overriding emphasis on the social dimension of the process (the Stocktaking report calls for more data) and their call for free higher education.

The Ministers' Communiqué

The Bologna Declaration (1999) conveyed an overriding focus on higher education as a means toward accelerated economic growth. While there was little objection to this emphasis at the time, concern over its narrowness surfaced early in the voices of commentators, students, and university administrators. Through the decade, the education ministers responded by framing the objectives of Bologna in far broader and more generous terms. At the conclusion of the decade, virtually all the major reports prepared prior to the ministers' conference in Leuven/Louvain-la-Neuve mirrored this expansion of vision. As we have seen, the Prague Declaration (EUA Prague, 2009), *Bologna With Student Eyes* (ESU, 2009b), and the Stocktaking (2009) report all give generous attention to higher education's capacity to educate individuals not only as contributors to the labor force, but as solid citizens and thoughtful adults.

The Leuven/Louvain-la-Neuve Communiqué (2009) sought to broaden the vision further through its references to "student-centred learning," its commitment to creating "active and responsible citizens," and its expression of concern with "the cultural and social development of our societies" (¶ 2, ¶ 3). In contrast with the declaration that launched the process, the ministers' statement invokes higher education's "full range of purposes": the preparation of students "for life as active citizens in a democratic society," the enabling of their "personal development," the creation of "a broad, advanced knowledge base," and the stimulation of research and innovation—all in addition to the initial focus on workforce development (¶ 4). And it makes it clear that such aims should be furthered through a process that includes students and faculty and that respects "the European values of institutional autonomy, academic freedom and social equity" (¶ 4).

Bologna clearly has come a long way from 1999 in practice and in concept, and the most dramatic indication of just how far lies in the attention paid by the Leuven/Louvain-la-Neuve Communiqué (2009) to an emphasis persistently urged through the decade by students: the social dimension. As we have seen, criticisms of Bologna from student eyes have regularly faulted the process for inattentiveness to issues of access and inclusiveness. But the communiqué claims this issue by its emphasis on achieving equity through providing broader access and support.

> Access into higher education should be widened by fostering the potential of students from underrepresented groups and by providing adequate conditions for the completion of their studies. This involves improving the learning environment, removing all barriers to study, and creating the appropriate economic conditions for students to be able to benefit from the study opportunities at all levels. (Leuven/Louvain-la-Neuve Communiqué, ¶ 9)

Moreover, in an apparent response to some governments' having cited the Bologna Process to justify transferring more of the costs of higher education to institutions and students, the communiqué endorses "public investment in higher education" as an "utmost priority" and defines the EHEA as an entity in which "higher education is a public responsibility" (Leuven/Louvain-la-Neuve Communiqué, 2009, ¶ 3, ¶ 4).

Taking Note of Accomplishments

Reports prepared prior to the ministers' meeting describe in detail the accomplishments of the Bologna Process in its first decade while attesting to significant shortfalls. For its part, the Leuven/Louvain-la-Neuve Communiqué (2009) focuses most directly on substantive achievement. At the conclusion of its first decade, the Bologna Process can claim

- that systems of higher education in Europe have become more comparable with one another and more compatible.

- that students have become more mobile and institutions have become more competitive in attracting "students and scholars from other continents" (¶ 6).
- that higher education has become more "modern" through the wide adoption of the three-cycle structure including in many cases provision for "intermediate qualifications linked to the first cycle" (¶6).
- that higher education has become more accountable through the adoption of European standards and guidelines for quality assurance, through the creation of a European register for quality assurance agencies, and through NQFs reflective of EHEA standards for student learning outcomes and workload.
- that the "transparency and recognition" of academic credentials have been enhanced through use of the diploma supplement and through increasing reliance on the ECTS (¶ 6).

Even in this succinct form, the record is considerable, and the ministers were no doubt well advised to emphasize what had been accomplished. After all, their next meeting under the auspices of Bologna would be to celebrate the record they had established.

Priorities

In light of the contributions to the ministers' deliberations from the EUA, the ESU, and their stocktaking group, the ministers' disinclination to dwell on widely shared perceptions of shortfalls and misdirections may seem perplexing. But the framing of the Leuven/Louvain-la-Neuve Communiqué (2009) may reflect a deliberate strategy: Maintain a positive focus in the public report while charging the BFUG with priorities directed to the concerns raised.

One of these priorities we have already noted. Furthering the social dimension of the process leads the list. The other broad categories are lifelong learning, employability, the teaching mission of higher education, research and innovation, internationalization, mobility, data collection, accountability, and funding. At the outset of the second decade of the Process, it is important to understand what the ministers mean by each.

Lifelong Learning

In the preamble to their communiqué (Leuven/Louvain-la-Neuve Communiqué, 2009), the ministers declare that their vision of a creative and innovative "Europe of knowledge" will depend on "the talents and capacities of all its citizens" (¶ 1). Hence the expansion of access to higher education must be accompanied by a strong commitment to sustained learning through the course of a lifetime (¶ 1). Such learning, offering "new skills and competences" as well as opportunities for "personal growth," must be available through a variety of means emphasizing access and flexibility (¶ 10). Access should be further enhanced by the value placed on prior learning, whether academic or experiential, and by greater consistency in the evaluation throughout Europe of academic credit. To this end, the ministers call for implementation by 2012 of qualifications frameworks "prepared for self-certification" (¶ 12) by every participating nation to meet the standards of the broad European framework—another deadline to replace the two earlier ones that had been missed.

Employability

Given the prominence of workforce development as a principal motivation for the 1999 declaration, the relatively modest statement in the 2009 Leuven/Louvain-la-Neuve Communiqué may give the appearance of a reduction in emphasis. To the contrary, providing students "with the advanced knowledge, skills and competences they need throughout their professional lives" (¶ 13) remains at the heart of the Bologna priorities, but the extent to which this priority depends on many others had become increasingly apparent. For example, it had become clear that raising entry-level qualifications would require tracking student learning outcomes through comparable curricular structures, a process that would in turn require far greater cooperation among faculty members, students, institutions, and employers. And encouraging students to enhance their cultural awareness and intellectual flexibility through geographic mobility had drawn attention to the importance of the documentation (diploma supplement, ECTS) and evaluation of academic credentials—reforms that in turn depend on curricula made comparable through the Tuning Process of articulating consensus on academic outcomes (discussed in chapter 10). In a sense, then, all Bologna priorities are about employability—just as they are all, in a sense, about accountability and the culture of trust that only effective quality assurance can sustain.

Teaching and Learning

Consistent with the tone of the Leuven/Louvain-la-Neuve Communiqué (2009) as a whole, the ministers' discussion of teaching and learning offers broad aspirations rather than detailed directives. But their aspirations embody substantive progress in framing comparable curricular cycles, in defining outcomes through the Tuning Process, and in raising expectations for accountability through the development of a European framework. Hence their expectation of "ongoing curricular reform geared toward the development of learning outcomes" rests on a record of accomplishment. Improved "teaching quality" at all levels should remain a priority of the Bologna Process, but one perhaps best left for the attention of higher education institutions (¶ 14).

Research

In the midst of the decade, university leaders had expressed the concern that the emphases of the Bologna Process—undergraduate education, lifelong learning, normative accountability, workforce development—could discourage research. In the Leuven/Louvain-la-Neuve Communiqué (2009), again without going into much detail, the ministers affirm the critical role of higher education in fostering innovation (¶ 15). Echoing an emphasis of the Prague Declaration (EUA Prague, 2009), the general objectives must include an increase in "the number of people with research competencies," the assurance that all doctoral programs include "high quality disciplinary research," an expansion of "inter-disciplinary and inter-sectoral" programs at the doctoral level, and attention to enhancing "the career development of early stage researchers" (¶ 15).

International Openness

Two ministerial charges reflect the early priority on international competitiveness. But there appears to be less of an edge in the Leuven/Louvain-la-Neuve Communiqué (2009) and an impression of greater inclusivity. While it may be overly optimistic to conclude that the ministers are inviting advice from academic colleagues previously excluded from the conversation, at least their tone seems more positive. For example, the communiqué calls on institutions of higher education to become more international in their activities and "to engage in global collaboration for sustainable development" (¶ 16). And as Europe becomes more attractive to international students through the reforms of the Bologna Process, competitiveness should be balanced by "enhanced policy dialogue and cooperation based on partnership with other regions of the world" (¶ 16). The second charge recognizes that an expansion of access to transnational education will depend on the maintenance of standards that reflect the international consensus expressed in UNESCO and the Organization for Economic Cooperation and Development (OECD) guidelines.

Mobility

If openness is the external expression of Bologna's international goals, mobility is the internal one. In the view of the ministers, mobility of students, "early stage researchers," and faculty within Europe should lead to improvements in academic quality, enhance research, promote an appreciation for the diversity inherent in other cultures, encourage "linguistic pluralism," and contribute to "personal development and employability" (Leuven/Louvain-la-Neuve Communiqué, 2009, ¶ 18). Without setting forth any additional directives, the ministers call on each country to work toward a goal: by 2020, 20% of European graduates should have studied in a country other than their own. To this end, the ministers ask that explicit opportunities for mobility be built into each of the three cycles and supported through jointly offered programs. They also call on one another to work toward improving the logistics of student mobility (funding, visa and work permit policies, program descriptions, and protocols for the evaluation of credits earned outside the home country) and of faculty mobility also (e.g., portability of pensions, working conditions standards, transparent career paths). Here, too, much is left for the BFUG to do. But the reiteration of this goal in the context of an international economic recession is not without significance.

Data Collection and Transparency Tools

In tracing the progress of Bologna, we have followed a number of efforts to improve data gathering and reporting with respect to higher education. The methods and purposes of such efforts have been various—and not always complementary. In their reference to "several current initiatives," the ministers appear intent on becoming more systematic. They urge that assessment mechanisms be developed "in close consultation with the key stakeholders," ask that "transparency tools" align clearly with the principles of Bologna, and they insist that the data gathered be comparable to shed real light on "the diverse profiles of higher education institutions and programmes" (Leuven/Louvain-la-Neuve Communiqué, 2009, ¶ 22).

Funding

One sentence is sufficient as a summary: "Public funding remains the main priority to guarantee equitable access and further sustainable development of autonomous higher education institutions" (Leuven/Louvain-la-Neuve Communiqué, 2009, ¶ 23). There was good reason to restate this principle. The decade that identified higher education as a central concern for an increasingly united Europe was also marked, particularly in its final years, by some unraveling of European unity with the rise of so-called Euro-skeptic parties. Moreover, some national efforts to modernize higher education by increasing regulation, decreasing state funding, and requiring that students and their families bear a greater percentage of the cost exacerbated the trend.

bout the first decade a somewhat more inclusive agenda for the second. The our documents we have examined in this chapter—EUA Prague (2009), ESU (2009b), Stocktaking (2009), and the Leuven/Louvain-la-Neuve Communiqué (2009)—all indicate specific arenas for renewed and more clearly focused effort.

Yet if the ministers and the various participant and observer groups that have contributed reports deserve credit for acknowledging the shortfalls, frustrations, and occasional misdirections in implementation, they have paid little attention to the possibility that deep systemic crevices and potentially injurious external forces may impede or even reverse continued progress under the aegis of Bologna. There may be solid strategic thinking behind this apparent myopia, but a full appreciation for all that Bologna has accomplished and for the compelling example it represents must include also an awareness of the threats, internal and external, that could stall or undermine the Process. We turn to those now.

To be sure, tuition levels in European countries still lie for the ı   a
below those in the United States and in many other parts of the   f
an apparent paradigm shift in countries such as Spain, France, ar
enough to bring students, faculty members, and many other citize
streets on strike and in protest. Notwithstanding the lack of a clea
to the students' call for free higher education, the ministers' draw
tion to the importance of public funding and institutional autonom
ing in the context of some trends in the other direction.

Follow-Up

As with their previous communiqués, the education ministers direct
BFUG to prepare a work plan to "take forward" the priorities of the Le
Louvain-la-Neuve Communiqué (2009) *and the recommendations d
reports* submitted prior to the conference (¶¶ 24–27). The BFUG will
to interpret this sweeping statement, for there are differences of emph
among the recommendations of the different reports, and the full pand
of all recommendations would overtax any effort at implementation. I
within this broad array of possible tasks, the BFUG can at least focus
several ministerial requests in particular, as follows:

- Defining the data collection methods and indicators being used fo
  measuring mobility and the social dimension.
- Framing recommendations for the accomplishment of balanced
  mobility within the EHEA.
- Monitoring the status of the transparency mechanisms in use to frame
  a report for the ministerial conference in 2012.
- Creating through existing structures the means for promoting the
  Bologna Process more effectively outside the EHEA.
- Conducting an analysis of the various national action plans with
  regard to consistent protocols for the recognition of academic credit.
  (Leuven/Louvain-la-Neuve Communiqué, 2009)

Looking Ahead

The most important decision made by Europe's education ministers during
the first decade of the Bologna Process was that the Process should be continued for another decade. And their directives to the BFUG give some idea,
but only a very limited one, of what the further effort may look like. Given
the lack of anything more definitive, we may infer from concerns expressed

To be sure, tuition levels in European countries still lie for the most part far below those in the United States and in many other parts of the world. But an apparent paradigm shift in countries such as Spain, France, and Italy was enough to bring students, faculty members, and many other citizens into the streets on strike and in protest. Notwithstanding the lack of a clear reference to the students' call for free higher education, the ministers' drawing attention to the importance of public funding and institutional autonomy is striking in the context of some trends in the other direction.

Follow-Up

As with their previous communiqués, the education ministers directed the BFUG to prepare a work plan to "take forward" the priorities of the Leuven/Louvain-la-Neuve Communiqué (2009) *and the recommendations of the reports* submitted prior to the conference (¶¶ 24–27). The BFUG will have to interpret this sweeping statement, for there are differences of emphasis among the recommendations of the different reports, and the full panoply of all recommendations would overtax any effort at implementation. But within this broad array of possible tasks, the BFUG can at least focus on several ministerial requests in particular, as follows:

- Defining the data collection methods and indicators being used for measuring mobility and the social dimension.
- Framing recommendations for the accomplishment of balanced mobility within the EHEA.
- Monitoring the status of the transparency mechanisms in use to frame a report for the ministerial conference in 2012.
- Creating through existing structures the means for promoting the Bologna Process more effectively outside the EHEA.
- Conducting an analysis of the various national action plans with regard to consistent protocols for the recognition of academic credit. (Leuven/Louvain-la-Neuve Communiqué, 2009)

Looking Ahead

The most important decision made by Europe's education ministers during the first decade of the Bologna Process was that the Process should be continued for another decade. And their directives to the BFUG give some idea, but only a very limited one, of what the further effort may look like. Given the lack of anything more definitive, we may infer from concerns expressed about the first decade a somewhat more inclusive agenda for the second. The four documents we have examined in this chapter—EUA Prague (2009), ESU (2009b), Stocktaking (2009), and the Leuven/Louvain-la-Neuve Communiqué (2009)—all indicate specific arenas for renewed and more clearly focused effort.

Yet if the ministers and the various participant and observer groups that have contributed reports deserve credit for acknowledging the shortfalls, frustrations, and occasional misdirections in implementation, they have paid little attention to the possibility that deep systemic crevices and potentially injurious external forces may impede or even reverse continued progress under the aegis of Bologna. There may be solid strategic thinking behind this apparent myopia, but a full appreciation for all that Bologna has accomplished and for the compelling example it represents must include also an awareness of the threats, internal and external, that could stall or undermine the Process. We turn to those now.

Falling Short

Why had the Bologna Process failed to meet its goals within its original time-line? There are two obvious reasons—and some less obvious ones. First, the ministers responsible for implementation of the Process had agreed along the way to additional action lines. So there was more to accomplish than origi-nally envisioned. Second, the number of participating countries expanded from 29 to 42 to include some with traditions of higher education distant from those of the European mainstream. So the goal of bringing comparabil-ity among national systems became a greater challenge.

Among the less obvious reasons was the necessity for cultural shifts "under-estimated in many ways" (EUA Trends V, 2007, p. 75). Then the economic downturn toward the end of the decade discouraged investment in higher education. And from the student perspective, a developing "gap between rhetoric and reality" had created confusion, fostered misunder-standing about "the real goals of the Process," and led to "pick and choose" approaches to the action lines at the national level. The result? In their view, "contradictions and inconsistencies." More specifically, "the focus on struc-tural reforms, a divorce between form and content, the misuse of tools, and reforms reducing student participation in institutional governance have led to a feeling of frustration and a reduction in support amongst the student body" (ESU, 2009b, p. 2). In sum, the shortfall of the Bologna Process in its first decade points to systemic issues that must be resolved if Bologna is to succeed.

Deeper structural issues have emerged as well. Despite efforts by the education ministers to moderate the stark pragmatic language of early Bolo-gna documents, a discontinuity has persisted between the initial economic focus of the Process and values shared by many members of the academy. And as Lorenz (2006) has observed, another structural issue arises from entrusting "the transformation of a great number of very diverse national systems of higher education into *one* competitive European 'educational market'" (p. 129) to nations that harbor a deep historical pride in their respective educational traditions and in the inimitability of their higher edu-cation institutions.

A Second Decade

Because 2010 had long been established as the deadline for full implementa-tion of the EHEA, because of the considerable accomplishments of the Bolo-gna Process to date, and because of the difficulties that have emerged with the onset of a global recession, the education ministers' meeting in April 2009 might have pronounced the Bologna Process a qualified success and brought it to a dignified conclusion. That they did not do so may be the single most persuasive reason for optimism as to even greater success over the long term.

A positive perspective on continuing the Process to a second decade with the intent of accomplishing all its action lines more fully over time began to emerge with the recognition in the European University Association (EUA) report that "the processes set in motion will neither be fully achieved nor come to a sudden end" by 2010 (EUA Trends V, 2007, p. 79). From the perspective of the authors, the efforts to implement Bologna had shown the need "for a more permanent process of societal innovation and change" but had allowed only enough time "to lay the initial foundations" (EUA Trends V, p. 75.) Hence they recommended that 2010 be regarded not as a terminus but as an interim station along the line. And others, including the European Students' Union (ESU), endorsed the idea. "A renewed and ambitious Bologna agenda" aimed at making "the original vision of the EHEA an unequivocal reality for all European students" would require another decade (ESU, 2009b).

But if the renewal of the Process for another 10 years was seen as essential to its achieving more of its objectives, no one expressed the view that additional time would by itself ensure success. To the contrary, even the most optimistic observers have acknowledged that the road ahead for Bologna is clouded with issues that must be resolved. The strongest supporters of the Process understand that its progress has been uneven, that resistance to some of its goals has emerged and may be growing, that there is some disenchantment even with what has been accomplished, and that enthusiasm for the Process may be difficult to sustain.

Looking forward, the question may be whether the issues concerning Bologna represent speed bumps or potholes. The homely metaphor is apt. Are concerns regarding the Bologna Process surmountable problems that may slow the rate of progress? Or do they represent genuine threats to its sustainability? Speed bumps may be approached with prudent deliberation, but potholes can be hazardous or even deadly if not filled—or circumvented.

Speed bumps and potholes fall into two broad categories: external and internal. The external challenges largely reflect Bologna's political origins. As the fortunes of the European Union (EU) shift, those of Bologna shift also. Despite the eventual ratification of the EU constitution in November 2009 with the approval of the final holdout, the Czech Republic, the rise of Euro-skeptic political parties in the latter part of the decade, confirmed most visibly in results of the European parliamentary elections in June 2009, may not bode well for pan-European initiatives in the long run. But even more ominous for European unity than the election results was the voter turnout of 43%, a low water mark "analysts across the European Union were identifying as frustration and waning support for European integration" (Castle, 2009, A5).

And Bologna has been further discredited in the eyes of some by its association with particular national higher education initiatives often unrelated to—in some cases antithetical to—its agenda. A conspicuous example may be found in Italian legislation offering a degree of autonomy to universities but requiring in turn an increase in institutional budgetary responsibilities. The result has been an increase in fees that has drawn sharp reactions from students. Finally, because of the extent to which higher education in Europe depends on public funding, a slow recovery from a serious global recession may continue to trouble its future.

Internal Issues

The issues internal to the Process arise in part from its structure, from its commitment to priorities that may be incompatible, from the range of governance assumptions within a large and now heterogeneous membership, even from the language used in official statements. Examples include the juxtaposition of academic ideals and a priority on economic development, the failure to distinguish clearly between using assessment for making institutional comparisons and for supporting institutional strengthening, and the contrasting priorities on expediting movement of graduates into the workforce on the one hand, and on ensuring their international competitiveness on the other.

Continuity remains a concern given the distributed model of leadership chosen by the ministers. And the lack of real enforcement authority in that model has drawn attention to inconsistencies in accomplishment within what is now a very large Bologna family. Concerns about the acceptance of reforms by employers have grown through the decade, as has impatience with lack of progress in pursuit of the social dimension of the Process. The language used in the official documents may continue to convey problematical messages. The relative lack of attention to technology is puzzling, and there is the possibility that a flat world may in time draw attention to parochial elements in Bologna's international vision. Even a cursory survey can suggest that Bologna has experienced and will continue to face some serious internal issues.

Sustaining the Process

As has often been observed, the Bologna Process was created as a voluntary undertaking with little in the way of sustained leadership or central authority. And it may be that avoidance of a costly central bureaucracy in favor of distributed authority has disarmed what might otherwise have been some formidable sources of opposition. Indeed, if we consider the growing pains experienced by the EU itself, we may surmise that a more formal bureaucratic approach would not have served Bologna well. Yet despite some effort to sustain the continuity of the process through the creation of a kind of coordinating authority under the aegis of the EU, itself a step fraught with the risk of alienating some participants, advocates for the Bologna Process have had to depend largely on the support of the Continent's education ministers and other political leaders and opinion makers and on the cooperation of national governments and institutions of higher education.

In that prudent course may lie paradoxically some explanation for Bologna's shortfall in its first decade and potential risks for the future. Even in a period of economic stability, significant disparities from one nation to another in fiscal and political support for educational reform will inevitably emerge. And that has been the case for Bologna. But an economic downturn can exacerbate such disparities and threaten even the degree of coordination and comparability that exists. When circumstances call leaders to attend first to economic and political issues, a voluntary process with important but slowly emerging benefits may be relegated to a back burner on the policy stove.

A Very Large Tent

In 1999 the 29 ministers who signed the Bologna Declaration represented for the most part nations identifying with western Europe, many of them already pursuing higher education reforms that would come to be identified with the Process. But with the growth of Bologna to 46 participating states, an initial vision of coherence and comparability has become more ambitious. By embracing many more members and their distinctive higher education traditions—Russia, Turkey, Albania, and Azerbaijan are among the new Bologna participants—the process has embraced also a much broader range of political, ideological, cultural, and geographical influences, and it is by no means clear whether participating nations will ever achieve anything like a comparable approach to the implementation of all action lines (EUA Trends V, 2007, p. 9).

For instance, some of the most recent signatories, with strong eastern European traditions of faculty authority, may have the most to gain from alignment with the Bologna standards, but they may also face the greatest tests (EUA Trends V, 2007, p. 9). And issues of institutional autonomy, so critical to the Bologna priorities concerning accountability and mobility, may be defined in some nations in terms very different from those shared for the most part by the charter cohort.

There is also in any international endeavor the risk that foes of change will take new energy for resistance from the relaxation of borders. As we may infer from the European parliamentary elections mentioned previously, there are influential voices on the Continent not friendly to European integration and therefore skeptical about the value of Bologna's mobility and comparability priorities. Just as the analogy of economic convergence may help to explain the thrust of Bologna Process reforms, the risks to coordinated fiscal policies may represent risks also for a process seeking greater educational unity. In short, while the expansion of the Bologna group has been heartening in some respects, the creation of an educational community stretching from western Ireland to the Bering Straits has made the achievement of Bologna's goals more of a challenge.

Knowns and Unknowns

There are many unknowns with regard to the future of the Bologna Process. But there are also many known issues that may present problems in a second decade. We know, for instance, that the degree of implementation of the action lines varies widely from one country to another. We know that in many countries little if any additional state funding has been provided to support implementation of the Bologna reforms. We know that in some participating countries there are initiatives that appear inconsistent with the Bologna emphasis on increasing access and student body diversity. And we know that in some cases reports of reform camouflage a lack of real change.

While a minister of education may confirm a commitment, for that commitment to become effective the minister's government must recognize it as a priority by providing the necessary funding and by framing policies required for its accommodation. And repeatedly through the Bologna decade, surveys of participating institutions have revealed deep disquiet about follow-through at the national level. At eight years into implementation, the "issues most often identified . . . concern insufficient institutional autonomy to implement reforms in the way in which they would be most effective, and insufficient government support for reform" (EUA Trends V, 2007, p. 19).

Two thirds of those responding to the EUA Trends V study indicated that their institutions had received no additional funding whatsoever to support implementation of educational reforms. Hence it is not surprising that some institutions have found their governments "more interested in the rhetoric of reform than in providing genuine support to institutions." A reliable recipe for consternation among faculty members and students thus emerges. On the one hand, ramp up expectations for new curricular structures, more aggressive quality assurance, and invigorated pedagogy. On the other, reduce state support, propose changes in professional status and benefits, and announce policy changes that suggest to some the privatization of public higher education.

And if diverse results on the extent of implementation are now appearing through comparisons of one country with another, inconsistencies can be found even within countries where some of the Bologna priorities have received more attention than others—and where some institutions have achieved real reform under the aegis of Bologna while others have made do with "more cosmetic and superficial implementation" (EUA Trends V, 2007, p. 19). For instance, some institutions appear to have approached implementation of the three-cycle structure as an end in itself, a to-do item for checking off rather than as a means to the larger ends of student mobility, employability, and access. And others, such as Ludwig Maximilians University in Munich, may have found a competitive advantage in a *failure* to comply fully. One student mentioned in an analysis by Aisha Labi (2009a) of Bologna skeptics told Labi that he had chosen the Munich university "because it still offered the five-year undergraduate diploma." He knew that "many of the other universities had already changed to Bologna degrees" and wanted to avoid them, saying, "The problem is that the people who employ students, they don't know much about the new degrees. So I think when they have a choice between an applicant who did the *Diplom* [the traditional German undergraduate credential] and one who did the new Bologna degree, I think there could be advantages for the guy with the old degree."

The depth to which the Bologna reforms are penetrating institutions and classrooms is a matter of particular uncertainty. In some cases, the problem may be one of awareness. Even if reforms are taking place, those engaged in them may not recognize them as somehow associated with Bologna or may not find it necessary to communicate what they are accomplishing to concerned stakeholders. On the other hand, there is also the risk that familiarity with the Bologna jargon has created a cadre of cognoscenti more capable of framing impressive progress reports than of making real progress.

Given that one of the priorities of Bologna has been to increase the transparency of educational programs and institutions, this risk may not be the least worrisome.

First-Cycle Degree Concerns

Wide variations in the practical impact of reform may represent another source of public confusion. As the example of the Ludwig Maximilians student suggests, implementation of the three-cycle degree structure has encountered resistance and created some lines of internal stress. In 2007 the EUA Trends V report determined that fully 82% of European universities had implemented the Bologna cycles, a "point of no return" according to one observer (Jaschik, 2007). But while some of the May Day 2009 demonstrators in Germany objected to the new degree structure in principle as a movement toward "vocational training in the university," others objected because the reform has been superficial, a tinkering with structure "rather than a proper reform of courses that would have come up with really new concepts" (Gardner, 2009). And in some cases the new cycles appear to be simply supplementing the old ones. Hence, again in Germany, according to the same report, "many institutions still continue to enroll students into the old degree programs" (EUA Trends V, p. 20). And in other countries as well, "very strong remnants of the old system" (p. 22) persist.

The old system still has its defenders, and at least some of them are also strong critics of Bologna. Speaking to *Chronicle of Higher Education* reporter Labi (2009a), the president of a leading technical university called Bologna "a disaster" for well-structured programs in the sciences and in engineering. The first-cycle degree is "just too short," and its brevity creates unnecessary pressures. "There is no time to think, to see relations between real fields." he said. And greater mobility, one of Bologna's explicit aims, may in fact be *negatively* affected by the first-cycle degree standard as "the shorter degree times and constant exams create powerful disincentives for students worried they will fall behind by taking time away from their home institutions."

The Social Dimension

A different kind of problem appears in the frequent but inconclusive references through the decade to the social dimension of the Bologna process. Prompted largely by persistent student expressions of concern, the ministers have periodically affirmed an obligation to expand access to higher education for all those well qualified to undertake it and to ensure that student bodies reflect the ethnic and economic diversity of the population. But as the spring 2009 declaration of the ESU observes, despite such commitments "on paper," few results have been observed "on the ground" (ESU, 2009b, p. 2). To the contrary, the students say "the financial situation of students has worsened; tuition fees have been introduced or raised in several countries and poorly implemented degree structures has [*sic*] brought inflexibility in admissions and progression between cycles" (p. 2).

A related concern is that the pursuit of the social dimension has occasionally prompted ill-advised defenses of quality, on the specious grounds that expanded access and increased quality are incompatible goals. Having heard such expressions, the authors of EUA Trends V (2007) charge Bologna institutions "to stress that widening access does not imply any reduction in quality" (p. 74). But governments surely have the largest role to play in this regard through their capacity to frame policies and provide resources. With little indication that real progress on the social dimension of the Bologna Process is likely anytime soon, it is difficult to anticipate how much will be accomplished during the second decade of the Process.

Dissonances

That not all Bologna's priorities have remained complementary and some may even have come to appear incompatible is not uncharacteristic of a complex process that is continuing to mature, but if real problems are to be avoided, such dissonances must be identified and addressed. One issue lies in the tension between insistence on the first cycle bachelor's degree as an appropriate entry-level credential and the emerging priority on encouraging many more students to undertake graduate study. Another continues to emerge from the uneasy balance between national authority, seen as necessary to ensure institutional compliance with many of the Bologna initiatives, and institutional autonomy, seen as necessary to ensure the necessary engagement by those most directly concerned: students, faculty, and staff members. And we have already glanced at the possible conflict between the emphasis on greater student mobility and on shrinking the first undergraduate degree to three years.

The significant latent conflict that we have noted between developmental and evaluative priorities of assessment and accreditation may be among the most problematical. To the extent that assessment arises from a faculty-driven commitment to improved effectiveness in the accomplishment of learning outcomes, measurements at the instructional and institutional levels can enhance institutional performance. And to the extent that assessment employs performance standards to measure and compare institutions and programs, the Bologna Process can contribute significantly to political accountability and public awareness. But as the ESU (2009b) declaration makes clear, the two emphases do not easily coexist—and the conflict between them may develop into a sticking point.

Why Change?

There may be some advantages to change "more evolutionary than revolutionary," the EUA Trends V (2007, p. 22) authors observe, but compromises and accommodations carry risks. Public understanding of the Bologna reforms will hardly grow broader if parallel degree structures continue to compete, for instance, and if some students find the choice among them uncomfortable. A confused emphasis on poorly distinguished evaluative and developmental assessment could result in less rather than greater transparency. Continued references to a social dimension with little to show in the way of real progress may prompt more general skepticism regarding the Process itself. And as such doubts arise, diehards may take heart and conclude that procrastination may offer a reliable defense against innovation. If the vision of reform should become progressively more accommodating and nuanced, why change? "If all these national particularities are cumulated, rather than presenting a picture of more convergent national systems in Europe, the picture is rather one of greater similarity at a superficial level, but significant diversity within and between national systems in all manner of details" (EUA Trends V, p. 21).

Mixed Signals

Later in this chapter (see pp. 114–115) we consider how the protests in higher education in 2008 and 2009 may complicate further implementation of Bologna reforms even though many of the demonstrations either have not referred to the Bologna Process or have associated Bologna with initiatives contrary to its agenda. That issue is largely an external one. But there may be an internal dimension to such unrest, a legitimate reason for the association of the Bologna Process with the issues that have more directly motivated the dissent.

A "discourse analysis" of the Bologna Process by Terhi Nokkola (2007) goes so far as to identify *globalisation* as "possibly the most important" force evident within the Bologna Process (p. 223). Indeed, she directly associates the Process with "a systemic, sustained effort at making higher education more responsive to the requirements and challenges related to the globalisation of societies, economy and labour markets."

In this regard, Gumport (2000) helps to define an important tension illuminated by the Bologna Process. On the one side, higher education represents a source of national pride and identity, a means for the creation of national leadership, a nursery for the birth and growth of new knowledge, a workforce training ground, a base for national culture, and an opportunity for individual fulfillment. On the other, higher education may be viewed also (or instead) as an industry accountable to standards expected of any other European economic enterprise—that is, the *commodification* argument. By this standard, if higher education is to support European competitiveness, it must operate according to sound managerial practices, achieve close coordination in its structures and processes, eliminate costly duplications and inefficiencies, and improve its revenues.

Amaral and Magalhaes (2004) take this premise a step further in determining that the language of the Bologna Process implies an intent to convert public benefits to private goods, and Nokkala (2007) agrees: "The Bologna Process documents create a conceptual understanding of universities and other higher education institutions as producers of knowledge and the skilled labour force needed by Europe to survive in global competition" (p. 227). Through close analysis of the Sorbonne and Bologna declarations and the first three ministerial communiqués, Nokkala traces a clear shift from a traditional emphasis on "culture, shared values, and intellectual pursuits," expressed through the vision of a "Europe of Knowledge," to the "more economic and innovation oriented contexts" (p. 233) that are the focus of the March 2000 Lisbon Strategy.

Some of the indicators are subtle. Nokkala (2007) observes a move from references to "universities" in the Sorbonne and Bologna declarations to the Prague Communiqué's reference to "universities and other higher education institutions" to the exclusive use of the term "higher education institutions" in the Berlin and Bergen communiqués (p. 240). Through this same period, she says, "the public good of higher education seems to take a new shape: the public benefits do not operate on an abstract level of general good but are specifically related to the aspirations of the states to become knowledge societies and economies" (p. 243). "Higher education has to be relevant, and relevance is increasingly defined in terms of the employability of graduates and direct contributions by the higher education institutions to the economic competitiveness of states and regions" (p. 243).

She observes also some effort in the Bergen Communiqué to mitigate the apparent drift to greater pragmatism. By emphasizing a continued commitment to the social dimension of the process, by restoring references to cultural values, and by explicitly reaffirming higher education as a "public good and a public responsibility" the Bergen Communiqué appears to seek a kind of balance between the vision expressed in Bologna's founding documents and the pragmatic imperatives of the intervening communiqués (Nokkala, 2007, p. 237). And as we have noted, the Leuven/Louvain-la-Neuve Communiqué (2009) continues this trend.

It may be possible to make too much of these issues of language, but any frank assessment of the future of Bologna must take into account what political leaders appear to be saying about higher education and the observable evidence that many students and faculty members disapprove of what they are hearing. While it is important to appreciate the extent to which the ministers and their advisers, such as the redoubtable Sjur Bergan, have begun to articulate a broader and more inclusive view, we cannot overlook the possibility that tensions created by earlier, more rigid statements may remain.

An Island in a Flat World?

The ministers who signed the Bologna Declaration in 1999 envisioned the realization in higher education of the Europe promised by the EU, one where boundaries between nations would become almost irrelevant in the face of shared economic, educational, and security issues. And the reforms prompted by Bologna have indeed contributed to that vision. But many nations outside Europe have also been moving toward more permeable boundaries. Hence a possible risk for Bologna is that a pan-European vision regarded in 1999 as border breaking may over time come to appear as Eurocentric, that is, as insular and parochial, continental rather than international.

Perhaps in a world with lowered borders the Bologna signatories will benefit from having been early trendsetters. But the economic and political gains that are envisioned in the Bologna declaration may in time accrue more directly to Europeans through their participation in a truly global approach to higher education. As a worldwide higher education common market continues to evolve, a process defined by its focus on a pan-European enclave could enter the history of higher education as a well-meant effort compromised from the start by the narrowness of its vision. Of course, the opposite risk is that some of the borders within Europe will begin to rise again as nationalistic movements gain strength.

Transcendent Technology

Although technology may represent the single most influential agent of change in contemporary higher education, the Bologna Process has appeared for the most part curiously inattentive. While many of the participating institutions have documented innovative investments in technology, biennial reviews of the Process have given little notice to ways in which technology might support further progress with respect to the action lines.

The growth of the Internet and the emergence of Internet II as a platform for communication and access to information represent one important front. The influence of distance education on pedagogy and on the articulation of learning outcomes is another. The opportunities that technology offers institutions for costs savings and efficiency gains, especially when cooperating institutions choose to consolidate basic processing functions, is yet another. And technology is exerting a profound effect on the assessment and documentation of quality. An information revolution still in its early stages represents an emerging opportunity for higher education, and those involved in any reform process aimed at achieving greater competitiveness should be paying careful attention.

Beyond its potential to expedite reform initiatives or render them more efficient, technology has the capacity to broaden them. For instance, the limited impact to date of the diploma supplement might well be enhanced through the additional depth and flexibility that an electronic portfolio could provide. Rather than focusing on the institution issuing the credentials, a portfolio could provide potential employers and graduate schools with a broad representation of the candidate's performance, recognition, and potential. Adelman (2009) has made this point well. In sum, there is no reason why Bologna should not exploit every advantage to enhance the likelihood of eventual success.

Innovation and Convention

As the final chapter suggests, the United States has an opportunity to build on the successes of Bologna and to avoid its missteps. Some of these missteps may appear in retrospect as a consequence of overreaching, trying to do too much too quickly. That some of the ambitious commitments of 2001 and 2003 could not be met during the projected time frame provides counsel on realistic scheduling. Yet Bologna's most serious limitation may arise not from being too ambitious but from not being ambitious enough.

For all its breadth and resolve, Bologna has worked almost entirely within the constraints of existing conventions. Because implementation of the three-cycle degree system has never reflected consideration of whether traditional degrees any longer effectively document academic performance and potential, it has been possible for some institutions to claim compliance through the simple expedient of dividing a five-year curriculum into two components. Similarly, guidelines for quality assurance in the EHEA reflect for the most part predictable and broadly stated expectations. The European Credit Transfer and Accumulation System (ECTS) receives, records, and reports academic credit based on the duration rather than the depth of study. The overarching outcomes framework for the EHEA, while commendable as the expression of a potentially influential consensus, has achieved currency in part through its high level of generality. And—an issue we consider in greater depth in chapter 10—the Tuning Process works within existing disciplinary silos rather than questioning the relevance of closely defined disciplines for an era when knowledge is multifaceted, associative, and not only multidisciplinary but transdisciplinary.

Perhaps given a second decade, the Bologna Process will reveal not only the commendable determination its advocates have demonstrated but a higher measure of thoughtfulness and creativity. Given the internal issues described in this section, both are likely to be required.

External Issues

The Bologna Process is at its heart more a political than an educational initiative. The immediate precursor to the Bologna Declaration of 1999, the Sorbonne Declaration of 1998, emphasizes (in the words of the ministers' meeting at Bologna) "the creation of the European area of higher education as a key way to promote citizens' mobility and employability and the Continent's overall development" (Bologna, 1999, ¶ 4). In turn, the Bologna Declaration aligns its priorities squarely with the "extraordinary achievements" of the European process (¶ 1). These reflect "a growing awareness in large part of the political and academic world and in public opinion of the need to establish a more complete and far-reaching Europe, in particular building upon and strengthening its intellectual, cultural, social and scientific and technological dimensions" (¶ 1). The aspiration to create a "Europe of Knowledge" thus reflects a social and political agenda in which higher education makes its contribution as "an irreplaceable factor for social and human growth and . . . an indispensable component to consolidate and enrich the European citizenship" (¶ 2).

Bologna and the EU

As we have observed, while the Bologna Process does not operate under the auspices of the EU, it has benefited considerably from the support of the EU and the European Commission (EC). After all, education ministers from EU nations were the charter signers of the Bologna (1999) Declaration. As the table on pp. 5–6 indicates, many of the nations now participating in the Bologna Process are EU members, and all EU members are Bologna participants. But the relationship between Bologna and the EU and EC is also a cause for concern. One reason is that the EU may grow more powerful. The other is that it may grow weaker. Either development could create problems for Bologna.

The concern regarding a more dominant EU and EC reflects the awareness that Bologna might come to be regarded as only one of several elements in the growing EC education portfolio. Why would that not be a good thing? From one perspective, at least, closer alignment between the EC and the Process could compromise through greater regulation the distinctive strengths many Bologna members attribute to their respective systems of higher education. In a 2007 report, the Education Select Committee of the UK House of Commons recommends caution regarding Bologna, lest a commitment to "comparability and compatibility" evolve toward the "standardisation of higher education systems across the European Higher Education Area" and "undermine the autonomy and flexibility of the UK system" (Commons, 2007, ¶¶ 3:33, 35, 42).

Citing the United Kingdom and Ireland as "the only countries in the EHEA with flexible, autonomous higher education sectors," the report finds "a very different culture across the rest of continental Europe where state-owned higher education systems are closely controlled by government through detailed legislation outlining degree structures, financial arrangements, credit systems, and even curriculum" (Commons, 2007, ¶ 3:71). Hence "the concern is that despite the official intentions or purposes, there is a possibility that the Bologna Process could move towards a more typical European-style bureaucratic, top-down, rigid and legislative process which would result in higher education sectors being forced to move towards standardised or uniform higher education systems" (¶ 36).

So we have further balances that Bologna must seek to maintain. On the one hand, without the support of the EU and EC, the Process could hardly continue to operate. Yet if Bologna's relationship to the EU and EC should become more dependent, some participating nations may become less cooperative. And if the Process appears insensitive to institutional specificity, it will alienate those whose cooperation is most critical, but if it becomes too protective with respect to a variety of missions and protocols it will compromise its guiding vision of increased consistency and comparability in standards and practices. So as it navigates its relationship with the EU and EC,

Bologna must continue to seek an equilibrium between achieving the benefits promised through its action lines and honoring the autonomy of higher education systems within the participating nations. Giving the impression of a "European-style bureaucratic, top-down, rigid and legislative process" (Commons, 2007, ¶ 3:36) may alienate participating nations, but too generous an accommodation of national and institutional cultures and practices may leave in place the very inconsistencies that Bologna was created to resolve and deprive the EHEA of any real meaning.

Paradoxically, there is also a concern that the EU may grow weaker, and that too could be problematical for Bologna. Like the Bologna Process, the EU must manage a continuing tension between achieving greater consistency throughout Europe and honoring national autonomy. As is the case with Bologna, growth through an expansion of membership can provide an impression of progress but create complications difficult to resolve. And for the EU and the Bologna Process, economic challenges exacerbate points of stress that can complicate international initiatives even in the best of times. For all these reasons, any look forward to the Bologna Process in its second decade must include an assessment regarding the prospects for the European Union.

Such an assessment must be cautious. The EU may deserve the recognition offered by Laurent Cohen-Tanugi (2005) as "the most progressive political experiment of our time" (p. 67). And the completion in 2009 of the protracted ratification of the Treaty of Lisbon, which creates a full-time European presidency and foreign office, should encourage EU supporters. But there were already signs of stress in the middle of the decade, well before the onset of economic recession. The effort to secure ratification of the treaty had to overcome French and Dutch resistance in 2004, the European Council's consideration of the 2007–13 EU budget ran into a dispute between the British and the French, and Cohen-Tanugi (2005) described "a growing malaise over the EU's operation and prospects" attributed to a witches' brew of "growing disenchantment with 'Europe,'" a "troublesome mix of left-wing radicalism, right wing sovereigntism, bipartisan populism, and anti-Americanism." What these trends share in his view is "a common aversion" to, among other things, "open borders" (pp. 55, 62). Most recently the ratification of the Lisbon Treaty prompted critics to assert "that the document encroaches on national sovereignty and threatens to turn the European Union into a monolithic superstate" (Bilefsky & Castle, 2009).

If the future of the EU rests on its ability to deliver economic growth to an increasingly unified Europe, its challenges in the near term are likely to prove considerable. And the most recent indicators are not encouraging. A front-page headline in the *New York Times* makes the point succinctly: "Dire Economy Threatens Idea of One Europe" (Erlanger & Castle, 2009a). Reporting on an emergency meeting of EU leaders, Erlanger and Castle suggest that the global recession may have given a free rein to "forces threatening to split Europe into rival camps." By way of emphasizing this prospect, they quote the foreign editor of *Süddeutsche Zeitung*, Stefan Kornelius: "The European Union will now have to prove whether it is just a fair-weather union or has a real joint political destiny" (Erlanger & Castle).

While approval of the European Constitution represents a promising step forward, June 2009 elections for seats on the European Parliament represent two steps back. Citizens eligible to vote largely ignored their opportunity to do so. Continuing a trend in which a high participation rate of 62% in 1979 fell to 48% in 2004, only 34% indicated an interest in casting a ballot. Why is that a problem? Citing the economic crisis and a "lack of political leadership" as reasons for voter apathy, Thomas Klau of the European Council on Foreign Relations observed, "The danger is that those who do bother vote for the more radical elements" (Erlanger & Castle, 2009b). And the election proceeded to bear out these projections, as parties critical of the EU gained power.

A Political Agenda

By closely linking their aspirations for higher education with a compelling vision of a once again dominant Europe, the education ministers attracted the attention of national leaders and ensured support for their process at least on paper and for the near term. And by continuing to link the reform of higher education to the economic strength of the Continent, the ministers have continued for the most part to enjoy the backing of the national governments—if not, for the most part, increased funding.

But there are disadvantages also to a resolute focus on economic development and European ascendency. As we have observed, such an agenda can lead to a Eurocentric perspective inattentive to instructive models and experiences elsewhere. It can alienate those who take part in or support higher education for its highly valued but less tangible benefits. And policies framed to reflect a political objective may be subject to shifts in that objective and vulnerable to any strains that threaten it. Hence as the European process has evolved to become increasingly respectful of discrete cultures, divergent development goals, economic disparities, and in some cases competing interests, the Europe of Knowledge originally envisioned by the ministers in 1999 now increasingly appears to favor inclusivity over consistency, coordination over comparability, equivalence over common practice. That evolution may in time prove to be a good thing and may in fact contribute to the flexibility and adaptability essential to an enduring reform. On the other hand, a paramount challenge for Bologna is the extent to which a compelling initial vision of coherence and comparability may assume a more complex and nuanced shape without becoming lackluster.

Bologna is not yet at that stage. Its accomplishments to date and the energy created by its 10th anniversary should help to sustain the momentum of the Process, and much of what has been achieved appears likely to withstand whatever challenges the second decade will offer. But any serious analysis of this effort must acknowledge that the link between the Bologna reforms and the pan-European ambitions will continue to provide a source of impetus and a threat to continuity.

Lisbon and Bologna

Another risk to Bologna as the prime mover of higher education reform in Europe may be found in initiatives that appear similar to those of the Process or that invoke the priorities of the Process but may be antithetical to its values.

For instance, the Lisbon Strategy (or Agenda) authorized by the European Council in March 2000 expresses the determination to make Europe "the most dynamic and competitive knowledge-based economy in the world" (Kok, 2004, p. 6). With three pillars—economic, social, and environmental—the strategy emphasizes investment in education and training. While clearly intended as a larger and more inclusive framework for a broad economic development agenda, the Lisbon Strategy advances educational priorities that pose a risk of confusion with those of Bologna. By one perspective that now appears as though it may prevail, Bologna is to be regarded as an educational initiative under the developmental umbrella of Lisbon. But Bologna came first and in many ways has proved more successful.

The risks of confusion intensified in the early part of the decade when the Lisbon Agenda did not lead to the anticipated results. In 2004 a review panel observed "slow progress" and "disappointing delivery" owing to Lisbon's "overloaded agenda, poor coordination and conflicting priorities" and to "the lack of determined political action" (Kok, 2004, p. 6). The panel report called for "urgent action" across five policy areas, two of them clearly related to—but not making reference to—Bologna. For instance, creation of "the knowledge society" in Europe would require far greater emphasis on research and development. That priority, with strong budgetary implications, would presumably attract talented scientists and other researchers. The aim? "Europe can thus build on its generally strong commitment to create a knowledge society to win potential world leadership" (Kok, 2004, p. 19). And, echoing another of Bologna's action lines, attention to strengthening the labor market would place a premium on "developing strategies for lifelong learning and active ageing" (p. 6).

The strategy might be regarded as an important context for the implementation of the Bologna Process, and some of its documentation acknowledges this. But Lisbon proponents can lose sight of the connection. As suggested above, the Lisbon Statement (2004), which discusses higher education, research, and lifelong learning, at no point so much as mentions the Bologna Process. Nor, when reaffirming priorities that echo those of the Process, does the statement acknowledge progress already made through the Process. In another echo, the statement observes that "developing a system of mutual validation of national quality assurance and accreditation processes would be an important step in the right direction." It calls also for a reduction in "the administrative obstacles to mobility within the EU that European researchers continue to face." And it calls on the EU member states "to urgently address the problem of funding for universities" (Kok, 2004, p. 20). All are of course explicit concerns of Bologna as well.

A 2005 communication within the EC emphasizing the link between higher education and Europe's economic growth does at last acknowledge the Bologna Process. Because "spreading knowledge through high quality education system [*sic*] is the best way of guaranteeing the long-term competitiveness of the Union," the EHEA must be completed on schedule (EC, 2005, p. 9). But in light of all that was being accomplished through Bologna, the communication's solicitation of ideas for increasing research and improving links between industry and the academy seems odd. And, again, as though there were no Bologna Process, the EC declared that it would "address the question of how to enable European universities to compete internationally" (p. 21).

In the fall of 2008, national coordinators for the Lisbon Strategy convened to consider next steps in the face of the emerging economic crisis. Again, the result of the meeting was reported in language closely aligned with priorities of Bologna. That is, Europe should invest in "human capital, knowledge and innovation" to support "European norms and standards" (EU, 2008). And again the report fails to mention the Bologna Process. As Terry (2008) observes, it can be helpful to recall that the Bologna Process "has developed in the context of a parallel EU education development called the Lisbon Strategy" (p. 126). But it would also be helpful if Lisbon Strategy discussions were to acknowledge the ways the accomplishments of Bologna have supported progress toward the strategy's broader economic development goals.

It would be especially helpful if there were no inclination to create structures that appear to replicate those already in place in Bologna. For instance, the European Qualifications Framework's (EQF) offering overarching rubrics similar to but distinct from those of the EHEA qualifications framework adds nothing to the cause of reform and creates a further possibility of confusion.

"Bologna" Reforms—But Not Really

With the approach of the end of the first decade of the Bologna Process, higher education reforms distinct from the Process appeared with increasing frequency. For instance, the German Excellence Initiative, announced in June 2005, earmarked nearly 2 billion for five-year grants to "make Germany a more attractive research location," to make the nation more "internationally competitive," and to bring attention to "the outstanding achievements of German universities and the German scientific community" (Excellence, 2008). If you seek any mention of Bologna in the program description or the press releases announcing grant awards, you will be disappointed. Similarly, in a sharply worded statement delivered on January 22, 2009, President Nicolas Sarkozy (2009) of France assailed academic research systems as childish and moribund, denounced French scientists for their lack of productivity, and announced that 2009 would be *the* year of reform in higher education—all without any mention of the Bologna Process.

These two examples may be sufficient to define the concern. An undertaking as ambitious as the Bologna Process can continue to move toward its objectives only to the extent that it commands respect as the principal driver for higher education reform. If it comes to be regarded as one of several similar initiatives, as a Continental agenda somehow detached from more pressing local priorities, or as a subordinate element within a broader agenda, the influence it must exert to accomplish its ends may be compromised, and a proliferation of action plans, initiatives, reports, declarations, and treaties may create a welter more likely to lead to confusion than genuine systemic reform.

We may also be observing some of the symptoms of policy fatigue. The fact is that most ambitious reform initiatives eventually run out of steam. Having shared the enthusiasm of those responsible for the initiation of

114 THE CHALLENGE OF BOLOGNA

reform, early advocates may leave office, discover fresh priorities, or face different challenges. (As of 2009, only one of the original signers of the Bologna Declaration was still in office.) The highest priorities of those who govern Bologna are, after all, the interests of their respective nations. Here may lie the explanation of why some policy makers in the latter half of the decade have announced plans for higher education reform with little or no mention of Bologna, even though the issues they seek to address are largely those already being pursued through the Process.

Guilt by Association

Supporters of the Bologna Process properly observe that the massive demonstrations protesting higher education reform in spring 2009 were for the most part directed at initiatives distinct from the Process. In Italy, for instance, in fall 2008, Italian students took to the streets—organizers claimed 500,000 at a rally in Rome—to protest new policies suggesting a so-called privatization of Italian higher education. Similarly, in Spain in December 2008, student protests targeted the Bologna Process as a means toward the "creeping privatization of state universities, in which . . . private interests such as those of employers are taking precedence over the common good" (Warden, 2008).

In France spring 2009 brought what one reporter described as "an unheard-of wave of protest by university staff and students" (Mullen, 2009). At one point, 25 universities were experiencing sustained student protests, strikes, and avoidance of classes (Mabut, 2009). And even when the semester ended, faculty members vowed "to continue the fight" (Labi, 2009b). The impetus for the demonstrations, which effectively crippled much of higher education, did not lie principally with the Bologna Process but with reforms proposed by Sarkozy. One initiative assigns authority to university presidents to modify teaching loads to reflect institutional priorities. Another, closely related, provides institutions with greater autonomy in managing their budgets. But the protesters have claimed that such autonomy is simply a prelude to the imposition of tuition and an American-style commercialization of higher education (Labi).

While these particular initiatives may have limited scope, the abrasiveness with which the president has promoted them appears to have aroused broad opposition to higher education transformation in general. At one point he belittled the study of "old literature." At another he suggested that criteria for evaluating research may be captured in a simple question: "How many patents have you put in for?" (Mullen, 2009). But if the president's proposals have generated opposition, it may be even more worrisome that he can offer a sustained and detailed scolding of higher education as though France had taken no role in the Bologna Process. The damage to Bologna created by these expressions of unrest could prove considerable. To the extent that such actions have necessitated compromises in standards and values, they may have a pernicious effect on the credibility essential to public support for higher education reform. It is difficult to reconcile the accountability aspirations of Bologna with the spring 2009 scramble in France to schedule examinations following what many describe as a lost semester. A student at the Sorbonne told an Associated Press reporter, "I don't want to take an exam that will give me a grade based on three weeks of class" (Ganley, 2009). Examinations "based on teaching done so far" will hardly contribute to Bologna's commitment to increased rigor and comparability (Ganley). Nor will the credentials students earn compare to those earned by students engaged through the full semester. University of Oslo history professor John Peter Collett told the reporter, "It is a real tragedy for the French university system" (Ganley).

In Germany, as we have noted elsewhere, May Day 2009 demonstrators protested that structural reform had gone too far—or perhaps not far enough. Concerns with the three-cycle system appeared in combination with issues regarding professorial status, student participation in governance, course availability, and tuitions. Again, many of these issues appear only tangentially related to Bologna. But in Germany as elsewhere, some of those in the streets and on strike have used Bologna as an incendiary rallying cry.

Why find cause for concern in demonstrations that are often poorly informed, misdirected, and unproductive? Four reasons. The first is that faculty and students piling chairs in the streets cannot further the sustained effort that continued reform will require. Second, ministers of education who must manage demonstrations will find themselves hard pressed to maintain oversight with regard to the Bologna action lines. Third, because the Bologna Process insists on a close integration of higher education and society, a schism between the two will hardly serve the cause. And because political leaders may respond unfavorably to protests from the higher education community, the education ministers may face an even greater challenge in securing the policy changes and funding Bologna will continue to need.

Economic Trials

In March 2000, at the inception of the Bologna Process, ministers meeting in Lisbon to frame economic and educational priorities congratulated themselves on a promising outlook. The EU was "experiencing its best macro-economic outlook for a generation," they observed. And Europe's continuing economic growth would for several years support implementation of the Bologna Process. The question was whether the cooperation and vision required for sustained progress would survive a serious economic downturn.

In 2008 the world's economies moved into a deep recession. Throughout the Continent, fears of a protracted slump forced reductions in higher education budgets. While the full impact of the recession on the Bologna Process will become clear only over time, initiatives requiring additional funding within the near term may require modification or postponement. Some further adjustment in the pace of implementation is probably inevitable. And though a protracted economic crisis no longer appeared inevitable as 2009 came to an end, any further reductions in higher education funding could continue to discourage attention to reform initiatives by requiring higher work loads of faculty, more pragmatism of administrators, and increases in—or the initial imposition of—tuition and fee payments.

The practical impact of changes in the cost structure of European higher education are problematical enough, but their political impact may prove even greater. Precisely because Bologna is closely aligned with national and European economic interests, efforts to modify the funding basis of universities may easily, if inaccurately, be associated with the Process. Hence the rallying cries in student protests have been *privatization* (government efforts to transfer an increased share of higher education costs to students), *commodification* (policies suggesting that higher education is regarded only as one of many economic assets), and *globalization* (concerns about loss of national identity, local economies, and educational autonomy). And there is a further dimension to this concern, in that increased globalization following Europe's economic recovery could call into question Bologna's sharp focus on the boundaries of Europe. As one observer commented, "the paradox of Bologna is thus that the EU's attempt to respond to globalised economic competition may be undermined and outpaced by this same competition" (Coleman, 2004).

There may be concomitant risks for the Bologna Process in the broader public arena. If advocates for Bologna should find the Process moving to the margins of political discourse, the reason may be not that their objectives are regarded as unimportant, but because compelling economic issues are claiming greater urgency. During an economic crisis and the ensuing upturn European governments tend to "focus inward as their citizens demand that national resources be concentrated on domestic recovery" (Altman, 2009, p.

9). Moreover, because the ministers responsible for the Bologna Process have promised Europeans economic gains through reforms in higher education, the apparent failure of Bologna to enhance Europe's prosperity, at least within recent memory, may discourage its supporters and arouse its critics.

The EUA Trends V (2007) authors urged governments "to examine whether they are really providing the support that institutions need, as well as ensuring that institutions have the necessary autonomy required to fulfill their missions" (p. 75). It is probably an understatement to suggest that in the aftermath of global recession a near term increase in governmental support for higher education is unlikely. And increased institutional autonomy, if coupled with an expectation for increased self-support, may provide a cover for national disinvestment rather than promote an increased capacity for reform.

A Global Reform

Those committed to the Bologna Process not only must continue to make the case that it remains a visionary, compelling, and realistic model for the reform of higher education in Europe. They also must continue to demonstrate that it represents the *preferred* model. And to sustain their original aspirations, through which European higher education would become once again the dominant model for the world, they must make the case to a global audience.

That effort is already showing some success. In November 2008 academic and political leaders met under the auspices of the Association of Southeast Asian Nations (ASEAN) to approve a deadline of 2015 for the completion of a higher education "compatibility and harmonisation agreement" (Powell, 2008). In the words of one commentator, the clear intent of the agreement is "to follow in the footsteps of the Bologna Process" (Powell). But the obstacles facing this effort in Southeast Asia would also be familiar to Bologna advocates: "fragmented bureaucracies, vastly different basic education systems and the perennial problem of nationalism, coupled with inadequate resources" (Powell).

By contrast, in Australia, which sent an observer to the ASEAN meeting, interest in the Bologna Process remains just that—interest, informed by awareness of competing models. In April 2006, a paper issued by the Australian Department of Education, Science and Training described challenges in international student recruitment and placement likely to arise from the Bologna Process. But two months later, in June 2006, the Australian Vice-Chancellors' Committee, representing the chief executive officers of Australia's universities, commended the effort to understand "the changes occurring in Europe" but added a caution: "It is equally important that Australia does not assume that full compatibility with the Bologna Process is the only option. Any engagement by Australia with Europe through the Bologna Process must not result in a diminution of the diversity of the Australian university system nor in its collaboration and cooperation with countries around the world . . . nor in any approximation to a one-size fits all approach" (Australia, 2006). One commentator concluded from the discussion of the vice-chancellors, "Australia should consider closer ties with Asian and North American universities before aligning with Europe's powerful new higher education bloc" (Illing, 2006).

Steering With Care

After several years of substantive process the Bologna Process reached in 2009 a problematical point in the evolution of any ambitious international scheme. A record of accomplishment was on the books, there was momentum encouraging further progress, and there was among the Continent's education ministers a widely shared commitment to a renewed effort through a second decade. Yet inconsistencies, flawed assumptions, and dilatory and selective approaches to implementation were also becoming more evident, and pressures on the Process from the outside were increasing. To make matters worse, a recession developed and the ensuing recovery appeared likely to take considerable time.

Yet what *cannot* be known with regard to the future may bear more heavily on the Bologna Process than what we do know. The extent to which participating nations will address patent irregularities in the implementation of the Bologna action lines cannot be foreseen, and the impact on the credibility of the Process from inconsistencies nation to nation cannot yet be assessed. Similarly, reaction to efforts in some participating Bologna nations to reform the cost structure of higher education may overshadow all but the most highly visible of the reforms sponsored by Bologna.

Bologna represents an exemplary effort toward higher education reform. Because its accomplishments give heart to all those who believe that higher education can and should become more effective and accountable, most observers share the wish that it succeed. But there are potholes on the Bologna road, and those that cannot be patched must somehow be circumvented lest the sturdy vehicle that began its journey in 1999 be unable to complete the course. At best, the ride ahead is likely to be rough.

8

THE CHALLENGE *OF* BOLOGNA
Access and Mobility

Through the course of the decade, the Bologna Process has pursued three closely related priorities: more vigorous educational mobility for European students and faculty members across national borders, increased success in the competition for international students, and the expansion of access to university study for Europeans. In terms of these priorities, "the diversity of cultures, languages, [and] national education systems," acknowledged in the Bologna Declaration (1999, ¶ 15), represents an impediment and an incentive, a source of complications for those seeking entry to higher education or attempting to pursue higher education in more than one country, but an invigorating stimulus to intellectual and cultural growth for students who can be mobile. Ideally, the Bologna aspiration "to consolidate the European area of higher education" (¶ 15) would lead to enhanced access and mobility without diminishing attractive and edifying singularities. While efforts to reach these ends have proceeded on different fronts at different paces, the steps that have been taken forward so far encourage a continuation of the journey.

Expanding Access

"By the end of the next decade, I want to see America have the highest proportion of college graduates in the world. We used to have that; we no longer do. We are going to get that lead back" (Obama, 2009b). Thus U.S. President Barack Obama reiterated in April 2009 an aspiration he had expressed three months earlier in an address to a joint session of Congress, one he shares with many other leaders in the United States. For instance, state legislators have expressed the similar conviction that the United States should seek to provide broader access to "a high-quality college education for all citizens" (State Legislatures, 2006, p. 10). And Senator Ted Kennedy (2007), writing in the *Boston Globe*, offered the reminder that this commitment is long standing. A primary impetus behind the momentous 1965 Higher Education Act was "the principle that no qualified student should have to forego college because of the cost" (Kennedy). If not entirely alone in this aspiration, the United States, beginning with the GI Bill, had led the world in voicing it.

And it had continued to do so until the last decade. But the Bologna Process has taken up the most characteristic and distinctive of U.S. higher education values. Through its pursuit of a social dimension, the Process emphasizes the expansion of access for demographic groups underrepresented in European higher education. The Process also maintains a broad commitment to lifetime learning, seeks to increase the availability of short-cycle degrees (similar to the U.S. associate's degree), and expresses a commitment to more systematic recognition of prior learning. There is also an increasing recognition of the potential for e-learning and a salutary interest in recognizing the dignity and viability of part-time study. Granted, Europe as a whole still has a considerable distance to go before improving on the U.S. commitment to college access, but as President Obama acknowledged, there is already a disturbing bellwether: Several countries in Europe have passed the United States in the percentage of college-going and graduating students relative to population (Obama, 2009a).

Moving in the Wrong Direction

How has the United States responded to the European challenge? Essentially by moving in the opposite direction. Paradoxically, through nearly a decade of significant national prosperity, many state governments pursued a continuing retreat from the nation's long commitment to higher education as a public good deserving of strong support. The story became familiar. Unprecedented increases in less discretionary categories such as corrections and Medicaid prompted lawmakers in one state after another to balance budgets by passing more of the costs of public higher education on to students. Hence the student share of such costs increased markedly as institutions faced with declining state support were forced to compensate by increasing tuition and fees. For President Obama's determination to restore the leadership of the United States in terms of educational accomplishment to be realistic, this trend must be reversed.

To be sure, in the United States and in Europe, the aspiration to expand the number of those attending and graduating from college confronts also several issues that are *not* financial—or at least not directly financial. Academic readiness for college is one, and there the U.S. statistics are discouraging. Because many high schools fail to offer adequate preparation for college study, students and institutions of higher education must invest in catch-up courses early in the college experience. For instance, fully 97% of students applying for entry to the University of New Mexico at Gallup require transitional courses before they enter the curricular mainstream. Parental encouragement and community support are also critical, and these factors can vary considerably.

Geography can play an important role as well. Adelman (2009) proposes that we learn from Europe "geocoding in fairly sophisticated ways." Once we acknowledge more directly that populations far removed from higher education participate less frequently, we can frame a more concerted approach. "When we examine the geo-demographics of those isolated rural populations, we will find ourselves in the arroyo seccos of New Mexico, the Mississippi delta, the central valley of California, the northwest counties of Minnesota . . . and can get to work in specific zip codes" (p. 228).

Encouraging Degree Completion

For many states, the work of higher education reform now includes a variety of strategies aimed at expanding college enrollments, encouraging the completion of degrees, and facilitating transitions between different educational levels.

One such strategy lies in the proliferation of state programs providing for dual or concurrent enrollment opportunities linking high schools and institutions of higher education. Through such programs, qualified high school students in their junior and senior years form an early bond with higher education, experience a smoother transition from high school to college, and enjoy the possibility of a more expeditious approach to the baccalaureate.

Another effort to increase enrollments in higher education appears in a renewed emphasis on the role of community colleges—a major thrust of the Obama administration in its first year. But if the objective of higher education reform is to increase the baccalaureate completion rate as well as overall higher education enrollments, the picture becomes more complicated. A 2009 study determined that Ohio students who begin their higher education careers at community colleges *with the intent of completing a bachelor's degree* are 14.5% less likely to do so within nine years than students who matriculate at four-year institutions (Long & Kurlaender, 2009, p. 42). According to the research, such students suffer a penalty.

How to build on the advantages offered by community colleges while addressing this alleged penalty? The recent Bologna Process emphasis on the expansion of short-cycle (that is, associate's) degrees may offer one answer. In Europe such degrees are typically the province not of autonomous two-year (i.e., community) colleges but of baccalaureate-granting institutions. That is sometimes the case in the United States. For instance, Northern Kentucky University offers associate's as well as bachelor's degrees, Western Kentucky University hosts the Bowling Green Community College (one of its six undergraduate colleges) on its south campus, and Stark State Technical and Community College in Canton, Ohio, adjoins a Kent State University regional campus (Kent State Stark) that offers associate's and baccalaureate degrees. But such instances are more the exception than the rule.

The closer partnership between two-year and four-year institutions proposed by Adelman (2009) may offer an alternate means toward neutralizing this so-called penalty by enabling two-year and four-year institutions to work more closely together in serving students who seek to apply their community college work to further study. That is, "entering students are admitted to both the community college and the Bachelor's degree granting institution simultaneously, are coached through both a period of habilitation to higher education, all the 'gateway' courses, and at least the foundation courses of a major while they are in the community college (having access to all the facilities and services of the four-year college during this period), then moving over to the Bachelor's degree-granting institution at whatever the Alliance Agreement has established as a minimum credit and performance threshold" (p. 204). In Ohio, such dual admission is already a reality in that community college students who intend to pursue a baccalaureate degree may seek simultaneous admission to a community college and a state university. To qualify, students must be able to satisfy the admissions requirements of the community college and the university, but those who do so are guaranteed admission to the public university of their choice.

By the expansion of such an approach, the United States would be able to build on the Bologna example, taking advantage of the strong traditions of community college education, through which two-year institutions pursue a proud, discrete mission, while promoting at the same time the advantages of a more intentional and fully supported transition from a two-year to a four-year education. The associate's degree should continue to enjoy real standing and not become a perfunctory progress indicator, but it may at the same time be developed into an even more resilient platform.

Another critical transition follows the baccalaureate. Again, with the example of Bologna in mind, four-year institutions in the United States might well give more of their attention to encouraging student persistence beyond the baccalaureate to the master's and other advanced degrees. If, as seems possible, the master's becomes the standard entry-level qualification in the European economy, students in the United States who pause after the baccalaureate may find themselves at a disadvantage on the world stage.

Once transitions are successfully made, the concern of course shifts to student persistence *within* an educational level. Here again the record in the United States is discouraging. Of students who enter higher education intent on the completion of a baccalaureate degree, barely half do so within six years. The result is often unsatisfying financially for students and their institutions. Hence, with an eye on the bottom line, colleges and universities tend to speak of retention, because students who discontinue their higher education before completing a degree represent a loss of revenue.

But a more appropriate perspective embraces instead the challenges of student persistence and success. This is not the place to review the many reasons students leave college, but from the perspective of Bologna, the central focus of the Process on defining at each degree level and within each discipline what students should know and be able to do pertains directly. When students understand the logic behind a curriculum and can perceive the connection between the courses they take and the objectives they have chosen, they are far more likely to persist. We know that. Yet many programs and courses fail to set forth explicit learning objectives that define a clear path to meaningful degrees. By following (and improving upon) the example of Bologna, U.S. higher educators would address a fundamental intellectual obligation: making clear what it is they are attempting to accomplish. More on this in the final chapter.

Rising Financial Barriers

The United States should identify and address all barriers to higher education. But as Senator Kennedy (2007) observed, there are none more formidable than financial ones. In his editorial, "Grant Access to Higher Education," he urged lawmakers to support the "400,000 qualified students a year" barred from baccalaureate education by financial constraints. In the same tenor, an earlier report from the Advisory Committee on Student Financial Assistance, which points to economic gains that would follow from supporting higher college-going rates, is titled "Access Denied" (Access, 2001). The report cites three factors as contributors to an "access crisis." First, while the issue of middle-class affordability has captured the political spotlight, the real impact of the rise in higher education costs has fallen disproportionately on low-income families. Second, as a result, the financial challenge faced by low-income students after the award of all student aid and loans has increased significantly. Finally, because of both these factors, low-income students often must pursue educational pathways that reduce their chances for success—working long hours at low-paying jobs while taking classes, attending only part-time, and assuming heavy loan obligations (Access).

A report published in December 2008 by the National Center for Public Policy and Higher Education made it clear that the concerns detailed in 2001 have not gone away. They have grown worse. The *New York Times* responded with an alarming headline: "Higher Education May Soon Be Unaffordable for Most Americans" (Lewin, 2008). The report found that college tuition and fees had increased 439% in a 25-year period in comparison with a rise in median family income during the same period of 147%. The president of the center, Patrick M. Callan, observed, "If we go on this way for another 25 years, we won't have an affordable system of higher education." And the report reflected figures *prior to* the 2008–09 global economic recession. "When we come out of the recession, we're really going to be in jeopardy, because the educational gap between our work force and the rest of the world will make it very hard to be competitive," Callan said. "Already, we're one of the few countries where 25- to 34-year-olds are less educated than older workers" (Lewin)

Making a Difficult Situation More Difficult

Financial issues are infringing on Bologna aspirations as well, of course. Even before the 2008–09 recession, there was little real investment in Bologna's social dimension. In fact, Europe's tradition of strong support for public higher education, making possible free or low-cost (but selective) admission to universities, was itself up for discussion—to the consternation of many students. But the question for the United States is not only whether the public investment in higher education is insufficient. That we know. An even more urgent question may be whether there are circumstances that exacerbate the problem of inadequate funding.

In an "anniversary visioning paper" written for Campus Compact, Bob Giannino-Racine (2008), executive director of the Action Center for Educational Services and Scholarships (ACCESS), calls growing barriers to access in the United States "a perfect storm." Rising costs, an increased preference for merit-based (rather than need-based) student aid, the persistence of legacy admissions, and institutional self-interest in targeting students most likely to influence institutional rankings have combined to raise the barriers against those who may have most to gain from higher education. As he concludes, "The haves continue to get the upper hand on economic growth, and the have-nots have to fight twice as hard—if not harder—to get their share of the American dream" (Giannino-Racine, 2008).

I suggest in the final chapter it may be time for U.S. higher education to follow the example of Bologna by defining more resolutely the social dimension of its own higher education policy and by considering new funding models that reward effective collaboration. By exploring and promoting alternate paths to higher education, Bologna has sought to add substance to the commitment to open up opportunities for those formerly excluded. The four emerging paths inviting nontraditional students to higher education—short-cycle degrees, enhanced support for part-time students, the development of online courses, and increased willingness to consider the award of credit for prior learning, broadly construed—are all promising, even though with the exception of a few success stories in particular nations, none has as yet produced dramatic gains in access (Adelman, 2009).

There may be a broader point for the United States to take away. Efforts to increase access to higher education in the United States have often been scattershot. A priority on increased financial aid one year may yield to legislation concerning credit transfer in another. Some states have developed a coordinated emphasis on expanded e-learning, while others rely on institutional entrepreneurship. From state to state, and often from institution to institution, there are widely varying standards with regard to the validation of experiential learning. And there are state and federal reporting requirements that can penalize institutions for emphasizing service to part-time students: Students who accomplish their specific educational aims through a few courses but do not take a degree may appear in the records as dropouts.

In sum, even as we recognize that Bologna's efforts to increase access may take some time to yield results, we may find a worthy example in its more comprehensive and coherent array of related aspirations.

Mobility

The discussions at the University of Paris in 1998 that led to the Sorbonne Declaration expressed at one point a nostalgia for an earlier era in European higher education, one in which scholars and teachers alike "would freely circulate and rapidly disseminate knowledge throughout the continent" (Sorbonne, 1998, ¶ 2), expanding their experience with different cultures as they gained in expertise of a chosen subject. By contrast, the four Sorbonne signers observed, "Nowadays, too many of our students still graduate without having had the benefit of a study period outside of national boundaries" (¶ 2).

Even in its earliest stages, the effort to reform higher education in Europe aspired to a continent without educational borders and barriers. Given appropriate support for the costs of relocation, scholars at all stages of maturity should embrace the opportunity to find new sources, new colleagues, and new experiences. And Bologna has drawn on existing initiatives and created new ones in an effort to bring this ideal closer to reality.

The results have been limited. While the 160,000 students taking part in Erasmus in 2007 doubtless gained much from their experience, that total is about 4% of enrollments in universities participating in Bologna. From the most recent perspective of the European Students' Union (ESU), there has in fact been very little progress. "Mobility is another aspect of Bologna with something of a gulf between perception and reality, and where the pace of real change is considerably less than ministers, politicians and HEI [higher education institution] leaders would have us believe. Despite the regular appearance of commitments to the contrary, the goal of making mobility the rule rather than the exception seems almost as elusive as ever" (ESU, 2009a, p. 8). And as we observed in a different context, there are concerns that another of Bologna's priorities, the three-year baccalaureate, may even discourage such mobility. Given the pace of the concentrated program, a junior year abroad may be a far greater challenge if the third year is the last in the degree program. These issues notwithstanding, there is good reason to regard increased student and faculty mobility as a continuing priority for the Bologna Process—and as an important aspiration for the United States as well.

The Lisbon Convention

As we have observed, about a year prior to the meeting in Paris that produced the platform that would lead to the Bologna Process, the Council of Europe and UNESCO convened a meeting in Lisbon to discuss principles for the evaluation of academic credits earned outside the country where the evaluation is sought. Now is our opportunity to give more detailed attention to the protocols developed at the meeting, remarkable for their vision and for their pragmatic address of the issues that had prompted the meeting in the first place.

The formal title of the document, "Convention on the Recognition of Qualifications Concerning Higher Education in the European Region," understates the weight of the principles it advances. These speak of the human right to higher education, to cultural and scientific motives for the pursuit of knowledge, to the diversity of education systems in Europe as an "asset" reflective of cultural, social, and other distinctions among European nations, and to the importance of institutional autonomy. The preamble also refers to Council of Europe (COE) and UNESCO conventions then in place as an intermediate platform for the convention that would supersede them (Lisbon Convention, 1997, ¶¶ 2–9).

The Lisbon Convention (1997) contains 11 sections, each of which incorporates several articles. A few emphases deserve mention for their significance to the Bologna Process and for the extent to which they may expose U.S. practice to critical scrutiny.

- Those who earn an educational credential in one country have a *right* to its *unbiased* evaluation in another. (III.1)
- The procedures and criteria employed in assessment and recognition should be "transparent, coherent, and reliable." (III.2)
- While those seeking the evaluation of their credentials have the primary responsibility for providing accurate and adequate information, the credentialing institution has an equivalent responsibility to respond promptly to requests for information, and the body asked to assess and recognize credentials bears the burden of demonstrating that the information provided in any given case is not sufficient. (III.3)
- Decisions on recognition should be timely, and reasons for refusing recognition must be clearly communicated to the applicant. (III.5)
- Unless significant discrepancies between preparatory programs can be demonstrated, the assessment of academic credentials should assume their practical equivalence. Specific expectations as to qualification for admission must be well and clearly justified. (IV.1–7)
- As support for recognition decisions, adequate information must be made available with respect to institutions, preferably on the basis of formal assessment programs, and national databases should list institutions of higher education, describe the programs each makes available, and indicate the admissions requirements for each program. (VIII.2 , IX.1–2)

From its inception, the Bologna Process has tracked adoption of the Lisbon Convention (1997) by participating countries as a prominent indicator of compliance with the priorities of the process. As of December 2008, there were 48 ratifications (or accessions) in hand from Europe and elsewhere, though there remained several perplexing holdouts among the Bologna group, including Belgium, Italy, and Spain. Among nonmembers of the COE, ratifying states include Australia, Israel, and New Zealand. The United States signed the convention in November 1997 and ratified it in 2003 (CEPES, 2007).

Where lies the challenge for the United States? First, ratification of the convention should have sent a positive message to students around the world that the United States agrees where the burden of proof should lie when foreign credentials are not accorded full credit: with the evaluating institution, not with the student. Second, while greater clarity regarding "the procedures and criteria employed in assessment and recognition" institution by institution would be helpful, broad national agreement on shared standards would be especially so—for international and domestic students alike. Many institutions and programs will retain specialized criteria for admission, but these could be far more clearly stated in comparative terms. Third, as consensus develops further on the learning outcomes specific to general education and to academic programs within and beyond the traditional disciplines, it should be possible to frame a variety of default transfer mechanisms allowing for the transparent and expeditious movement of academic credit. Finally, an accurate and detailed database should make it possible for anyone to discover at once the admissions requirements for an academic program in the United States. Such initiatives would represent effective responses to Bologna to be sure, but, far more important, they would address significant issues of access that should be resolved for U.S. students, Bologna or no Bologna.

The Diploma Supplement

One complication in facilitating the mobility of students and, for that matter, of graduates, has been the inscrutability of credentials earned through higher education. The diploma supplement is meant to address that issue (Gateway, 2008). With its origins in UNESCO discussions in the 1970s, the supplement emerged as an instrument recommended by the 1997 Lisbon Recognition Convention and became the object of a firm mandate through the Bologna Process in 2003. In fact, the need for such a supplement has become even more evident as the Bologna priority on student mobility has exposed difficulties in the transfer of higher education credentials. And its broader potential usefulness has become more apparent as well. Even as the diploma supplement promotes increased mobility, it promises to facilitate student movement from one degree level to another, even within the same institution, and to promote the cause of lifelong learning.

As the name suggests, the document should accompany and complement an academic diploma by providing essential information according to a common "transparent" format. In its Bologna incarnation, it describes "the nature, level, context, content and status of the studies" that the degree recipient has completed (Diploma, 2006). In essence, the supplement enables a student seeking recognition to present evidence of the alignment of educational credentials with the credit expectations of the European Credit Transfer and Accumulation System (ECTS), the disciplinary outcomes developed through faculty consultations across national boundaries (see a discussion of the Tuning Process in chapters 10 and 11), and with broad educational outcomes statements of the European Higher Education Area (EHEA) qualifications framework. And from the perspective of the institutions, the supplement should smooth the evaluation of student and faculty credentials, provide the convenience of a widely accepted template while protecting institutional autonomy, promote the employability of graduates, and increase the institution's visibility abroad (Diploma).

The Berlin Communiqué (2003) provided the strongest thrust for the diploma supplement through its objective that by 2005 every student graduating from a European institution of higher education would be granted such a supplement at no cost. That goal was not met by 2005, nor has it yet been met.

Implementation has been irregular, with the result that recognition and understanding fall far behind projections. So, again, while the United States may find much that is worthy in the principle of the Bologna reform, there may be an opportunity to build on the European experience.

Adelman (2009) offers a useful criticism of the supplement: In its present form, it testifies more directly with regard to the student's home institution than on behalf of the student (p. 94). Drawing on his extensive experience in the analysis of student records, Adelman sets forth requisites for a more informative instrument, and, as the modest proposal on pp. 187–201 in my final chapter suggests, any effort to improve on what Bologna has accomplished might well begin with his suggestions.

By the way, another model for the support of improved mobility may be found in the Europass offered under the auspices of the Lisbon Strategy primarily as a support for international employability. With origins in the certification of vocational education, the credential has broadened considerably to include language competencies, employment history, and a record of education and training. A U.S. version of the diploma supplement might well draw upon both European precedents.

As we have seen, this is by no means the only arena in which the U.S. might improve on the European example, but it may be one of the most immediately approachable. All that is needed for a modest enhancement is agreement nationally on what might be included and what forms of validation would be appropriate. And a diploma supplement focused more directly on the student, as Adelman (2009) has suggested, rather than principally on the institution, would be a step forward. Surely a working group of registrars, provosts, and faculty members would be able to develop standards for such a supplement to U.S. degrees. And with some creative help from professionals in information technology, there seems to be no reason why the supplement might not be compiled and maintained electronically and thus rendered far more flexible, adaptable, and capacious.

Progress in this regard would address a number of concerns. Those pressing for enhanced institutional accountability might find in uniform diploma supplements a valuable database for validating broad institutional goals. Those faithful to the ideals of a liberal education could find in such supplements evidence for the accomplishment of those ideals. Employers would gain a more reliable measure of applicants' potential, graduate schools would be better able to assess capability for advanced study, and students would obtain a credential capable of expressing their accomplishments in more than one dimension.

Credit Where Credit Is Due

An important step on the road to Bologna, the ECTS has offered the Bologna Process a significant leg up on the intent to bring consistency and clarity to the recording and assessment of academic credits. First piloted in 1989–90 as a companion to Erasmus, ECTS has developed into a comprehensive program for the recording and valuation of credit. But the standards of the process have had the additional virtue of encouraging participating institutions to become more explicit about what students study and what they accomplish. Hence, participating institutions may describe their degree programs through Web-based catalogs, specify the intended learning outcomes for each of the courses offered, and clarify workload expectations corresponding to academic credits—all positive steps (ECTS, 2009).

In practical terms for students studying abroad—or planning to do so— ECTS facilitates the recognition of the credits they have earned and can serve as a neutral bank for student credit "deposits." Institutions benefit from the increased transparency of credits earned at other institutions and from the ease with which agreements for student exchange and the articulation of credits may be developed. A further benefit has arisen from the prompt provided by ECTS for institutions to frame more transparently the curricular structures that ECTS reports.

ECTS does not stipulate recognition decisions. Those remain the responsibility of authorities: professors involved in student exchange, university admission officers, recognition advisory centers (European Network of Information Centres [ENIC] and National Academic Recognition Information Centers [NARIC]), ministry officials, and employers. But it is not difficult to imagine the evaluation of academic credits in time becoming virtually automatic except in idiosyncratic cases.

Here again the United States may be moving in the wrong direction. While the transfer of academic credits within the United States has never been as straightforward as it should be, regional accreditation has provided at least a rudimentary basis for consistent evaluation. But by directing that the accreditation status of academic institutions may no longer serve as a sole determinant in the evaluation of academic credits presented by a student seeking to transfer, the 2008 Higher Education Act may have made such evaluation more, not less, complicated.

A U.S. Clearinghouse

How might the United States respond to this element within the Bologna challenge? Through the American Council for Education, the Council for Higher Education Accreditation, or some other broadly representative organization, higher education institutions might collaborate on developing a clearinghouse for academic credits modeled on the ECTS. The discussion of standards, the framing of criteria, and the definition of exceptional cases requiring discrete analysis would not be easy, but it would be valuable.

And not only in itself. As is the case in Europe, a consideration of what academic credit means and how it should be valued necessarily involves discussions directed toward qualifications frameworks. But the advantages of a central repository for earned academic credits appear so compelling that they may serve as an incentive for the broader discussion. Such advantages should include increased efficiency and reductions in costs for institutions and students alike. Fewer courses taken unnecessarily to satisfy arbitrary admissions requirements would save students time and money and promote the more effective use of existing resources. And by modeling its program on that of the Bologna Process, the United States would not only ease the transfer of credits from one U.S. institution to another but also assist students seeking recognition abroad of credits earned here.

What are the impediments? Institutions would have to commit to thorough self-assessment at the program and course level: What outcomes do courses offer, how much work do they require, and how long does that work take? That information would support the publication of transparent catalogs enabling the comparison of participating institutions. And states would have to surrender a measure of their autonomy for regulating the transfer of credits into their institutions from out of state and within their borders. But the advantages in our taking this page from the Bologna book could be considerable.

Other Cross-Border Efforts

Still further support for mobility appears in guidelines for cross-border higher education developed through the work of the Organization for Economic Cooperation and Development (OECD) in cooperation with UNESCO (Guidelines, 2005). The objectives of the OECD guidelines are to protect students from misleading information, from inadequate accommodation, and from the pursuit of credentials of marginal value; to promote the transparency of qualifications and, hence, their "portability"; to support fair, reliable, and expeditious procedures for the recognition of credentials; and to "increase mutual understanding" through the greater cooperation of national quality assurance and accreditation agencies (Guidelines). These objectives are familiar, for they seek to express in more explicit operational terms the values inherent in the Lisbon Convention and in the work by ENIC/NARIC. While the OECD publication (Guidelines) refers neither to the Bologna Process nor to ENIC or NARIC nor to the Lisbon Convention (1997), the text of the guidelines reflects close collaboration with UNESCO and complements the priorities of Bologna.

Lessons Worth Learning

The variety of approaches to the expansion of mobility within European higher education may remind us that a proliferation of conferences, reports, studies, and declarations from a number of acronym organizations can create a sense of indeterminacy and complicate further action (Guidelines, 2005). But the range of the efforts under way testifies as well to a level of commitment to mobility that U.S. higher education should observe.

There is little evidence of that commitment in the United States at present. To the contrary, as we have observed, financial issues continue to prompt state universities to impose disproportionate tuition increases on out-of-state students and to motivate some state legislators to propose quotas for such students. Perhaps real progress on increasing the mobility of college students and faculty members across national and state borders will have to await a fully accomplished economic recovery. But it is worth considering the possibility that just as mobility in a broader sense "is intertwined with the Nation's economic growth" (U.S. Department of Transportation, 2009), restrictions on educational mobility may constrain that growth. When a student living near a state border cannot cross it to secure an education without paying a substantial penalty, are the economic interests of the nation well served?

Arguably, mobile students may become mobile members of the workforce, more willing to move in response to the emerging needs of a dynamic economy, and thus more readily become contributors to an increasingly critical economic agility. Moreover, institutions that attract students from other nations and states create richer learning environments for domestic students. The more deeply rooted in the provinces, the less provincial a college or university can afford to be. And students given the opportunity for study in a different country or state learn one of higher education's most important lessons, the intellectual stimulus that may be found through confrontation with different environments, different cultures, even different food. While encouraging college students to enjoy greater mobility has never been a particular priority for U.S. higher education, perhaps in light of Bologna it should become one.

Competing for the World's Students

Internal mobility represents one element in the Bologna commitment to expanded access. Making European higher education more competitive internationally is the other. While not yet one of the more productive elements in the Bologna Process, the European determination to attract a larger share of the world's students represents another challenge for the United States.

There are ways the United States may make itself progressively *less* competitive in this respect. We can maintain daunting visa policies and create widely publicized embarrassments for notable scholars seeking entry. U.S. institutions of higher education can continue to regard the evaluation of credits earned abroad as a privilege granted to international applicants rather than, as in the terms of the Lisbon Convention, their right. We can maintain cumbersome and inconvenient application processes and require hefty fees.

We can offer dilatory responses to applications and couch them in idiosyncratic language. We can question without compelling reason the quality of the academic credentials being presented and place the burden of proof for their positive evaluation on the applicant. And, most importantly, U.S. colleges and universities can fail to provide clear, accurate, and detailed information about their programs. In short, we can continue to defy through our practices principles conveniently expressed through the Lisbon Convention that the United States has at last ratified. But only at considerable risk.

Here, again, a good track record in the past may inspire some complacency about the future. If one source of international students becomes less productive, another will surely develop. That has been the case in the past. But that has not been the trend of late. The Bologna Process may not create finally the student magnet that its advocates have envisioned, but their determination should remind us that we will continue to face an earnest challenge from Europe—and from Australia, from India, and perhaps within a decade or less, from an increasingly competitive Pacific Rim. If the United States continues to make itself progressively less competitive for the world's students, the consequences in reduced and less-diverse enrollments may become apparent within a short time, but the period required for recovery could be considerable.

9

THE CHALLENGE *OF* BOLOGNA
Structure and Sequence

A
t what age students attend university, for how long, to what purpose, and for what part of the year are not only structural and logistical issues. College costs, for students and for institutions, track the length of time required to earn a degree. The efficiency with which higher education prepares graduates to enter the labor pool or the professions, the depth of preparedness sought through each curricular level, and the capability of the university to address values beyond those of career preparation are all closely linked to such conventions. Moreover, differences in academic calendars, degree designations, and curricular structures from one nation (or one state) to another can create confusion, discourage student mobility among institutions, and complicate the evaluation of educational credentials.

For many centuries, the universities of Europe have preserved such differences as distinctive traditions. As a result, wide variations in the designation of academic degrees, in the recognition of intermediate learning stages, in the definition of outcomes associated with the various credentials, in the length of academic programs, and in standards for admission have remained the norm. But a premise of Bologna is that the Continent can no longer afford the costs of such idiosyncrasy. An interest in greater comparability, if not uniformity, with respect to such matters has been a priority of the Bologna Process from the start.

That priority has reflected also the European education ministers' view that higher education may be out of touch with employers' needs, that academic programs should become more efficient in leading students to timely completion of desirable and easily understood credentials, that the educational process as a whole may be more expensive than necessary, and that movement along the ramps from one level of higher education to another may be poorly defined and out of step with national priorities.

Within this initiative appear several related interests. In the context of national imperatives to increase educational efficiency, to limit costs, and to focus on improving the European labor force, the Bologna Process has sought through structural reform also to enhance the intelligibility of higher education, to increase points of correspondence among related degree programs as an encouragement to transfer of credits, and to define clear links between earned academic credentials and explicit, measurable learning outcomes. Further, advances along these lines would promote a broader priority of Bologna, the increased competitiveness of European higher education for the world's peripatetic students. While the Bologna pursuit of increased comparability among academic structures may not encompass all the action lines, any progress made on this front contributes to progress on many others.

And there has been progress—or at least there was during the first part of the decade. In fact, the increasing rate of apparent compliance with this priority has been for many audiences the most conspicuous of Bologna's accomplishments. The highly detailed study of the Bologna Process by Laurel Terry (2008) is thus aptly subtitled, "It's So Much More Than Degree Changes." And for several reasons the structural reforms of Bologna, in particular the adoption of a three-year standard for the baccalaureate degree, have come to represent one of the Process's clearest challenges to the United States. Even if other elements of the Bologna Process should prove more substantive over time, the potential appeal of an expedited bachelor's degree has captured the attention of U.S. leaders in higher education and government.

A (Qualified) European Success

The Bologna commitment to "the adoption of a system of easily readable and comparable degrees . . . based on two main cycles, undergraduate and graduate" rests on a clear and pragmatic rationale. The accomplishment of these objectives would "promote European citizens employability," produce a three-year undergraduate degree "relevant to the European labour market as an appropriate degree of qualification," and enhance "the international competitiveness of the European system of higher education" (Bologna, 1999, ¶ 8). Moreover, a common degree structure offering discrete and compact courses of study—a three/two-year structure rather than a five-year structure—would make it possible for students who leave higher education after three years to enter the workforce with a credible credential. Perhaps as another benefit, students who had found five-year programs intimidating for one reason or another would now be encouraged to pursue a more manageable course (ESU Policy, 2007).

These are important objectives for the expansion of educational opportunity and for the enhancement of workforce qualifications. Yet from the perspective of the ESU, recent efforts to implement the three-cycle system represent "the most notable loss of momentum" observed in the Process. Following considerable activity in the middle of the decade, implementation "has scarcely advanced in recent times." The ESU criticizes in particular "an attitude of something being completed if it is technically 'in place', regardless of quality or the extent to which it is operational and delivering on its original purpose" (ESU, 2009b, p. 10). That is, rather than create new programs that promote employability and enhance international competitiveness, some nations and institutions appear to have divided existing curricula to fit the new framework and used the Bologna vocabulary to create an impression of compliance. Indeed, despite the considerable progress that has been made, a bewildering range of programmatic combinations and credentials remains.

Of even greater concern is the possibility that the three-cycle initiative may be producing results precisely contrary to those intended. The Bologna action line specifically envisions a three-year baccalaureate that qualifies its recipient for entry into the labor force. But, according to the ESU (not to mention the Ludwig Maximilians undergraduate quoted in chapter 7 on p. 100), students instead have found it necessary "to follow longer periods of study in order to reach a position of sustainable employment" (ESU, 2009b, p. 10). As standardization of the second cycle (master's degree) creates a further incentive for baccalaureate recipients to proceed to graduate study, Adelman's (2009) prediction may well come true: "the Master's will become the preferred exit point for 'undergraduate' education in virtually all fields, academic and occupationally-oriented, across the Bologna universe" (p. 203). Hence for students and employers alike affirmations regarding the sufficiency of the three-year baccalaureate may increasingly appear less relevant.

On the other hand, where the three-year baccalaureate is most successful in preparing graduates for labor force entry, there appears to be a negative impact on another of Bologna's priorities. While a move throughout the Continent to a common structure should facilitate the mobility of college students across institutional and national boundaries, anecdotal evidence suggests that the urgent pace characteristic of a three-year baccalaureate in fact discourages study abroad. In addition to the issue mentioned earlier (the inconvenience involved in finding space within a concentrated program for extended study abroad) students able to enter the labor force or begin graduate or professional study with a highly focused and demanding three-year degree may have little incentive to explore the attractions of greater mobility.

Even if the Bologna Process cannot claim full victory on this most conspicuous of its action lines, what it has achieved can instruct U.S. higher education in important ways. Beyond the claimed and to some extent debatable advantages of the three-year baccalaureate, implementation of the three-cycle structure has encouraged the clarification of higher education sequences, prompted the development of more lucid academic program designations, and promoted greater attention to employer expectations and economic priorities. Regardless of the eventual fate of the three-year degree in Europe, whether as a genuine employment qualification or as a platform leading to a virtually obligatory master's degree, related improvements occasioned by the efforts to implement this priority should summon U.S. higher education to understand, define, and address a meaningful and timely challenge.

What to Leave In, What to Leave Out?

If Europe can create closely comparable academic structures, increase public understanding of higher education, cut the costs of education through more efficient (i.e., less time consuming) academic programs, and make its programs more competitive internationally in the process, why should the United States not attempt to do so? And even if Europe should stumble on this path, might it not still be the right path?

That was the point made to the American Council on Education in February 2009 by Republican Senator Lamar Alexander (2009) of Tennessee. Speaking at the annual meeting of the American Council on Education, he called on U.S. colleges and universities to regard current American baccalaureate degrees as inefficient, cumbersome "Detroit gas guzzlers." Automobile manufacturers in the 1980s "should have been figuring out how to build smaller, lower-cost cars that were more fuel efficient," he said. By analogy, U.S. higher education should now seek to produce "a low-cost, high-quality three-year curriculum for a college degree." He concluded with the observation that tight budgets arising from an economic crisis may represent the ideal environment for innovation and change (Alexander).

Although he did not invoke the example of Bologna to underscore his call for a leaner, less expensive, more resourceful approach to a college education in the United States, the Senator might also have commended to his audience the benefits of the greater uniformity sought through the Process. Given its focus on the preparation of a well-qualified workforce, Bologna seeks to distinguish far more straightforwardly between vital and optional curricular elements, to frame a closer alignment between educational results and employer expectations, and, as appropriate, to calibrate educational encouragements and incentives according to the needs of the economy. In a sense, the three-year baccalaureate degree may prove most important as a synecdoche for a broader range of related reforms. In Europe and the United States, the question of how greater efficiency might be achieved leads to far-reaching and perhaps more significant issues related to the changing environment, values, and priorities of higher education.

Prior to his death in 2007, the influential higher education analyst George Keller identified increases in tuition and fees as primary motives for undertaking "structural redesign," but observed in the posthumously published *Higher Education and the New Society* (2008) that other important prompts in this regard include advanced preparation for college on the part of some students and the high percentage of college graduates who proceed to graduation or to professional study. On the one hand, students who have completed entry-level courses before college should be able on arrival to take advantage of opportunities to expedite their progress; on the other, students bound for further study in graduate or professional programs may have less need for concentrated undergraduate study in a major. In addition, students beyond the traditional age for college (as a majority of college students now are) may require less time as undergraduates for social and intellectual maturation.

In fact, such factors have already prompted a number of experiments in the United States. Had these precedents proved more successful, Alexander (2009) might have found them worth citing. But the record has been mixed. Examples from the 1990s include Oberlin College and Stanford University. The presidents of both announced support for a three-year baccalaureate program, but the idea did not prosper at either school. Some institutions have taken the idea further. Upper Iowa University, also a private institution, announced a three-year option early in the decade. Five students signed up. None graduated in three years. None has signed up since. And Waldorf College in Iowa has discontinued three-year programs that did produce some graduates (Pope, 2009).

More successful—at least in terms of moving from idea to implementation—may be Hartwick College in New York, which now offers students in selected majors an opportunity to earn a bachelor's degree in three rather than four years. But no curricular or pedagogical reforms appear to be involved; participating students are simply accelerating their progress toward a traditional 120-credit-hour baccalaureate by taking 40 credits a year (Hartwick, 2009). Other examples of institutions making three-year programs available to some students include Judson College in Alabama and Seattle University. But the three-year baccalaureate is not the sole or even as yet the preferred pathway to the degree in any of these institutions. And this approach does not suggest in any of these institutions genuine reconsideration of the elements associated with the baccalaureate or the traditional means of providing these elements. The question such programs pose is simple: Can students complete the same work in less time?

At least the European three-year baccalaureate is meant to introduce a different paradigm, one resting on the assumption that students begin their college educations with the essentials of a liberal education already accomplished and with their professional goals clearly established. That assumption may be questionable, but the resulting model challenges the United States to consider its own assumptions and to defend or revise them as necessary.

One of these assumptions is that colleges in the United States should enable students to make more fully informed choices regarding their career interests before they pursue those interests through dedicated academic programs. In other words, effective general education programs allow students to explore several curricular options before they choose a major. Hence the vice president for enrollment management of Upper Iowa University explained to a reporter that a three-year degree "would be attractive to someone who knows right now what they want to do with the rest of their lives." He then conceded that "most students don't have it all figured out right now, and that's fine" (Pope, 2009).

By contrast, European students for the most part are expected to begin college study with a sense of direction. They may amend that direction, and many do, but they typically embark at once on a program of study related to the direction they have chosen. Hence a three-year baccalaureate in Europe is not an accelerated version of a U.S. baccalaureate; it is meant to be more highly focused, to require more extensive secondary school preparation, and to qualify many of its degree recipients for graduate study at an advanced level. As Adelman (2009) observes, "One can count the number of U.S. high school graduates who qualify to be directly admitted to most European *universities* on one's fingers and toes" (p. xii).

The other important assumption in U.S. higher education is that a liberal education comprising an effective general education, correlated learning and experience, and study in the major offers the most secure approach to success in employment and satisfaction in life. The Bologna Process offers a challenge: Defend this assumption. As I suggest in my Modest Proposal in chapter 11, the three-year baccalaureate may hardly represent an example for us to follow, but it should prompt us to be more intentional about what we seek to accomplish, more communicative in explaining the means we employ, and more resolute in measuring and declaring the results of our efforts.

The Four-Year Bachelor's Degree

If the European three-year baccalaureate should emerge as a well-worn stepping stone to a virtually obligatory master's degree, rather than as a credential prompting early entry to the labor force, some observers will dismiss the action line as a repackaging of the status quo. Yet the three-year baccalaureate might nevertheless represent a prominent option for the United States, albeit for reasons different from those that have prompted the Bologna experiment. In other words, Senator Alexander (2009) may well be onto something. Increased use of the advanced study option at the secondary level, the offer of dual credit (high school and college) for concurrent enrollment in the junior and senior years of high school, movement toward a flexible 12-month academic year, and the development of more flexible curricular structures based on better defined learning outcomes are all options that might in many cases lead to a three-year baccalaureate that preserves (and even advances) the values of informed curricular choice and liberal education.

But discussion of this direction should be informed by an awareness of the historical roots of the four-year baccalaureate in the United States and by an understanding of the fairly robust arguments in its favor, at least for American students. As suggested above, the differences between Europe and the United States in terms of structuring the baccalaureate degree transcend merely counting the years required in each case.

For one thing, European education, from primary through tertiary levels, has historically operated as a series of filters. Screened according to demonstrated ability and documented potential, students are directed to tracks presumably most clearly aligned with their interests and abilities. By this assumption, European students identified to proceed to university-level studies have received at the secondary level preparation comparable in some ways to the first year or two of a baccalaureate program in the United States. Hence a three-year European baccalaureate, based on a presumption of accelerated preparation at the secondary level, could at least theoretically ensure learning outcomes comparable with those associated with four-year programs in the United States and elsewhere.

The four-year baccalaureate in the United States has developed according to two very different assumptions, however.

The first of these assumptions is that higher education in the United States is not a preserve restricted to the extraordinarily talented. We have already noted President Barack Obama's (2009a) view that "every American will need to get more than a high school diploma" and his corresponding goal that "by 2020, America will once again have the highest proportion of college graduates in the world." His vision is one of regaining the momentum established by several decades of expanding access that began with the GI Bill. That invitation to enter the doors of the nation's rapidly growing colleges and universities to many millions who otherwise would not have found their way to college then stood in sharp contrast with the far more stratified systems of higher education in Europe.

The second assumption is that U.S. higher education offers not only preparation for a productive and remunerative career, but also essential grounding for an informed, responsible, and satisfying life. "General" or "liberal" education, as this traditional component of a U.S. baccalaureate program is called, represents in many respects a U.S. invention. First the province of small colleges seeking to preserve a credible niche in a higher education landscape increasingly dominated by professional schools and state-supported research universities, general education is now regarded as an essential element in virtually all baccalaureate curricula and as a prerequisite for entry to professional programs in disciplines such as law, medicine, and theology.

Indeed, regional accreditation agencies require such programs of accredited institutions. For instance, *The Principles of Accreditation,* published by the Southern Association of Colleges and Schools (2008), specifies that an accredited institution "identifies college-level general education competencies and the extent to which graduates have attained them" (p. 32). And many professional accreditors in areas such as business and engineering also demand that students in their degree programs meet general education requirements.

Though the electives provided in some European undergraduate degree programs may allow a degree of breadth in individual instances, there are few programs comparable in European higher education to effective—that is, coherent, substantive, and compelling—general education programs in the United States. Indeed, pursuit of the Bologna Process action lines to date has emphasized the differences between the two systems.

As the Process continues into its second decade, these differences may become even more pronounced. Or the Process may expand to encompass a broader vision. In a policy paper, the ESU urged that the Bologna Process reflect "all fundamental objectives of higher education," including "personal development," "preparation for life as active citizens in a democratic society," and development of the capacity for "critical thinking" (ESU Policy, 2007, ¶ 16). Sjur Bergan's (2009) observations prior to the Leuven/Louvain-la-Neuve ministerial conference offer a view of similar breadth. But whatever the course of reform in Europe, we must continue to learn what we can from Bologna's implementation of its first-cycle degree and to take from that example the obligation to defend what we do not seek to change—and to change what we cannot defend.

Most obviously, U.S. higher education must demonstrate more convincingly that the enormous expansion of access in the latter half of the 20th century is in fact producing a better educated and more capable workforce. Can a guarantee of "some higher education" for everyone lead to a more efficient and effective educational system than one that assigns students at specified transition points to curricula differentiated according to demonstrated ability? And, presuming a credible positive response to this question, should U.S. higher education be further modified to respond even more effectively to the full spectrum of talent and ability within the population?

These are largely issues of accountability addressed in chapter 10, which is devoted to effectiveness, but they are given some urgency by concerns that egalitarian values implicit within U.S. higher education have not led to a proportionate expansion in opportunity and capability. A U.S. Department of Education (1999) study takes up the charge that "many marginally qualified or unqualified students" are attending college, fail to complete degrees, and "do poorly in the labor market." In fact, the evidence compiled by the Department of Education largely discredits such negative assumptions. While there are of course obvious disadvantages to dropping out of college without a degree, standardized test scores suggest that U.S. college students today "are about as able now as they were in the past." And though some students do take longer than in the past to finish their degrees, "noncompletion" has increased "only modestly in the last several decades" (U.S. Department of Education). These indicators offer a more constructive context for reform but do not lessen its urgency. The department's study itself suggests that improving the efficiency of higher education, by encouraging broader pursuit of Advanced Placement credits for instance, should represent a priority.

Perhaps less obviously, U.S. higher education may also find it necessary to defend on the world stage its singular conviction that all college students deserve and should receive some form of a liberal arts education. There are persuasive efforts in this regard—studies of general education that attest to its value in an economy ever more dependent on graduates who will continue their learning, adapt rationally and creatively to changing circumstances, work effectively with others, and contribute as responsible citizens to society. But such efforts must produce results demonstrating that a general education curriculum adds value otherwise not likely to be provided and that such value well justifies the additional year a traditional U.S. baccalaureate requires. And the case must be made to an international as well as a domestic audience.

Vocabulary Matters

There are other ways the accomplishments of Bologna may press U.S. higher education to consider its structures and sequences. While Europe has a large task in moving toward a common nomenclature (across multiple languages) and consistent expectations for its degree programs, U.S. higher education is not without its own challenges in this regard. The associate's degree, for instance, ordinarily signifies academic preparation of about two years. And the associate of arts typically provides a platform for continued study through transfer to a four-year or graduate institution. But some terminal degrees instead offer prompt access to vocations. One measure of the largely unsuccessful effort to impose some order on U.S. higher education's bewildering nomenclature may be found in the growing use of the term *technology* to designate levels of capability appropriate for giving assistance to practitioners but not for independent practice: legal assisting technology, human services technology, and so on.

Similar conundrums appear elsewhere. Once presenting a simple distinction between the bachelor of arts (often requiring the study of a second language) and the bachelor of science (usually not requiring a second language), the bachelor's degree now appears in a variety of recondite forms pointing to areas of specialty and differing levels of aspiration. Again, some are terminal, that is, intended for immediate application in the workforce. Others may signify a professional credential (bachelor of architecture, bachelor of science in nursing), a focus on performance rather than on theoretical study (bachelor of fine arts), or even a first graduate degree (bachelor of divinity). Wikipedia, a barometer of public awareness if not always a reliable reference, lists more than 50 different abbreviations of the bachelor's degree.

More recently, the bachelor's, master's, and doctoral levels have all become even more difficult to understand because of the emergence of the so-called professional doctorate, the use of the doctoral title to refer to an initial practitioner qualification. For instance, while the bachelor of laws, or

LLB, indicates in most countries the professional qualification for the practice of law, in the United States the analogous credential is now most often the juris doctor (JD) degree. In 1990 the bachelor's degree in pharmacy became the PharmD. Even more recent are the doctor of physical therapy and doctor of audiology degrees.

Many other examples could be given to support an obvious conclusion: We have made it more difficult for U.S. citizens to understand academic credentials, and we have complicated enormously the task faced by those in other nations attempting to understand our academic programs and the qualifications promised by our various degrees. As a task force appointed by the Higher Learning Commission (HLC, 2006) of the North Central Association of Colleges and Schools observed in its report on the professional doctorate, "While the various professions have defined the nature of each program, there seems to be no obvious consistency among the various degrees as to length of study; rigor, substance, or content of the program; or the ultimate utility of the degree to the person who earns it" (p. 1).

A Step to Consider

What might be done to create greater intelligibility without infringing on the autonomy and specificity of the various academic disciplines and the institutions that accommodate them?

One step that may be worth considering is a reversion to two bachelor's degrees—arts for liberal arts graduates, and sciences for those pursuing more technical degrees, combined with a parenthetical reference to the specific discipline and (to take a page from Bologna) a lucid diploma supplement describing the course of study, the competencies so assured, and the experience gained. The Bachelor of Integrated Studies might then become the BA (Integrated Studies), the Bachelor of Organizational Management would appear as the BA (Organizational Management), the Bachelor of Journalism would become the BS (Journalism), and so on. A modest step, to be sure, but an example of a reform that would cost little while helping to ameliorate the present inscrutability of higher education in the United States.

Another move toward greater clarity might come through the creation of a credential distinct from the doctoral degree that would designate the completion of an entry-level professional course of study. Some possibilities? *Practitioner* or *master of practice* might serve. The confusing welter of doctoral degrees that in fact designate an initial qualification to practice a profession might be clarified considerably with a common credential, MP,

combined as in the case of the bachelor's degree with a parenthetical designation and a supplement providing more detailed information.

Encouraging Progression

One concern within the Bologna Process has been the facilitation of student
progress. Expressing the recognition that a competitive Europe will require
far more graduates educated at the master's and doctoral levels, the Process
has sought through various means to encourage smooth transitions from one
degree cycle to the next. Here, too, because of "poor implementation . . .
and inadequate understanding" Bologna has not yet documented much success (ESU, 2009b). But the objective is one well worth pursuing in Europe—
and well worth emulating in the United States.

Crucial to the effort in Europe has been the far clearer delineation of
what is meant by each cycle. To this end, the European Qualifications
Framework of the EHEA provides five broad categories, each of which may
be defined relative to a particular cycle. While clearly important as elements
in what Adelman (2009) succinctly describes as Bologna's intended
"accountability loop," their considerable breadth may limit their role in promoting overall clarity and coherence. Nevertheless, European agreement on
even very general rubrics offers a useful point of departure for the development of qualifications frameworks at the national level. Yes, only a few
nations have made considerable progress while others have made little, and
the available results at the end of Bologna's first decade present considerable
disparity and discontinuity. But the process of clarification must begin some-
where, and the Bologna Process has made a good start.

No less critical to Bologna's aspirations has been an interest in guaranteeing access to the second cycle for graduates of the first. While student
experience has so far not confirmed the broad availability of such a guarantee, the principle should challenge the prevailing U.S. convention. In the
United States, the degree cycles typically stand as a pyramid, with a broad
baccalaureate base leading upward to a far narrower master's degree section
and to a small highly specialized peak for doctoral candidates. Programs are
largely discrete. A student receiving a baccalaureate degree from an institution in most cases must then apply for admission to a graduate program *in
the same institution.* By contrast, Bologna proposes to create a conduit students may pass through easily from one curricular structure to the next. If
an important motivation for education reform in the United States is to
maintain economic and educational competitiveness with the rest of the

world, an expansion of access to master's study and an increase in the number of students proceeding to that level should be among the priorities. In the final chapter of this study, it is so defined.

The third dimension of this move toward greater clarity has been work at the disciplinary level to define learning expectations. We will examine the Tuning Process in the next chapter as a significant precedent especially in terms of enhanced effectiveness, but Tuning has implications also for academic structure. If U.S. faculty in each discipline were to reach agreement on what students in each discipline should know and be able to do at each stage, they would achieve also far greater clarity on what recipients of associate's, bachelor's, master's, and doctoral degrees should know and be able to do. And the ability of the academy to persuade qualified students to advance from one level to the next would be considerably enhanced.

Yet as noted elsewhere Bologna may have a choice to make in this regard also. If a renewed emphasis on the importance of the master's degree has compromised an emphasis on the sufficiency of the baccalaureate as an appropriate entry-level qualification, renewed insistence on the baccalaureate could overshadow the priority on progression through the degree levels. Europe may already be making its choice in favor of enrollments at the master's level. The United State may want to do so also.

These issues of implementation notwithstanding, as Europe continues to manage and reorder its priorities, there is an implicit summons in the Bologna Process for U.S. higher education to give closer attention to the sequences that students follow en route to their respective callings. Efforts by institutions to compete more effectively with one another have doubtless led to innovations that attract students. But the consequence of innovation has been an enormous proliferation of programs, degrees, credentials, terms, expectations, and sequences. And confusion in the marketplace rarely encourages an expansion of opportunity.

Learning From Bologna

There is much good work going on in the United States to frame consistent degree structures according to rational curricular principles. Whether that work will satisfy those who look admiringly at the gains Europe is achieving will depend ultimately on the extent to which justifications of current U.S. best practices can be framed on objective and persuasive grounds and on the willingness demonstrated by the academy to look beyond the status quo. Similarly, whether Europe will continue to prompt U.S. higher education to examine itself, to consider adopting (or adapting) its examples, and to justify in other cases its own models will depend on Europe's ability to demonstrate that the goals of its structural reform—faster student progress toward degrees, lower educational costs, employer acceptance, greater mobility, stronger graduate enrollments—are in fact being realized. But when all of these variables are taken into account, it will require considerable self-assurance and perhaps some degree of insularity to argue that U.S. higher education has nothing to learn from Bologna's accomplishments in terms of structure and sequence.

THE CHALLENGE *OF* BOLOGNA
Effectiveness and Accountability

The designation of intended educational outcomes, assessment of the extent to which they are accomplished, and effective use of the information that is obtained to improve learning represent essential elements in a complex undertaking ordinarily described by a simple term: accountability. In Europe and in the United States, demands for more detailed accountability—in effect for better information about what universities do and how well they do it—have been expressed by political leaders, by students making educational choices, by accreditors, and by institutions of higher education themselves. And there has been a substantive response to such demands.

A corresponding impetus has arisen from the recognition that steps taken to enhance accountability may improve the educational process itself. To the extent that higher education becomes more clearly intentional through the articulation of broad outcomes for each degree cycle, more detailed definition of programmatic outcomes, and broadly consultative development of outcomes for each discipline, learning should improve. Faculty members should pursue more clearly understood learning priorities, and students should understand more clearly the contexts and purposes of the learning they are pursuing.

Europe and the United States have shown some leadership in accountability, and each could learn from the other. However, while there has been more activity in the United States over a longer span of time, the Bologna Process may offer the more instructive model.

Bologna: A Coherent and Comprehensive Approach

A commitment to the measurement of effectiveness lies at the heart of the Bologna Process. But in tracking the first decade of the Process, as we have observed the emerging emphasis on different elements in this commitment, we have not been able to appreciate the full extent of their interconnectedness. Because the coherence of the Bologna approach to accountability may represent its most edifying characteristic, we should first attempt a bird's-eye view of what Adelman (2009, p. 24) describes as the "accountability loop," from the definition of learning expectations to the restructuring of degree programs.

This loop begins with the effort to define what students should know and be able to do at each degree level. To this end there is a qualifications framework for the EHEA, the structure of Dublin Descriptors (n.d.) rubrics approved in 2005 to guide the development of frameworks nation by nation. In turn, the Tuning Project, a distinct undertaking initiated by the European academy, seeks to advance expectations of outcomes discipline by discipline. The logical next stretch of the loop is some means of recording what students have accomplished, that is, a credit accumulation system based on understanding what such accomplishments signify, and an accompanying means (the diploma supplement) of providing the student with a more informative portable credential. Because mutual trust across borders is critical to the functioning of such a system and to the greater mobility that it is intended to achieve, the effectiveness of the various programs offered through degree structures comparable from one country to another must be demonstrated with credible and consistent indicators. Thus the accountability loop is complete—or will be, as information obtained along the way informs continuous improvement.

Problems can arise when movement along the loop takes place at different speeds, or when some making the journey focus on some elements and not others—what European students describe as the à la carte approach to Bologna. And Bologna might have made greater progress through a consideration of experience beyond the borders of Europe. The principle of peer review, for instance, now emerging within the Bologna Process, is already well established in the United States. And the U.S. example of value-added assessment might be more fully applied by Bologna in the pursuit of its social dimension. But Bologna has defined an integrated and coherent approach to accountability that should continue to guide its further progress. Unfortunately, the same cannot be said for the United States.

Bologna's Accountability Agenda: Process and Progress

The intent to build a commitment to quality assurance through the development of "comparable criteria and methodologies" appears among the first six action lines set forth by the Bologna (1999) Declaration. The three major biennial perspectives of the BFUG Stocktaking (2005, 2007, 2009), of the EU Trends reports (1999, 2001, 2003, 2005, 2007), and of the ESU *Bologna With Student Eyes* reports (2003, 2005a, 2007, 2009b)—that have tracked efforts with regard to this central objective have found evidence of considerable progress. And as we have noted in several contexts, while Bologna has undertaken some important initiatives, it also has drawn on efforts already under way in Europe, lent its support to activities aligned with its priorities, and recognized progress accomplished by allied European entities as evidence for the incremental realization of its aims. Most important, it has endeavored to gather such initiatives into a coherent whole that can make sense even to those not working in higher education.

One example of an initiative that long predated Bologna—but has since been taken up by the Process—arose in the 1950s and 1960s from the growing workload involved in the evaluation of educational credentials. So long as there was little movement of students among the universities of Europe, those engaged in assessing credentials could look deeply into curricula to determine the equivalence (or not) between presumably comparable programs of study. But with an expansion in mobility, detailed analysis became impractical and had to give way to recognition of programs judged comparable, a trend that emphasized the importance of reliable information about them. In turn, the 1992 Council of Europe (COE)/UNESCO agreement led to the Lisbon Recognition Convention (Lisbon Convention, 1997). Though intended to support mobility, the agreement was significant also for its focus on standards governing the evaluation of educational attainment. It became evident during the Lisbon Convention discussion that a much clearer focus on "provisions for assuring the quality of . . . teaching and qualifications" (Lisbon Report, 1997, p. 3) would be required.

A Three-Stage Platform

The signal contribution of the Bologna Process to the achievement of this clearer focus has been the loop defined by Adelman (2009) in considerable detail. The coherence of the ideal with its three distinct levels of defined qualifications is powerful, and some nations are already enjoying the benefits of implementation—especially those that were engaged in the work of accountability prior to Bologna.

The European Level

The first of the qualifications levels, "the framework of qualifications for the European Higher Education Area [EHEA]," offers an umbrella that defines in general terms the degree cycles (Framework, 2005). Adopted by the ministers at their 2005 meeting in Bergen, this overarching document maintains a high level of generality. But if the categories it describes (depth of knowledge and understanding, the ability to manage scholarly protocols, capability in the use of data, scholarly independence) make sense, they suggest a cumulative vision of higher education from one level to the next, and they represent a consensus that has gained favor. Excepting the Association of American Colleges and Universities (AAC&U) statement on the essential learning outcomes, these are goals that have largely evaded the United States. In practical terms, the European framework lives up to its name. It offers a broad but secure scaffold on which the Bologna nations may construct more focused and detailed national curricular structures.

The National Level

The second level, nation by nation, is intended to incorporate discrete national approaches to accountability, those developed prior to Bologna and those being prompted by Bologna. How are the two levels related? According to the 2007–2010 Bologna Process Web site's statement on the "Overarching framework of qualifications of the EHEA," the continent-wide EQF sets "'outer limits' within which national frameworks should be situated," accommodates diversity "within those limits," "ensures compatibility between national frameworks," and offers for European higher education a "common face" (Bologna, 2009, ¶ 7). By contrast, national frameworks, "closest to the operational reality," are the purview of the national system of higher education, are intended to facilitate movement "within the system," offer the ultimate determination as to "what qualifications [degrees] learners will earn," and describe how the different qualifications are related (Bologna, 2009, ¶ 8).

Some national frameworks, well under way prior to Bologna, are robust. For example, long-standing interest in quality assurance in the United Kingdom became explicit in 1990 with the creation of the Academic Audit Unit. In 1997 the Quality Assurance Agency for Higher Education (QAA) began its work "to provide independent assessment of how higher education institutions in the UK maintain their academic standards and quality" (QAA, 2009). As in the United States, responsibility for the documentation of institutional effectiveness rests principally with universities, but they undertake such documentation guided by statements that describe what graduates at different levels must know and be able to do. In turn, the QAA "reviews and reports on how well [the institutions] meet those responsibilities and encourages continuous improvement in the management of the quality of higher education" (QAA).

As is the case with accreditation agencies in the United States, the agency is funded not by the government but by institutional dues. In 2008 the QAA undertook an external compliance review and a process of self-certification so that it might maintain its membership in the European Association for Quality Assurance in Higher Education (ENQA) while demonstrating alignment between its framework for higher education qualifications and the overarching EHEA framework. The resulting 65-page report offers a remarkable vision of an academy that is self-aware and focused on learning. If the standard it offers prompts other Bologna participants to respond similarly, the accomplishment of the Process in terms of accountability will prove formidable.

The United Kingdom and a few other countries (Denmark, Germany, France, and Ireland, for instance) are so far the exemplary exceptions in the Bologna family. Although most countries participating in the Process appear to be engaged in the development of a national framework at some stage, most of those at an advanced stage have been working on accountability for a long time.

Their efforts can guide those of their colleagues in Europe. And, despite some differences in structure, nomenclature, and process, they share important principles that can guide the United States. First, their approaches embody a sequential and cumulative view of higher education: One degree level builds on competences ensured by the preceding one and prepares students for advancement to the next. And the frameworks begin the effort to create meaningful rubrics for the crediting of student performance in terms of the extent and sophistication of the work required. Finally, these frameworks suggest a welcome ownership of accountability by the nations that are developing them.

The possibility that such diversity might lead to confusion may be mitigated through stronger oversight from the ENQA. As we have noted, the Bergen Communiqué (2005) adopted ENQA standards in calling for expanded cooperation among national quality assurance authorities. Although this initiative did not seek a common system of accountability, it did call for pan-European recognition of national decisions regarding accreditation and quality—another expression of Bologna's characteristic balance between seeking greater uniformity and comparability throughout Europe while conveying respect for local prerogatives. Whether the benefits of greater consistency and uniformity can be realized without the assertion of a strong central authority remains to be seen, but the principle set forth offers a useful point of reference.

The Tuning Project

The third level of the outcomes frameworks involves the disciplines, where the Tuning Project—an apt metaphor that suggests orchestral instrumentalists aligning their pitches with the A440 of the oboe or piano—convenes faculty members and others to define learning outcomes for specific disciplines. If the ENQA may be cited as representative of the external thrust of the Bologna Process emphasis on quality assurance, Tuning may be regarded (with some reservations) as preparation for its internal thrust. Initiated in 2000 by several European universities in response to (but independent of) the launch of Bologna, the principle objective of Tuning has been to translate the expectations of the three-cycle program structure into disciplinary terms. The primary object of the project is to secure agreement on those terms, discipline by discipline, but Tuning also considers the comparability of degrees and the maintenance of a transparent and widely accepted register of academic credits (Tuning, 2006).

Explicitly disavowing interest in degree program "uniformity" and in "any sort of unified, prescriptive, or definitive European curricula," the Tuning approach "has been developed by and is meant for higher education institutions" (Tuning, 2004). Indeed, the name was chosen to suggest the value assigned to programmatic diversity in European higher education and to emphasize an interest in seeking affinities among programs, encouraging convergence where appropriate, and building shared understanding of differences where convergence appears unlikely. Unlike European assessments of educational systems to ensure compliance with national expectations, ordinarily a purview of governments, Tuning has instead engaged members of the academic community in discussion of "educational structures and content." If Bologna is comprehensive reform, bringing into closer comparability the higher education systems of Europe, Tuning is particular reform, concerned with "the comparability of curricula in terms of structures, programmes and actual teaching" (Tuning, 2004).

Even beyond Tuning's estimable accomplishments in areas such as chemistry, where European standards for the bachelor's degree now stand to guide programs and interpret them to the public, the method it embodies deserves some attention. At the heart of the project is listening. Through consulting with employers, graduates, and their colleagues, the Tuning colleagues build up lists of appropriate generic competences and gain along the way a sense of the extent to which students are achieving them through current programs of study. They then formulate competencies specific to the discipline. The ECTS comes into play at this point because a common register of academic credentials depends for its credibility on their comparability and trustworthiness. Estimates of student workload in terms of hours required for the defined courses and competences thus complement the expectations that have been defined. And these issues in turn drive consideration of the pedagogies appropriate to the competencies desired and the time allocated to their accomplishment.

A measure of the thoroughness and detail characteristic of the Tuning project may be found in many of the subject-specific descriptions. For example, there are more than 30 items in the list for the discipline of history (Tuning, 2004). These include references to specific bodies of knowledge (knowledge of ancient languages, of local history, of "one's own national history," of "European history in a comparative perspective," and of "the history of European integration") and expectations as to broader intellectual proficiencies (ability to define research topics, to "identify and utilize appropriate sources of information," and to "organize complex historical information in coherent form").

As Adelman (2009) observes, what Tuning has accomplished challenges the United States to go beyond the "global labels" attached to broad learning outcomes to "focus on what is directly taught, i.e., subject matter that reflects the training and organization of our faculties" (p. 54). Of course, as the Tuning example suggests, it can be helpful to achieve consensus on global labels first so there can be a common base for subsequent efforts to focus in greater detail on subject matter.

The outcomes to date, available for review on the Tuning (2006) Web site, include an overview of each discipline so far included in the Project, profiles describing the content of the different degrees offered, suggestions of occupations for which program graduates should be well suited, descriptions of learning outcomes and competences associated with each program, some reference to appropriate quality enhancement programs, and a list of subject specific skills and competences that should be associated with each discipline as a whole. The results of Tuning now appear also in a series of publications offering "reference points for the design and delivery of degree programmes," discipline by discipline. The first cover European studies, chemistry, physics, and occupational therapy. More are forthcoming.

As Adelman (2009) observes, there is wide variability in the quality of what Tuning has accomplished. Some of the statements of competencies are vague. Some are arcane. And some may inundate with detail those who most need guidance: faculty members, students, the public. But beyond what it can document as evidence of its success, the Tuning process offers to those outside Europe the example of its process, one of "joint reflection and debate . . . reaching out and involving thousands of colleagues, students, graduates, employers and other stake-holders" (Gonzáles & Wagenaar, 2008, p. 1). In short, by responding to the Bologna Process through a principled and coherent university-based initiative, those responsible for the design of Tuning have gained an influential voice in Bologna and have assumed a share of authority for that part of the reform effort most clearly of concern to institutions, faculty members, and students. Perhaps more than any other enterprise in the early stages of Bologna, Tuning has enabled its participants to gain a sense of ownership for the reform of higher education—a vital engagement that the Bologna Process in its early stages did not encourage.

Two more recent developments have been the incorporation in Tuning of the third, or doctoral, cycle and the expansion of the Bologna umbrella to include thematic networks (a European Commission program that antedated the Bologna Process), each intent on pursuing a Tuning-like process within a discipline. So far, discussions of the doctoral level have remained fairly general, largely because of the specificity of particular disciplines with regard to structure and curriculum. Moreover, at this level students are more likely to initiate their own projects than to pursue shared assignments. Hence, Tuning has committed to learning "how doctoral programmes are organized and what they look like at subject area level by comparing the situation in the different European countries" (Tuning, 2004). Thematic networks, on the other hand, are grant-funded groups, typically within a discipline, that seek to advance a particular field through pan-European consultations with the guidance of Tuning authorities.

In sum, as with so many of the elements addressed by the Bologna Process, the concern with greater effectiveness and accountability has required not so much the creation of a new culture as an effort to align many distinct cultures. That is surely a strength of the Process to date, but it represents also a challenge. The greater the diversity of principle and practice, the less transparency. But as we shall see later, Tuning has already exerted a beneficent influence on the United States by prompting a pilot effort in three states.

Eurydice and the European Center for Higher Education (CEPES)

An important contributor to the effectiveness and accountability agenda of Bologna appears in Eurydice (2009), a program founded in 1980 by European Commission member states to provide educators and policy makers with reliable information on higher education. On the basis of what Euryd- ice had already accomplished, the Bologna Process was able to launch its concern for improved quality assurance on a firm platform of data. In addi- tion to its role in information gathering, Eurydice represents also Bologna's interest in the use of information to promote greater understanding of and cooperation within European higher education.

Eurydice (2009) has provided Bologna with continuing points of refer- ence. Its value in this regard can be best appreciated by accessing its open, free, convenient, and frequently updated database, intended to provide "a comprehensive source of information on education systems in 31 European countries from pre-primary to higher education" (Eurydice, 2009). In addi- tion, Eurydice has served also as an important source of reports used by the biennial Bologna conferences to assess progress country by country with respect to the action lines. In the fall of 2008, Eurydice was reorganized as a network under the auspices of the European Union's (EU) Education, Audiovisual, and Culture Executive Agency.

In its quality assurance efforts Bologna relies also on several other important sources of information. As mentioned in chapter 3 on pp. 39–40 in our tracking of Bologna's implementation, CEPES (2008) focuses on the cooperative study of higher education. The center provides direct sup- port to Bologna by following legislation concerning higher education, country by country, and by serving as a clearinghouse for effective quality assurance practices. Again, Bologna offers the example of making good use of existing resources rather than building from scratch ones dedicated to its agenda.

The United States is similarly well provided with respected sources that gather and interpret information regarding higher education. Two worth particular mention—one governmental, the other private but non- profit—are the Institute of Education Sciences (IES) at the U.S. Depart- ment of Education and the National Center for Higher Education Management Systems (NCHEMS). In addition, state agency reports, accreditor information caches, media publications, and commendable efforts by associations representing subsets of the U.S. academy organize information for the benefit of potential students. Lacking, however, is a neutral bureau or agency comparable to Eurydice and CEPES, one charged with selecting information about higher education of greatest pertinence to the academy and to the public, working to ensure its credibility, trans- lating that information to make it as accessible as possible, and presenting it to make it compelling.

ENQA

We observed the role of ENQA in the development of national qualifications frameworks, but this important association, one of the four official consulting members in the Bologna Process, merits separate attention for the range of its work beyond the frameworks. ENQA also convenes state-based quality assurance agencies for discussion of common interests, sponsors quality assurance forums, offers information about best practices, and works with national quality assurance projects in light of the overarching framework approved for the EHEA.

Its recent projects include a study of the diploma supplement "as seen by its users," a survey of quality procedures in European higher education, a study into the feasibility of a "convergence of national quality assurance systems in Europe," and a broad survey of "Quality Procedures in European Higher Education" (ENQA Past, 2009).

Through such efforts, ENQA operates as an invited collaborator to provide direct support for improved quality assurance through the development of recommended methods and metrics. That important role began to emerge at the Prague meeting in 2001, when the Bologna ministers asked ENQA to take a lead role in creating a framework for pursuing greater accountability. Then, at their meeting in Berlin in 2003, the ministers offered ENQA a double mandate: (a) to assist quality assurance agencies with the development of a peer review system and (b) to take the lead in creating a consensus on principles of quality assurance. In 2005, as we have seen, the ministers meeting at Bergen approved the recommended guidelines for quality assurance and invited ENQA into consultative membership (Quality, 2005). Finally, at their meeting in London in 2007, the ministers endorsed the ENQA recommendation for the creation of a European Register for Quality Assurance Agencies (EQAR, 2009). From its initial role as a helpful ally, ENQA has in short order become integral to the Bologna Process.

Accomplishments

Through the Bologna Process many of the nations of Europe are making progress with regard to accountability in and for higher education, particularly with respect to the Continent's relative lack of experience with assessment and accreditation prior to the 21st century. Indeed, what has been achieved in a decade calls into question the far more deliberate pace apparent in U.S. higher education over the course of nearly three decades.

In sum, on the basis of its three major biennial surveys—the EUA Trends (1999, 2001, 2003, 2005, 2007) reports, the perspective expressed in the iterations of *Bologna With Student Eyes* (ESU 2003, 2005a, 2007, 2009b), and the Stocktaking (2005, 2007, 2009) reports—the Process has supported and begun to prompt a broadly acknowledged paradigm shift from an emphasis on what is taught (and how) to what is learned (and how). On this, as on virtually all of the Bologna reforms, the actual depth of penetration can be discouraging, but substantial positive change seems apparent from a number of indicators. Reliable information concerning higher education has become more widely available, a growing awareness has emerged regarding the need for consistency in program evaluation and in the documentation of competences associated with program completion, and, increasingly, even at the institutional and faculty levels, it is acknowledged that curricula from program to program should reflect a widening consensus on learning outcomes and permit assessment with regard to the accomplishment of those outcomes.

Accreditation of Programs

Although much has been accomplished, much remains to be done. One issue in particular, programmatic accreditation, appears likely to emerge as an emphasis during the second decade of the Process. The importance of such accreditation relative to many of the other priorities of the Bologna Process has become apparent in the context of progress toward greater consistency in framing educational outcomes, enhancing mobility, and ensuring the comparability of credentials at the degree level. Indeed, sustaining progress in these areas may increasingly depend on a concomitant growth of confidence in the reliability of the credentials acquired through the new degree cycles in specific programs and presented across borders for appraisal and validation.

On this front, some attention to the lengthy experience with programmatic accreditation in the United States would probably serve the Bologna Process well. The tentative efforts in Europe toward the creation of systems of peer review, for instance, would probably progress more rapidly if time-tested protocols developed by U.S. agencies were invoked as points of departure. The extensive experience in the United States with selecting, assigning, training, and evaluating peer reviewers might spare European colleagues missteps. Similarly, because U.S. agencies have managed for many years the delicate balance between visibility and disclosure on the one hand, and the confidentiality necessary for candid reviews on the other, the precedents created could be useful points of reference. But there appears to have been little interest—at least officially—within Bologna.

Issues of Authority

One emerging impediment to further substantial progress toward pan-European accountability lies in Bologna's lack of real authority. As in its other arenas, what influence the Bologna Process has been able to exert has two sources: alignment of Bologna priorities with projects continuing under the auspices of the European Commission, and the convictions of a continually changing cast of national education ministers.

The Tuning Project illustrates the point. There are now clearly stated expectations with regard to what students are expected to know and be able to do in a number of disciplines. But the follow-through is not all the framers envisioned. Practical uses of the Tuning consensus at programmatic and institutional levels are not yet well documented. And there are as yet only limited indicators that programs are incorporating these expectations into statements of measurable outcomes, assessing their accomplishment of those outcomes, and using what they learn to make improvements. Already an example of earnest effort applied to the right ends, Tuning may experience a loss of momentum now that the enthusiasm of the early adopters has met the challenge of broader extrapolation.

Here too the United States might learn from—and improve upon—Bologna. By pursuing a more creative vision of learning outcomes, one less restricted by conventionally defined disciplines, those engaged with a U.S. version of Tuning might well revitalize the efforts of their European colleagues. The final chapter of this book in fact proposes that the United States build on its Tuning pilot efforts in three states to create a broad platform for a forward-looking quality and accountability initiative.

A Question of Priorities

In sum, the Bologna Process has accomplished much with regard to accountability, and it has sought to do so through a coherent and inclusive approach. But because that approach has evolved over time into a vision more encompassing and more complicated—for example, consider the emergence of competing overarching frameworks for the EHEA—one part of Bologna's challenge may recall a current U.S. dilemma, the lack of a clear message about what is most important. Assessment, evaluation, accreditation, quality assurance, peer review—the vocabulary of the effort itself points to a mix of initiatives that can present conflicting aims and methods. And confusion can produce inertia. With the end of the first Bologna decade, the potential for continued progress remains compelling, but the risks of fragmentation and inconsistency appear unlikely to fade anytime soon.

The U.S.: Competence, Commitment, Complexity

To appreciate the challenge of Bologna in terms of effectiveness and account-ability, we must observe what is taking place in the United States. There are many fronts in this effort: commercial (e.g., *U.S. News & World Report*) and higher education association (Association of Public and Land-Grant Universities [APLU] and American Association of State Colleges and Universities [AASCU]) initiatives that provide the public with comparative information on institutions, reforms in the practice of regional accreditation, collaboration between professional accreditors and academic associations on improvements in general education, state report cards—a long list.

Add to such efforts various state initiatives to allocate funding according to institutional performance, the public information efforts of agencies and associations previously mentioned, and related efforts in many institutions to measure the effectiveness of their programs for a variety of purposes. A picture of an earnest and widespread but poorly coordinated commitment begins to emerge. Despite the international advantage that might have accrued to the United States from its experience with assessment and accountability spanning several decades, consideration of that experience suggests instead there is much to be learned from Bologna.

A Long-Standing Commitment

In the current sense of accountability as a balance of evaluative and developmental assessments supporting comparison and strengthening of institutions, the United States stepped out first in the early 1970s. Institutions such as Northeast Missouri State University (now Truman State) and Alverno College in Wisconsin gained national attention by clarifying learning objectives, measuring the pursuit of these objectives from year to year using an idiosyncratic variety of tests, and using the findings from outcomes assessment to implement improvements. Soon a number of institutions with less-selective admissions standards began to use such means to demonstrate that they were taking their students further than more prestigious institutions. They were adding more value.

In the 1980s political pressures arising from tuition increases and an economic slump (conditions similar to those at the end of the 21st century's first decade) prompted regional and specialized accreditors to call for greater accountability and to clarify expectations of assessment for *all* institutions and for many programs. Through the 1990s, requirements that institutions and programs prepare plans for assessment evolved into expectations that such plans begin to show results. Most recently, in response to new calls for heightened accountability, U.S. higher education has implemented a variety of involuntary and voluntary protocols and sources—governmental, institutional, even proprietary.

Unfortunately, extensive activity through the long term does not guarantee leadership—or necessarily even improved accountability. For in this arena as in others, more can be less. There is much going on in the United States, but so long as that activity appears fragmentary, discontinuous, and opaque to the public, we have far to go—and much to learn from what Bologna is attempting.

Enabling Comparisons

One purpose of accountability is to support individuals in making informed choices among competing institutions of higher education. Three examples of U.S. efforts in this regard may suggest the range and limitations of this pursuit.

Since September 2007, College Navigator (IES, 2009), sponsored by the U.S. Department of Education through its National Center for Education Statistics, has provided information through its Web site on roughly 7,000 institutions from all categories: public, private nonprofit, and proprietary. The site lists programs available, degrees awarded, tuition and fees, retention and graduation rates, information on financial aid, reports on campus safety, and information on accreditation.

The National Association of Independent Colleges and Universities (NAICU) provides similar information about more than 700 participating private institutions through the University and College Accountability Network (U-CAN, 2009). The NAICU site makes a particular effort to be colorful, coherent, and concise. No entry is more than two pages.

Finally, there is the Voluntary System of Accountability (VSA, 2008) sponsored by the American Association of State Colleges and Universities (AASCU) and the Association of Public and Land-Grant Universities (APLU). While only 325 public institutions are represented in the list of participants, they account for 70% of all bachelor's degrees awarded in the United States each year. And the VSA is particularly significant in another way. It is the only public system of accountability and comparison that provides information about learning outcomes on the basis of student examinations chosen by institutions from a list of approved alternatives. While the examinations were developed independently of the VSA, they have become closely associated with it through the endorsement of the sponsoring associations.

The Collegiate Assessment of Academic Proficiency (CAAP), developed by the American College Testing (ACT) program, the long-established source for the widely used college readiness examination of the same name, offers six testing modules, each directed to an academic skill such as reading, mathematics, science, and critical thinking. Institutions may administer any or all of these modules to a student sample of any credible size to measure what their students have gained through general education—and to compare the performance of their students against national norms.

The other major national player in testing, Educational Testing Service (ETS), has developed the Measure of Academic Proficiency and Progress (MAPP), recently renamed the ETS Proficiency Profile. The test is meant to assess four skill areas, critical thinking, reading, writing, and mathematics "in a single, convenient test" (ETS, 2009). While the Proficiency Profile can be used to demonstrate the performance of an institution's students relative to national norms, like the CAAP, it can also be administered longitudinally, that is, to the same student cohorts at different points in their college careers to measure, presumably, how much students are learning.

A third instrument that has become closely associated with the VSA is the Collegiate Learning Assessment (CLA) offered by the Council for Aid to Education (CAE), a nonprofit group more frequently associated with tracking private support for higher education. Unlike the CAAP and MAPP, the CLA focuses not on individual students but on institutions. Rather than "another high-stakes test for individual students," the CLA focuses on "how the institution as a whole contributes to student development" by aggregating student performance on open-ended questions to suggest "the institution's role in promoting learning" (CAE, 2009). Funded by eight prominent U.S. foundations, including the Carnegie Corporation and the Ford Foundation, the CLA has been adopted by more than 200 colleges and universities. That is a small fraction of U.S. institutions, of course, but because the priorities and methods of the CLA represent a marked departure from more conventional tests they have prompted considerable interest.

A November 2008 study by the Social Science Research Council, which attempted to demonstrate whether the CLA offers an effective measure of student learning, followed 2,300 students at 24 institutions (not identified) and concluded that it does (Arum, Roksa, & Velez, 2008). The analysis offers a number of interesting findings about factors bearing on success in higher education, including the value of studying in groups (less than the value of individual study), the importance of faculty communicating high expectations, and the greater effectiveness of some fields (math, science, social science, humanities) in ensuring learning than others (education, human services, business).

But in the context of the advances made through the Bologna Process, perhaps the most interesting finding was that of significant differences among institutions in their effectiveness as educators. The study found "29 percent of variation in longitudinal growth in CLA performance" (Arum et al., 2008, p. 5). If one motive for greater accountability is to support individuals in their choice of an institution based on educational effectiveness, the CLA as part of the VSA may represent a genuine watershed. On the other hand, as one commentator observed, the CLA may do little to assuage concerns about the finding that the most prominent elite institutions are more effective as educators than those that attempt to educate students who present inadequate preparation. For good or ill, research identifying "the greatest gains at institutions with a well prepared student body in a traditional curriculum" challenges some premises of earlier value-added claims (Jaschik, 2008).

Hence the risk is that an instrument developed so that institutions might find reliable information to support their improvement (developmental assessment) might well yield findings prompting invidious comparisons (evaluative assessment). That is, "however sophisticated an analysis the CLA's creators envision, many politicians will look for a number, and may not credit the college making arduous but important gains with disadvantaged students" (Jaschik, 2008).

Improving Regional Accreditation

At the heart of the commitment to accountability in the United States lies regional accreditation. By affirming that colleges and universities meet standards and expectations developed in their respective geographic regions, the six accrediting agencies offer assurance to the public that accredited institutions meet at least minimal expectations. And there are of course considerable advantages for the accredited institution. Acceptance by other institutions of the credits it awards is one. Eligibility to distribute federal student financial aid is another. Indeed, the revocation of accreditation by a regional accreditor often means the end of the line for a faltering institution.

Given the extent to which the six regional accreditors share broad interests in the assessment of learning outcomes, in the pursuit of continuous improvement, and in the increasing preference for analysis of outcomes (graduation rates, alumni performance, etc.) over documentation of inputs (volumes in the library, compensation of the faculty, etc.), we might offer to the world a conspicuous commitment to quality assurance based on peer review, a tradition until very recently distinctive to the United States. But the six regional accreditation agencies, despite their concurrence on essential principles, maintain distinct expectations, express idiosyncratic cultures, and operate different processes. Even when the agencies appear to be making progress along the same lines, they do not develop and communicate a coherent public message. The positive side to this conundrum is that the regional accreditors find stimulus for genuine innovation in responding to the interests and needs of their specific regions. The negative side is that a compelling story of principle and effectiveness may be lost in a welter of idiosyncrasies.

One example of an important leading practice emerged at the turn of the century in the North Central Association's Higher Learning Commission (HLC). The HLC now invites strong universities to maintain accreditation through a closely monitored continuing relationship rather than through an extensive reaccreditation process every decade or so. Under this alternate approach, known as the Academic Quality Improvement Program (AQIP), brief annual reports and an occasional quality checkup visit by a small team replace a voluminous self-study and an intrusive campus visit of several days by a large team. AQIP (2009) looks above all for an effective institutional commitment to continuous improvement. In April 2009 the HLC announced that it was considering the extension of certain assumptions behind this approach to all accredited institutions in its region. It will increase the rigor and limit the volume of compliance documentation, and it will emphasize an institution-by-institution focus on opportunities for improvement.

By so doing, the HLC will align itself with regional peers such as the Southern Association of Colleges and Schools (SACS) and the Western Association of Schools and Colleges (WASC) in distinguishing more clearly between monitoring institutional compliance with quality standards and supporting institutions in becoming more effective. SACS still maintains a reputation for its rigor of its "must" statements, but its revised process now focuses on an academic institution's preparation of a Quality Enhancement Plan (QEP). The QEP identifies important issues at the institutional level, emphasizes the accomplishment of learning outcomes, documents the institution's readiness to implement its enhancement initiatives, and points to criteria to measure the accomplishment of goals. In contrast with the massive documentation once required for SACS reaccreditation, the QEP is limited to 75 pages (SACS, 2008).

WASC review teams make two visits to institutions under periodic review. The first is to assess the institution's capacity for improvement and the quality and extent of its preparation for comprehensive evaluation. The second visit is intended to measure and affirm the institution's educational effectiveness. Both are intended to offer guidance as well as appraisal.

Such new approaches to regional accreditation—and examples could be drawn from the other regional agencies also—have earned favor with many institutions of higher education as less intrusive, more respectful of institutional time, and of greater benefit. But there have been questions at the federal level on the reliability of such approaches in documenting institutional quality and detecting institutional problems. And here the challenge of Bologna could work in either of two directions. To the extent that the Bologna Process encourages innovation in quality assessment in its participating nations, giving its support to processes similar to those being introduced in the United States, it may strengthen the hand of those promoting a more constructive, formative approach to institutional accountability in the United States. But if Bologna over time must admit a more forceful exercise of European or national authority to ensure greater consistency and transparency, that example could revive calls in the United States for a similar application of federal and state authority.

Getting the Word Out

A record of reform and innovation, however rich and varied, may exert relatively little influence unless it is known and understood. One skirmish illustrates the risks involved when the ineffective communication of a myriad of undertakings may be easily ignored.

First, interest appeared in expanding the federal role in accreditation. That became evident in the lengthy and tortuous effort between 2003 and 2008 to complete reauthorization of the Higher Education Act (HEA). Although earlier renewals by Congress of this landmark 1965 legislation had proved largely routine, the debate this time became highly partisan. And issues of accountability were at the heart of the matter.

Second, while the HEA legislation was still being debated in 2005, Department of Education secretary Margaret Spellings convened a national commission on the future of higher education in the United States. Prominent among its areas of focus was an interest in improved accountability and effectiveness. Its call for thoroughgoing reform in accreditation was dramatic, but the information it obtained on reforms already under way was either inadequate or deemed unworthy of attention (Commission, 2006). In its September 2006 report, *A Test of Leadership: Charting the Future of U.S. Higher Education,* the commission complained of "a remarkable shortage of clear, accessible information about crucial aspects of American colleges and universities, from financial aid to graduation rates." It found higher education data systems so "limited and inadequate" they denied "policymakers . . . reliable information on students' progress through the educational pipeline." It therefore called for "improved accountability" in the form of "more transparent" information about college costs and student success. Such success must be measured "on a 'value-added' basis" and must be offered to the public "in aggregate form to provide consumers and policymakers an accessible, understandable way to measure the relative effectiveness of different colleges and universities" (p. 4).

The final act in this three-part drama occurred just a few months following the release of the commission's recommendations when the Department of Education proposed a negotiated rule-making process that focused in large part on issues of accountability and assessment. As one reporter saw the effort, Spellings "decided to try to use accrediting agencies and the government's process for recognizing them to compel broader change within higher education" (Lederman, 2009). In essence, the process appeared intended to codify demands that accrediting agencies become more demanding with regard to the measurement of student learning outcomes. Explicit standards must apply.

The effort sparked resistance on several fronts. Although the commission's call for more comparative information and for greater transparency may have appeared reasonable in itself, accreditors and higher educators objected to an expanded federal role in the development of standards for institutional and programmatic performance. It was thought that such a role could lead to a far stronger federal influence on policy making in institutions. But there was resistance also from Congress. Because rule making typically follows rather than precedes the passage of legislation, objections arose from both sides of the aisle, and the process ground to a halt.

Senator Alexander (2009), who was instrumental in thwarting the rule making, at the same time called on higher education to use its reprieve wisely by expanding in practical terms its commitment to improved accountability. Reiterating that veiled warning more clearly in the February 2009 speech to the annual meeting of the American Council on Education in which he called for three-year degrees, he urged in particular a more innovative and responsible approach to the documentation (and limitation) of college costs.

As a coda to this fascinating process, an *Inside Higher Education* headline asked, "Margaret Spellings, Where Are You?" (Lederman, 2008). Covering the annual meeting of the HLC, Lederman found himself impressed by the depth and range of the commitment to practical on-campus applications of outcomes assessment. "Walking from meeting room to meeting room . . . and scanning the program, it was impossible not to be struck by the fact that a good half of the hundreds of sessions have embedded in their titles the words 'student outcomes,' 'assessment,' or 'accountability'" (Lederman). Despite the volume of political rhetoric to the contrary, he found that "colleges have not been sitting idly by while Rome burns (and other nations gain on the United States in educational achievement)."

Taken together, the accountability initiatives of the past three decades have strengthened considerably the capacity of higher education to measure its performance and to provide reliable measures of quality assurance. But such initiatives are almost never taken together, even within the academy. For example, a peer reviewer who moves from the north central to the western region of the United States and undertakes the work of accreditation will discover a myriad of unexplained and perhaps unnecessary differences in the extent and detail of his or her new regional accreditor's expectations, in its processes of review and appeal, and in its management of documentary analyses and on-site visits. And if those in academe are largely unaware of the many different threads in the tapestry of regional accreditation, to take only one arena in the concern for accountability, it should not be surprising that political leaders and their constituencies are for the most part unappreciative of the significant gains that have been made in quality assurance.

Specialized and Professional Accreditation

Specialized and professional accreditation in the United States can also offer salutary examples of dedicated and productive assessment. Through the volunteer efforts of peer reviewers, many disciplines—for example, teacher education, journalism, the arts, chemistry, nursing—have implemented significant reforms in how they define and measure learning goals. Student accomplishment is now more persuasively documented, outputs receive more attention than inputs, and pedagogy often gets as much attention as research. With the exception of some disciplines in the liberal arts and social sciences, virtually every academic program now has its own accreditation agency, and some, such as business, education, and audiology, support more than one. But among these agencies a wide range of criteria may be found, and their processes and expectations, largely inscrutable to the public, are often obscure even to those directly served.

Through their collaboration within the Association of Specialized and Professional Accreditors (ASPA), leaders in programmatic accreditation are beginning to make progress toward greater visibility and coherence. A *Code of Good Practice* adopted in 1995 represents the specialized accrediting community well and offers guidance to accrediting practice (ASPA Code, 1995). But no one would claim that the message has become clear or that a significant increase in public understanding has developed. Here, too, much remains to be accomplished.

Learning From Bologna

While Bologna would benefit from considering several elements in the long U.S. experience with accountability, the United States may have more to learn from the approach Bologna has taken and from what has and has not happened.

For instance, while in some ways reductive, the rigorous language that characterizes learning expectations in Tuning (2004, 2006) documents should encourage us either to abandon broad, abstract terms in favor of more concrete language or to substantiate inexact terms with explicit examples. There are several possible points of departure in place: work by AAC&U to define a consensus on learning outcomes for general education, the standards developed by specialized and professional accreditors for the evaluation of programs within their purview, and certification standards designed by state authorities and professional organizations to protect the public from incompetent practitioners in areas such as engineering, law, and health care.

But while these are important efforts, they do not yet address the most prominent priorities of the Bologna Process. They do not add up to a widely accepted and acknowledged outcomes framework that defines at least in general terms what academic degrees signify. Nor do they approach what the Tuning Project promises, the development of a consensus discipline by discipline on what students should accomplish by the time they receive a degree at a particular level.

Here again are lessons to learn from Bologna. The overarching framework for the EHEA represents not the imposition of authority, but an effort "to make sense of diversity" by providing broad guidance for the development of more detailed national frameworks. It is a "reference point," not a directive (Bergan, 2007, p. 163). Similarly, by vesting responsibility with accomplished and respected faculty members for the development of curricular expectations, the Tuning Project has disarmed much of the resistance that might greet centralized bureaucratic action. And the progress already made by Tuning within selected disciplines might offer disciplines in the United States useful guidance. Expectations developed in the United States would doubtless differ in some respects from those set forth in Europe, as a current Lumina Foundation project is demonstrating, but such differences can be examined, justified if possible, and if not justified, at least openly declared.

Another way progress toward enhanced accountability in Europe may be instructive lies in its timetable. Starting almost from scratch, the Bologna Process has accomplished nearly as much within a decade as the United States has managed to accomplish in the last 30 years. That is not to say that Europe can yet match the United States for depth of experience. But there is much to be learned from the biennial foregrounding of the European accountability imperative, from the impetus arising from frequent progress reports expressing different but often reinforcing perspectives, and from the repeated emphasis in the biennial ministers' meetings and in other conferences on the necessity for sufficient resources and autonomy to support accountability.

And, as we have seen, there may be much to learn also from the European commitment to the development of a sophisticated and widely accessible database for higher education. In addition to the agencies mentioned previously, an important step in this direction appears in a project managed since 2000 by the National Center for Public Policy and Higher Education and supported by private grants. The most recent iteration of this project, Measuring Up 2008, offers state-by-state report cards that register improvement and regression regarding performance on key indicators. Such indicators include the preparation of high school students for college, the affordability of higher education, rates of persistence through degree attainment, and measures of higher education's contribution to state economies. And in turn, these state-by-state reports may prompt some generalizations. Hence the most recent report suggests "despite our historical success in higher education, the preeminence of many of our colleges and universities, and some examples of improvement in this decade, our higher education performance is not commensurate with the current needs of our society and our economy" (Measuring, 2008).

This commendable effort and those of the IES, NCHEMS, and other sources offer a solid base for continued development, but we have not yet committed to what Bologna seeks, which is a deep, reliable source of data that can effectively interpret for the public and policy makers the most

important questions of all: How much learning is taking place in U.S. institutions of higher education, and how can the process of learning be made
more effective?

The Council for Higher Education Accreditation (CHEA) Initiative

CHEA, created by U.S. universities to provide enhanced credibility at the
federal level for independent, peer-based accreditation, counts 3,000 colleges
and universities as members and has offered its recognition to 60 accreditors,
institutional and programmatic. Through an initiative (CHEA Initiative,
2009) announced in September 2008, CHEA has taken a lead role in
responding to concerns about accountability.

Within an overall intent to provide a foundation for the next generation
of accreditation, the initiative has two goals. The first goal, "to further
strengthen accreditation, thereby enhancing public confidence and trust in
peer/professional review and self-regulation," reflects the recognition that
accreditation should provide "a clear and unequivocal signal that an institution or program is reliable, legitimate and meets threshold expectations
of quality performance" (CHEA Initiative, 2009). The second goal, which
considers the federal role, "is about partnership and balance" between the
appropriate expectations of the federal government and "appropriate independence" for both institutions and accrediting agencies (CHEA Initiative).

Nowhere does the CHEA communication refer to the Bologna Process, but there are at least three oblique influences worth tracking. First,
as political leaders become more fully aware of Bologna's aspirations and
accomplishments, the advice of Senator Alexander (2009) and others
regarding the need for greater accountability in the United States may
assume a fresh urgency. Second, if the European commitment to the creation of national outcomes standards continues to bring results, interest in
the development of an equivalent consensus in the United States is likely
to grow. Finally, if a larger governmental role in European accreditation
should appear to yield actionable results in a period of significant economic challenge, the U.S. higher education community may face an activ-
ism at the federal level greater than any seen so far, even as Bologna's
preference for conferring greater autonomy on institutions and accrediting
agencies might offer a counterthrust.

It appears possible, therefore, that the CHEA initiative may offer U.S.
higher education some direction toward a more constructive and less defen-
sive examination of current accountability processes, and that the Bologna

Process may provide an additional incentive for serious and sustained engagement.

The Fruits of Experience

That the United States has much to learn about accountability from the Bologna Process in Europe seems clear. But as we have seen, such learning can take place in the context of a record of accomplishment that itself deserves respect. And there are values embedded in U.S. practice we may wish to preserve in any reform.

First, U.S. higher education created the principle of peer review as the standard for the accreditation of academic programs. From the regional accreditation of institutions to the accreditation of professional programs by specialized agencies, reviews are conducted by trained, objective peers of those being reviewed. Every regional accrediting association has in place methodical approaches to ensuring that reviewers are knowledgeable regarding current standards and practice and principles in their approach to evaluation. And as mentioned above, the ASPA *Code of Good Practice* directs members to "focus primarily on educational quality," distinguish between "what is required for accreditation and what is recommended for improvement of the institution or program," and "concentrate on results" (ASPA Code, 1995, ¶¶ 1, 2, 5). Europe may well adopt the principle of peer review. The United States should not relinquish it.

Second, accreditation in the United States has remained independent of the government as a process for the academy to examine itself and offer to the public and to policy makers the results of its examinations. Hence accreditation provides an internal impetus for sustained quality and an external assurance that graduates meet established standards. The current CHEA initiative endorses this fundamental value.

Third, accreditation has tracked—and in some instances anticipated—important trends in the academy. For instance, the first significant pressure on institutions to create assessment plans came from regional accreditors such as SACS and the North Central Association and from professional accreditors such as the National Council for the Accreditation of Teacher Education (NCATE). As much as 20 years in advance of growing federal demands for accountability, regional accrediting associations were making the renewal of institutional accreditation contingent in part on the presentation of a credible plan for internal assessment. The academy must continue to give close attention to accreditation as an important source of innovation and continuity.

Finally, the shift of emphasis in higher education assessment from inputs to outcomes (student learning, graduate employment, employer satisfaction) has been embraced, endorsed, and stipulated by programmatic and institutional accreditors. That shift should also inform academic life in all other respects, from the construction of an individual course syllabus to the reconsideration of an institutional mission statement.

In Europe and in the United States, then, a substantial effort is under way to achieve greater accountability in higher education. Because the stakes for both are high, both should take advantage of what the other has to offer. Because of its long experience, the United States may still have an edge—but one unlikely to last for very long unless we learn what we can from Bologna and build on it for the benefit of our students and institutions of higher education.

MEETING THE CHALLENGE
Improving on Europe's Example

The Bologna Process represents a challenge to U.S. higher education because its priorities are largely those we should be pursuing more assiduously and more effectively. The Process focuses on the needs of students. It promotes a critical shift in the educational paradigm from a focus on what is taught to what is learned. It reflects the capacity of higher education to create opportunity and support social justice. It respects the obligation of higher education to account for itself and to interpret itself in broadly understandable terms. The Process seeks also to increase cultural awareness and educational depth by promoting the movement across borders of students and educators, and it expresses a commitment to improve the documentation of educational attainment to facilitate such movement.

If European leaders were to terminate the Process, there would be cause for regret, but the challenge of its initiatives would remain. We can take instruction from what Bologna has done well, just as we can find caution in its limitations, errors of judgment, and misapplications. But a revitalized commitment to higher education reform in the United States should reflect U.S. priorities and express less a determination to compete with Europe than to do those things that ought to be done and to do them more successfully.

In addition to its action lines, Bologna's approach is itself in some ways instructive. From the start, the Process has identified a limited number of interdependent, easily understood, and compelling priorities for the most part well aligned with reforms already under way. And the judiciousness of its organizational model, a rotating voluntary authority depending on participating states to pursue shared initiatives and report progress accurately, appears in how much has been accomplished within a relatively short time.

In the three preceding chapters, we focus on the Bologna priorities according to broad categories. We acknowledge what has been accomplished in Europe, remark on considerable progress evident in the United States, and consider possible lessons to be drawn from the European experience. Now, from a perspective that includes European and U.S. accomplishments, we should be able to glimpse the outline of a comprehensive agenda for change that builds on the best of Bologna, protects important values of U.S. higher education, and holds out the possibility of a new American resurgence as a leader internationally in higher education. But we should do so for one reason: Such leadership would offer the promise of substantive improvements for students and institutions of higher education in the United States and lead to an expansion of the opportunities we offer at home and to the world. In short, we should take on the challenge of Bologna to serve the cause of learning more fully.

In this chapter we consider the requirements of an effective approach to meeting the challenge posed by the Bologna Process and improving on it. And we give careful attention to the ways the Bologna Process should—and should not—guide our effort. We must be frank about the impediments that stand in the way of a coordinated undertaking in the United States, and we should imagine a process that could circumvent such impediments or turn them into advantages. Finally, with the requirements of such a process in mind we can anticipate in light of Bologna and of current U.S. priorities what a reform agenda might look like.

The intent is to provide not a finished blueprint but a set of preliminary drawings. Nor is there a presumption that such drawings represent in any sense a proxy for the discussions that higher education leaders in all arenas are having in response to Bologna. But a broad, detailed, and ambitious proposal for the coordinated and concerted reform of higher education in the United States might be a useful prompt to such discussions. And that is what the final paragraphs of this chapter seek to offer.

Is There a Challenge?

The Bologna Process may challenge the United States through its focused and effective reform of higher education—on several fronts at least. But while Bologna has created a model for coordinated reform that the United States cannot afford to ignore, there is a more direct summons arising from issues in U.S. higher education's own backyard. We have already examined many of these issues, but a few reminders may be helpful.

For instance, access and mobility, which the Bologna Process seeks to expand, are contracting in the United States. Rising costs of attending college and a financial support system that has not kept pace with needs are discouraging well-qualified students. Moreover, public institutions strapped for resources are imposing disproportionate tuition increases on out-of-state students, thereby discouraging mobility even within the borders of the United States. And as these barriers are growing for students who are well prepared, an even more formidable barrier is evident in P–12 inadequacies that leave some students poorly prepared. We have already noted a regional campus in New Mexico where nearly all entering students require further basic preparation at the high school level before joining the academic mainstream. But 60% of students enrolling at *all* two-year colleges require some remediation, according to one study, as well as 20% to 30% of students beginning study at a four-year or graduate institution (Dillon, 2009). And these issues are likely to become more acute if college enrollments continue to grow.

There is also the broader issue of the competitiveness of the United States in the world and the role of higher education in sustaining or rebuilding national leadership. A 2006 report from a commission charged by the National Conference of State Legislatures offers a discouraging overview. With one eye on the United States and another on the competition, the commission states flatly that the American higher education system "no longer is the best in the world." Other countries now "outrank and outperform us" (State Legislatures, 2006, p. 1). Notwithstanding many distinguished U.S. institutions, "we do a poor job overall in our mass education production." Meanwhile, "other countries are significantly improving their higher education performance" by "prioritizing higher education" and by regarding it as integral to economic development" (p. 1). From the perspective of the state legislators, we are not.

No less an authority than Leslie H. Gelb (2009), president emeritus of the Council on Foreign Relations, observed even more recently that "the United States is declining as a nation and a world power" and called on Americans to be "clear-eyed about the causes and courageous about implementing the cures" (p. 56). The causes? "The country's economy, infrastructure, public schools, and political system have been allowed to deteriorate" leading to "diminished economic strength, a less vital democracy, and a mediocrity of spirit . . . conditions not easy to reverse" (pp. 56–57).

Although Gelb's (2009) primary focus is on foreign policy, we need not stretch far to align his diagnosis with that of the legislative commission. While other countries "are prioritizing higher education in their national public agenda" and "approaching higher education reform as part of a national economic development strategy," higher education in the United States "is not preparing students for the 21st century global society" (State

Legislatures, 2006, p. 1). Or as Jamie P. Merisotis (2008), president of the Lumina Foundation for Education, observes, "The United States is one of only two countries whose younger generation is less well educated than the one that preceded it." He warns that "we stand to lose a great deal—as a nation and as individual citizens—if this trend continues".

Higher education contributes to and feels the impact of all the factors of decline cited by Gelb (2009), the State Legislatures (2006), and Merisotis (2008). But to recognize this is to acknowledge several related paradoxes. For instance, even as graduates educated in developing fields of knowledge and experienced in university-based research can help to fuel the economy, economic downtowns often exert a disproportionate impact on colleges and universities. Another two-sided coin? Higher education must cope with the results of inadequate K–12 education, but colleges and universities educate the teachers who provide that education. Another? Although U.S. higher education is likely to suffer from the consequences of a protracted economic decline, the premise of the Bologna Process—and of this study—is that higher education can accept a role of leadership in national resurgence.

But the primary issue is not whether the Bologna Process represents a threat to higher education in the United States. If Europe finally achieves its Bologna objectives, the answer will be clear: yes—and for a long time to come. But the goal of the United States is not to "beat Finland," as Merisotis (2008) has remarked. "What really matters is that the rest of the world is roaring ahead with investment in higher education as a critical national goal while the U.S. is stuck in neutral. In short, we've become complacent." So the *more* critical issue is whether the United States can take important lessons from Bologna, mobilize its own commitment to comprehensive higher education reform, leverage strengths distinctive to American higher education, and regain over time its ascendency as the world's premier higher educator.

Meeting the Challenge: What Is Needed

Our review of Bologna's three broad arenas of reform considers how U.S. higher education is pursuing the transformation of higher education in ways similar to those of Bologna. At many different levels—state systems of higher education, associations of public institutions, accrediting agencies, individual colleges and universities, organizations representing disciplines—there is no dearth of focused and productive activity directed toward strengthening accountability, clarifying learning objectives, promoting student persistence, improving documentation of credentials, increasing financial support, and simplifying student lending.

In terms of curriculum and pedagogy, there are projects directed at active learning, service learning, critical thinking, undergraduate research, and writing and mathematics and foreign language across the curriculum. There is a new emphasis on greater coherence in general education, on the educational benefits of cultural diversity, on integrated science instruction. First-year seminars introduce students to university education, and capstone experiences offer seniors an opportunity for synthesis and practical application.

At the institutional level there are new initiatives in terms of faculty peer review, the use of examinations to extend (as well as measure) learning, and the application of responsibility-centered management to encourage efficiency and entrepreneurship among academic units. Accrediting agencies are experimenting with new approaches to continuous improvement, and states like Ohio are again taking up the cause of performance-based funding.

Yet for various reasons the substantive improvements arising from this activity are far from impressive, at least so far, with the result that many political leaders and opinion makers regard higher education as uninterested in reform and innovation. A study by the National Center for Public Policy and Higher Education and by Public Agenda observes that "as far back as the 1990s, more than six out of 10 government and business leaders believed that higher education was too bureaucratic and resistant to change, and that colleges needed to become leaner and more efficient" (Immerwahr, Johnson, & Gasbarra, 2008, p. 5). Now? "These attitudes have, if anything, intensified" (p. 5).

As we have observed, the charge to the Spellings Commission revealed a profound lack of awareness of initiatives already under way to address many of the concerns that it expressed. And the National Center study enabling college presidents to discuss increases in the cost of college, concerns about access, and the documentation of quality has suggested that many even at the chief executive level are unaware of how much reform activity is taking place. Although significant changes are regularly occurring in the practice of accreditation, in state expectations of institutional performance, in demands in the disciplines for defined learning outcomes, and in defining core elements of the baccalaureate, for instance, one president taking part in the discussion unaccountably attributed to the academy a strong aversion to change of any kind: "People are almost pathologically nervous about it" (Immerwahr et al., 2008, p. 16).

To take stock: In the United States extensive activity is directed at strengthening higher education on many fronts, but there is only limited awareness at any level of all that is going on, and there is virtually no discussion of an approach to reform that would be aggressive, coordinated, coherent, and comprehensive. Even those most fully engaged in the work of reform, while productive in their own niches, sometimes show little awareness of other arenas. And the result is often what we would expect: piecemeal reforms, poorly coordinated with related efforts and ineffectively communicated.

What is required? An approach to strengthening U.S. higher education that may recall the Bologna Process but that learns from Bologna's shortfalls to ensure even greater productivity. In light of Bologna, its accomplishments, and the snags it has encountered, U.S. higher education should undertake a concerted effort, one that addresses critical interrelated priorities through a coordinated process. Its goals should express a broad consensus that reflects awareness of progress already being made and that embodies awareness of and respect for values that reform should not compromise. The process should embody a clear and realistic timeline with consequences for dilatory performance. And secure funding must be provided to support the development and implementation of genuine reforms that meet rigorous criteria.

Guidance From Bologna

The Bologna Process offers a useful example in several respects. A manageable range of closely related priorities has guided the pan-European effort. The goals of Bologna fit on a business card. In addition, though the earliest stages of the Process were the province of only a few higher education ministers, the Process soon expanded to include a wide range of stakeholders. Bologna also committed to an aggressive timeline and to the methodical maintenance of its agenda through the work of a follow-up group and the review of that work in ministerial conferences every two years. We have seen the results.

But we can also take caution from what we have seen. For all its worthy aspirations, Bologna represents an insular, limiting, and incomplete vision of higher education closely tied to the present and future of the EU. A corresponding effort in the United States should by contrast become genuinely international from the start rather than continental. There is much to be learned from throughout the world, and an undertaking that seeks to provide international leadership must not ignore good practice and rich experience relevant to its priorities. Second, we may observe that Bologna stumbled at the start by offering the appearance of a top-down, bureaucratic initiative. The United States can avoid this misstep by looking to the higher education community to develop, initiate, and sustain the reform. Third, and most important, a U.S. reform effort should reflect an appreciation for higher education that embodies deeply held values highly relevant to personal and societal as well as economic development.

For instance, a commitment to providing a liberal education for all college students may represent the single best means available by which U.S. higher education can regain and advance its long-standing reputation for preeminence—both educationally and economically. For there is growing evidence to suggest that the pragmatic benefits of a liberal education— intellectual agility, a capacity for independent learning, an engagement with the advantages of diversity, and an enthusiasm for collaborative effort, for instance—are closely aligned with effectiveness and fulfillment on the job. Indeed, the "essential learning outcomes" commended by the Association of American Colleges and Universities (AAC&U Outcomes, 2007) could hardly be more closely directed to genuine challenges emerging in the 21st century. Knowledge of "human cultures and the physical and natural world," gained through study across the college curriculum, should be "focused by engagement with big questions, both contemporary and enduring." Skills, both intellectual and practical, should be honed through practice "in the context of progressively more challenging problems, projects, and standards for performance." Growth in "personal and social responsibility," prompted through education in intercultural competences and ethical reasoning, should be "anchored" through engagement with the world. And experience in "integrated and applied learning" should enable students to demonstrate what they have learned through its application "to new settings and complex problems" (AAC&U Outcomes).

Issues of access also must inform an inclusive reform effort. While economic pressures—increases in tuition without corresponding increases in student aid—have led to a retreat on this front, our commitment to opening the doors of colleges to all students who may benefit must remain an important value—as the 44th president of the United States has urged. Any realistic reform effort must of course take on the intractable issues of the so-called iron triangle: costs, access, and quality. But the point of departure for addressing this challenge lies in the same values that created the land-grant colleges, the GI Bill, and the unprecedented expansion of higher education in the 1960s. There is far to go, to be sure, but the U.S. starting line offers an advantage over its competitors.

And the United States has a potential advantage as well with regard to diversity. Even as the Bologna Process has shown little progress in the pursuit of its social dimension, the United States has continued to document the educational advantages that accrue within a diverse educational environment, celebrated the gains that a diverse society offers its members, and enriched its national leadership by drawing on an ever wider range of cul tures and ethnic backgrounds. A comprehensive program of higher education reform in the United States should build on this important value as a significant competitive advantage internationally.

Impediments

Our survey of different innovations and reforms taking place at all levels of higher education in the United States can suggest elements in a platform for comprehensive reform. But such awareness suggests also one of the complications that has so far discouraged the development of a coordinated approach. The complexity of higher education in the United States—its many sectors, its various sources of support, the rich mix of distinctive institutional cultures and mission, the bewildering assortment of organizations that reflect its multiplicity—has so far weighed against any effort to hold a broadly inclusive discussion of comprehensive, multifaceted reform, much less to move toward the synthesis of opinion and commitment that a thorough reform effort would require.

Another limiting factor is the role of the federal government so far as higher education is concerned. Where federal support has been invested in higher education, through initiatives such as the Morrill Act, the GI Bill, the 1965 Higher Education Act and its renewals, and various programs for providing support for research and student aid, advocates for higher education have been vigilant against compromising the authority of the states and the relative autonomy of institutions. And attempts to expand federal authority over higher education, as with the spring 2007 attempt at negotiated rule making by the Department of Education, have met with bipartisan opposition. This distinction of roles is an important legacy, but it could create a complication for an effort to mount an all-embracing higher education reform in the spirit of Bologna. Most notably, a unified and coordinated action would require a reliable source of sustained funding, and if that source is not a federal one it must be found elsewhere.

The issue of leadership becomes even more complicated when the wide variation in the exercise of state authority over public and private higher education becomes apparent. States that manage higher education through governing boards, for instance, may impose statewide control over degrees that institutions may grant, conduct on-the-ground reviews of institutional performance, and control closely the costs of providing instruction discipline by discipline. Those that operate with coordinating boards, however, may delegate such decisions to the boards of trustees appointed for each institution.

And the extent to which states regulate the operations and offerings of private institutions within their borders varies widely as well. It seems unlikely that a concerted national effort to mount comprehensive higher education reform will arise easily from this assortment of authorities, structures, and protocols.

Within the academy itself, the picture is no less complicated. With the possible exception of the American Council on Education, which describes itself as "the unifying voice for higher education," higher educators have organized themselves into a bewildering array of agencies and associations serving a variety of interests and niches. There are national organizations representing large and not always discrete sectors; some institutions join both the Association of Public and Land-Grant Universities (APLU), which for the most part serves large public institutions, and the American Association of State Colleges and Universities (AASCU), which serves mostly smaller ones. There are organizations for the most prestigious research universities (Association of American Universities [AAU]), for universities serving metropolitan areas (Coalition of Urban and Metropolitan Universities [CUMU]), for community colleges (American Association of Community Colleges [AACC]), for Jesuit colleges and universities (Association of Jesuit Colleges and Universities [AJCU]), and for a myriad of other mingled or sharply delineated sectors.

Then there are organizations operating on behalf of virtually every discipline as well as agencies that offer disciplinary accreditation. There are regional accrediting associations, of course, and there are different groups that bring together state higher education directors, accreditation agency executives, diversity officers, business officers, legal advisers, and academic advisors.

Some organizations draw from many sectors. The AAC&U brings together faculty members and administrators from institutions that emphasize the liberal arts, the Council of Colleges of Arts and Sciences attracts liberal arts deans from both state and private institutions, and the Society for Values in Higher Education convenes individuals from across the higher education spectrum to focus on ethical issues.

While there are occasional alliances, as shown in the collaboration by AASCU and APLU on the Voluntary System of Accountability (VSA, 2008; see chapter 10, pp. 162–164), these organizations for the most part operate within their respective niches, often unaware of one another's interests and priorities unless grounds for some disagreement or some shared threat should arise. Any successful effort to secure significant higher education reform in the United States must draw on the considerable resources of these organizations, for their leaders and members may well represent the single most dedicated, experienced, and creative force that higher education can offer. But to convene such individuals in an effort to coordinate comprehensive and visionary reform will not be easy.

To these impediments add those arising from a volatile economy, from legislatures intent on directing funds only to citizens of their respective states, from critics who assail higher education without bothering to consider evidence of reform, from those in higher education who dismiss the Bologna Process without understanding what it has accomplished, and from federal bureaucrats who believe there is a single appropriate source for coordinated national efforts, namely, the District of Columbia.

The question, then, is not whether there are impediments to a thoroughgoing reform of higher education in the United States, but whether there is a process that might enable those committed to such reform to use these impediments to their advantage where possible, and where that is not possible, to circumvent or disarm them. There may be.

A Process for Change

Productive discussions often begin with a proposal offered for consideration. In the spirit of offering preliminary drawings, we might imagine the structure of an effective process. Such an approach would give careful attention to Bologna, from the strategic errors apparent in the Sorbonne statement to the elements of an effective implementation strategy: biennial conferences, detailed stocktaking, incremental charges to a follow-up group, and a readiness to cement alliances with groups working toward comparable goals.

But in a departure from Bologna, the impetus for comprehensive higher education reform in the United States would arise not from government officials but from the academy. As a first step, a respected university president or, better, a coalition of college and university presidents and provosts representing all sectors of higher education, should meet to plan a Higher Educators' Congress. This gathering would include faculty members, students, administrators, university board members, state higher education officers, foundation representatives, and members of the public. The objective for the congress would be clearly defined: concluding a commitment to and a plan for comprehensive higher education reform. And the agenda would be framed to achieve this objective.

A congress planned to inform, invigorate, and mobilize its participants might well begin with a thorough briefing on the Bologna Process. What prompted it? What have been its aspirations? How have they been pursued? How successful has it been? What is its present status? What can be learned? Perhaps participants would benefit from reading this book!

No less important, however, would be a frank discussion with regard to U.S. higher education. What are the prompts that call for a dramatic and extensive reform effort? Why is such reform urgent? What are the arenas in which reform appears most needed? And where is the most progress already occurring? What would be the risks of not responding to the Bologna challenge? And what are the obstacles to success if a comprehensive response should be framed?

After a thorough briefing and plenary discussion, participants in the congress would be assigned to committees to study particular concerns such as outcomes frameworks, nomenclature, national documentation of academic accomplishment, interstate mobility, and the like—explorations, in effect, of the Bologna action lines from a U.S. perspective. With the benefit of these studies, the congress would reconvene to reach a shared understanding of how the major issues of U.S. higher education reform are related to one another. On the basis of these considerations, the participants would proceed to frame a strategy of reform that first recognizes and incorporates existing efforts and then identifies gaps and the means of addressing them.

As its final action, the congress should appoint an implementation oversight committee to manage the major reform initiatives prior to a subsequent meeting in three years. Each initiative would be assigned a director and codirector who would accept responsibility for convening the ensuing discussions and developing action proposals for the next congress. Initiatives ratified by that congress would then be regarded by all participating institutions and organizations as obligations. And it would be clear that participating institutions must agree to move forward with implementation of all proposals, thereby avoiding the problems created by the à la carte approach taken by some Bologna participants.

In a further contrast with Bologna, there would be no fixed term for the reform process. Instead, the congress would define criteria to measure progress relative to each initiative and invite proposals for assessment relative to such criteria. An executive group similar to the organizing committee would manage liaison with state and federal agencies, oversee the appointments necessary to further the operations of the undertaking, manage the documentation required for tracking pursuit of the approved initiatives, and seek sufficient resources. Such an approach would incorporate lessons learned from Bologna, positive and negative, while offering a serviceable platform for the accomplishment of real change.

On the premise that U.S. higher educators would find it possible to agree to an organizational approach likely to prove effective, to frame a realistic timeline, and to secure private and public assurances of adequate support, we can proceed to consider—for the sake of argument—some emphases that might characterize the agenda for U.S. higher education reform in the near term. As with Bologna, the agenda should be brief but compelling, and it should promise change meaningful to students, visible to the nation, and attractive to the world.

Toward a Modest Proposal

Those engaged in framing a comprehensive reform agenda would begin with several advantages. The first is that the United States is well positioned to build on the accomplishments of Bologna. As we have seen, with respect to many of the European initiatives, the United States already can point to considerable progress. And the United States now has the advantage of observing what has worked well and might be adopted (or adapted) and what needs rethinking. Second, compared with Europe, the United States has even more to gain from the reform of higher education. The unchallenged capacity and diversity of its higher education resources, properly leveraged, should enable the United States to regain the leadership it has risked and to use that leadership for the benefit of its own students and of higher education internationally. Finally, reform grounded in U.S. values and principles can and should inform an international vision of higher education that combines access to economic opportunity with a deep respect for the intellectual and creative potential of students.

Advice From Adelman

We should add to this list of advantages the lucid and constructive proposals outlined by Clifford Adelman (2009) as a capstone to his thorough study of the Bologna Process. His advice deserves careful attention, because it reflects his discriminating analysis of reform in Europe and his substantial experience as an analyst of U.S. higher education. While a brief overview cannot do justice to the detail of Adelman's suggestions, the following list suggests their substance:

- Higher education must articulate "clear and discrete criteria for learning and thresholds of performance" at the system, institutional, and disciplinary levels. To this end, Adelman advocates a Tuning-like approach to "organizing all the departments in at least each major discipline" in each state for the development of "qualification frameworks for each degree in a specific field." To this end, pilot Tuning efforts in Indiana, Minnesota, and Utah, a project sponsored by the Lumina Foundation to secure consensus on outcomes within selected disciplines, will offer critical guidance. Adelman would manage this process state by state because "state systems set the criteria for awarding degrees at public institutions" (p. 194).

- Institutions of higher education should offer all graduates a " 'legible' U.S. Diploma Supplement" that describes the purpose of the degree that has been awarded and the requirements in the major field, recounts the student's higher education history, aligns student accomplishment with the relevant qualifications framework where one is available, and lists "markers of student achievement" such as academic honors, service projects, and documentation of proficiency in a second language (p. 195).

- With Tuning-like outcomes criteria in place and diploma supplements provided to graduates, states will be in a position to develop "generic and not discipline-specific" qualification frameworks for the various degree levels that "offer stronger distinctions between degree levels" than those evident in Bologna (p. 199).

- Higher education should create an accounting system in which academic credits become "meaningful and indisputable." Conceding the unlikelihood that "every academic department in every institution would . . . work through calculations of estimated workload for the average student in every course offering" (p. 200), Adelman proposes instead building " 'credit-level' descriptors" (p. 202) relative to the qualifications frameworks. Faculty members would assist academic advisors in counseling students by calculating and making known the workload requirements of the courses they teach.

- A serious commitment to improving access to higher education for underrepresented populations should make use of "geo-demographics" to identify less-conspicuous prospects, primarily in rural areas, and to "get to work in specific zip codes" (p. 203).

- Every discipline must "rethink its undergraduate presentation" (p. 204) so that completion of the master's degree becomes an expectation for the typical college career. Otherwise, an increasing preference of European students for second-cycle degrees may give them a significant competitive advantage globally.

- Associate degree students who matriculate at a community college should receive simultaneous admission to a baccalaureate institution, enjoy access to the services of both institutions, and follow a seamless path from one to the other. (As noted earlier, Ohio is one state where this is now possible.)

- Institutions might choose to offer an intermediate credential attesting to the completion of all baccalaureate requirements except for those required by the major.
- Higher education should improve the lot of part-time students by offering more generous access to funding, by distinguishing continuing part-time study from intermittent enrollment, and by refusing to stigmatize students who cannot reasonably carry full-time academic loads.
- Community colleges, in particular, should offer inviting centers for the consistent evaluation and crediting of prior learning.

Estimable goals! For several reasons that I outline in the next section, we may want to consider a somewhat different sequence for the most critical priorities and to advance a different order of priority for some others. But any plan for the reform of U.S. higher education that overlooks the constructive initiatives proposed by Clifford Adelman (2009) is likely to prove inadequate.

The Modest Proposal Defined

Although there are important differences in emphasis, the suggestions that constitute the following modest proposal should not be regarded as differing in intent from those advanced by Adelman (2009). Both have the same objective: a U.S. system of higher education made stronger by its attentiveness to what has been and is being accomplished in Europe. But these suggestions give more attention to values distinctive to U.S. higher education, are meant to express a vision more compelling in some ways, and offer a sequence meant to prove more inviting. They are directed by and large to the nation as a whole rather than to the states. And they give full credit to impressive U.S. reform efforts already under way. This modest proposal finally reflects the belief that the United States has an opportunity not only to follow the example of Bologna, as Adelman has persuasively proposed, but to build on the best elements of Bologna a genuinely transformative national higher education reform more germane to the needs and opportunities of the United States.

In sum, the suggestions that follow do not have in mind a victory "over Finland." They envision a victory over the status quo.

Make access a priority. For reform to prove meaningful, the United States must reclaim the conviction that higher education represents a public value as well as an individual advantage. A social dimension has many facets, but the simple test must be whether students not advantaged but qualified to undertake higher education are enabled to do so in ways that make their success possible. And if the United States is to pass that test in the near term to remain competitive internationally, the development of secure and reliable funding is essential. We identify higher education as a national priority, but so long as students in one state enjoy far greater access to higher education than those in another, so long as some well-qualified students must accept full-time employment in order to pay tuition, and so long as place-bound students with documented potential have little prospect for continuing their education, we are creating rhetoric rather than reform. We are providing in such cases only an illusion of access.

There are ways to improve access that do not cost a great deal of money. We can make what aid is available more transparent to potential students through a national clearinghouse for information. As President Obama proposed in July 2009, we can direct increased support to community colleges as efficient preparatory educators. We can invest in distance learning and explore what it will take to persuade more students to take advantage of it and to persist in it. We can support more effective high school-to-college transitions by funding collaborations that join secondary school systems, community colleges, and four-year and graduate institutions. We can work with employers to create opportunities for student work that are genuinely cocurricular and that complement learning. And we can support institutions that frame offerings to meet the needs and the schedules of their students.

The challenge of Bologna may draw our attention in this regard to progress already under way in the United States. European efforts to develop short-cycle degrees as stepping-stones to the baccalaureate closely resemble the already substantial commitment in the United States to the associate's degree. From 1990 to 2006, the number of associate's degrees awarded annually grew by more than 60%, from 482,000 to 713,000. Indeed, according to the Institute of Education Sciences (IES, 2006), associate's degrees now account for about one fifth of all degrees granted. But Adelman's (2009) point that we could do a far better job of persuading recipients of associate's degrees to continue their education is well taken.

Similarly, Bologna's belated discovery of part-time students, its embryonic interest in assessing and crediting prior learning, and its growing understanding of the potential value of distance education all reflect arenas where the United States has long been active. Here too, however, the United States has no reason for complacency. Most record-keeping protocols still focus on full-time students, educational fees often support amenities part-time students do not use, and distance education more often offers flexibility to enrolled students than access to potential ones. Moreover, even where our efforts are moving us in the right direction, they may not offer an advantage if they are poorly understood, unpredictable, and different in degree and kind from one state to the next—and that is often the reality.

So meeting the challenge of Bologna may be less a matter of initiating new programs than of coordinating existing ones through agreement on common standards and through promotion of their availability and effectiveness. For example, while many states are ostensibly committed to increasing the percentage of their citizens who complete associate's and bachelor's degrees, there appears little consensus on the most effective means of accomplishing this objective. If the United States is serious about reversing its decline internationally, it should support an effort by higher education across the 50 states to create a coherent, multifaceted access platform. In addition to the initiatives described above, the elements of that platform should include in particular a consistent approach to granting academic credit for prior learning, adequate financial support for pursuit of the associate's degree, expanded availability of such degrees through distance education, flexible programming that acknowledges work and family responsibilities, and record keeping that conveys a deep understanding of part-time students.

And we can avoid exacerbating barriers to access that lie within the purview of higher education. While rising costs may constitute the most formidable barrier, admissions practices in some cases limit access to those who stand most to benefit. An increased preference for merit-based student aid may enable an institution to enroll a more highly qualified class and earn it an increase in magazine rankings, but capable students dependent on need-based aid are likely victims. Similarly, legacy admissions can contribute to an institution's bottom line by encouraging the generosity of alumni, but the practice can perpetuate a history of preferential treatment for the well connected. While it might be difficult for prestigious colleges and universities to suspend such practices unilaterally, a statement of consensual policy at the level of the AAU could produce a profound change in practice.

Yet for all that we can do with limited resources, the impact of higher education reform will depend finally on the public will to invest in the education of the next generation. In the Bill for the More General Diffusion of Knowledge introduced in the Virginia House of Delegates in 1779, Thomas Jefferson argued that the "publick happiness" depends on society's willingness to call to a liberal education "those persons, whom nature has endowed with genius and virtue . . . without regard to wealth, birth or other accidental condition or circumstance" (Jefferson, 1984). Society's willingness to meet this obligation remains the overriding issue.

Create a lucid national hierarchy of learning outcomes. Higher education is virtually the only profession that does not routinely define what it seeks to accomplish. Even if we believe there are benefits of higher education that transcend literal statement, there is value in seeking to elucidate intangibles. The object of this initiative should be to develop a national consensus on learning outcomes at four levels: the baccalaureate degree, the different academic majors, course sequences in each major and in general education, and the general education program itself. While there are practical merits to beginning with disciplinary outcomes and the diploma supplement before moving to qualification frameworks at the degree level, an approach leading first to a consensus on what the baccalaureate should represent might prove at least equally plausible and perhaps more compelling. With such a statement in place, the disciplines might be in a better position to frame their respective contributions to this overarching measure.

This approach also draws on the strategy laid out in the section "A Process for Change" (pp. 183–185) to move beyond state-specific reforms to develop a genuine consensus in the United States. While advances in the states according to the Adelman (2009) proposals might be more readily obtained and would certainly represent an advance over the present, the 50 qualifications frameworks created through a state-by-state effort could themselves create uncertainty and discourage mobility.

With a consensus on the baccalaureate in place, institutions of higher education would be well positioned to consider their curricular sequences. Of course, many disciplines are cumulative by necessity. Just as each course in a flight training sequence requires and relies on knowledge and skills gained in previous courses, so in many of the sciences, health care disciplines, and in a number of technical areas, students must move through a prescribed sequence supporting the development of the competences required for professional practice. But that model should represent a flexible standard for all disciplines, including those in the liberal arts. Students majoring in English or history should understand just as fully as mathematics or aeronautics majors how foundation courses lead to progressively advanced levels of analysis and application.

And the same expectation should apply, though perhaps on a less course-specific basis, to programs in general education. There too students should understand the overall learning outcomes intended by their institutions and the contributions different courses make to those outcomes. Indeed, Stanley

Katz, professor of public and international relations at Princeton University, has observed that a "focus on cumulative learning outcomes" can inspire "a renewed commitment to general education and to the role it plays in ensuring that students are liberally educated rather than narrowly trained" (AAC&U Poll, 2009).

In the effort to define the learning outcomes of all course sequences and of the courses that constitute them, the Tuning approach should prove useful and, as noted previously, is already informing pilot processes in Indiana, Minnesota, and Utah. Faculty members, students, and state education officials are collaborating on developing learning standards for education, history, chemistry, physics, and graphic design. Jamie P. Merisotis (2008), president of the sponsoring Lumina Foundation, describes the approach in each pilot as "a faculty-led discussion about what students need to know" notwithstanding the alternate approaches that might be followed.

But in contrast with this commendably down-to-earth approach, an eventual move to a *national* Tuning discussion to define learning outcomes for all disciplines might more fully capture the imagination of the academy and the general public. Instead of making the familiar trek to state houses or flagship university meeting rooms, faculty members and others would join colleagues from around the country to represent their disciplines in a scholarly undertaking of unprecedented significance.

Such an initiative could be a prominent and highly positive outcome of the proposed congress. As an alternate approach, national organizations such as the American Council on Education, AAU, AAC&U, and AACC, working in collaboration with private funding sources, could collaborate on organizing and guiding this initiative. With sufficient support, a coordinated effort could produce substantive results within an aggressive timeline. And once the outcome frames are in draft form, the United States could work under the auspices of UNESCO or some other agency to bring higher educators from around the world to the table. The goal of these discussions, which could draw on Tuning efforts in Europe, the United States, Latin America, and elsewhere, should be a provisional global agreement relative to learning outcomes, discipline by discipline. A "flat world" deserves nothing else. The draft agreement would be progressively refined over the course of a decade, then revisited every decade thereafter. Its adoption could not be mandatory, but nonparticipating nations and institutions would probably find themselves at a serious disadvantage in ensuring mobility to their own students and in recruiting international students.

Clarify and ensure the benefits of a liberal arts education. The Bologna standard of the three-year baccalaureate assumes that many students enter higher education possessing the cultural and social capabilities a baccalaureate degree should ensure. Conversely, U.S. higher educators for the most part assume that many of the vital but less-tangible capabilities developed through liberal education—intellectual agility, social skills, ability to work in teams, understanding of examined values, enjoyment of diversity, appreciation for culture, and so on—are most effectively developed among students who have completed secondary education. There are good reasons for so believing, but we must be better able to make that case beyond our borders.

Part of the effort must be the identification and elucidation of explicit learning outcomes for general education programs through the U.S. adaptation of the Tuning Process. But there must also be a further effort to document in detail the tangible benefits of a comprehensive liberal education—which would encompass general education, the major, and even cocurricular and noncurricular educational experiences. There are heartening indications in a survey of AAC&U members that "campus leaders are focused both on providing all students a broad set of learning outcomes and assessing students' achievement of these outcomes across the curriculum" (AAC&U Poll, 2009). While reflective only of institutions professing an explicit commitment to the values of a liberal education, the findings, that "nearly 80% of colleges now have a broad set of learning outcomes for all students and more than 70% now assess outcomes across the curriculum beyond the use of course grades," may indeed suggest "an important shift in focus for American higher education away from measuring progress by students' seat time and accumulation of credits toward clarifying more transparently what students are expected to learn" (AAC&U Poll). Yet notwithstanding such positive findings, only 5% of those responding are willing to claim that "almost all" of their students understand the learning outcomes invoked to measure their performance.

To make a familiar point once again, if we cannot ensure that those within academe understand the principles being developed through higher education reform or the progress being made, we can hardly expect those not within the fold to do so. We must be able through refined outcomes statements and ever more resourceful assessment to argue effectively before an international constituency that a liberal arts education confers benefits on individuals and society that are identifiable and valuable—and unlikely to be achieved through condensed degree programs that may assume but do not provide for liberal learning. By mounting a defense of its vision of the baccalaureate and interpreting that vision persuasively to the international higher education community, the United States would assert on the world stage that students presenting an American baccalaureate degree possess clearly

defined competencies and capacities that incorporate but improve upon outcomes set forth through the Bologna process.

Create a common standard for the accessible documentation of educational
results. A persistent motif in discussions among college presidents and at academic conferences in the United States is that higher education must tell
its story more effectively. Developing a standard nomenclature and clearly
articulated learning outcomes in the form of qualifications frameworks are
two of the three important elements in this storytelling obligation. Meaningful accountability is the other.

The commitment to achieve such accountability must take into account
the myriad of activities already taking place in the United States in this
regard—a decided advantage for the most part but a complicating factor as
well. Here again, more can appear as less. For there is so much happening
on so many levels to so many different purposes that a coherent image of a
self-critical academy intent on improvement has failed to emerge. The result?
Higher education can appear complacent and moribund—when it is anything but.

Bologna cannot be our arbiter in this regard, but the evolution of the
Process prompts two observations that may offer guidance. The first is that
agreement on principle—on what should be measured and documented and
by what standard the results should be made known—need not require standardization of method. So long as there is rigorous attention to the comparability of data, a national system of academic assessment may not be required.
But it must be possible to derive comparable national data from the different
methods that are employed. The second is that the process of reform does
well to rely on independent bodies to provide support, offer oversight, and
attest to compliance. Because the United States has long vested major
responsibility for accountability in volunteer peer reviewers, such confidence
is well justified. But, again, accrediting bodies must work in tandem so that
their findings and recommendations are comparable and easily understood.
This priority applies to professional as well as regional accreditors.

In addition to serving the United States well as points of departure for
its efforts, these principles point also to important ways U.S. higher education can improve on Bologna. We can distinguish more clearly between
developmental and evaluative assessment, so that both may operate more
effectively to provide their respective benefits to the academy. We can take
advantage of voluntary accountability efforts to build a culture of collegial
self-examination and disclosure. While Adelman (2009) correctly observes
that indicators provided through current voluntary efforts do not yet amount
to "accountability" (p. xi), they do embody a collaborative process that could
over time support a far more revealing and substantive approach. And even

as we expand such initiatives and undertake new ones, we can do a far better job of integrating the results of assessment currently operating at various levels to create a composite portrait of what higher education is learning about itself and the ways it is (or is not) becoming more effective.

Here, Europe may offer a useful example through the European Association for Quality Assurance in Higher Education (ENQA), which focuses primarily on institutional efforts to maintain continuous improvement, and the European Quality Assurance Register (EQAR), which seeks to provide recognition for accrediting organizations that embody European standards. Together, these offer several advantages the United States might enjoy more fully: They provide a clearinghouse for information on effective practice, they offer a platform for the collation of differing assumptions regarding accountability, and they articulate standards likely to enjoy increasing authority. Higher education in the United States would serve itself and the public well by drawing on deep reservoirs of experience in the assessment and accreditation communities to develop and articulate more authoritative standards and expectations. Here again, there is less of a need to create additional capacity than to coordinate existing capacity in ways that make information more accessible and useful.

But there must also be a shift in the criteria employed. Analogous to the change in emphasis from what is taught to what is learned, our concern with student enrollments and retention, for instance, should yield to a far stronger emphasis on student persistence and attainment. The capacities of entering students should be measured more carefully so that the educational value added by the institution can be documented in meaningful ways, and the kinds of support provided to encourage success—inclusive advising, entrepreneurial financial aid, creative student work opportunities, pragmatic career counseling, crisis interventions—should be documented as well. And we must take care that our performance criteria respond to the breadth of the higher education landscape, where nontraditional students (often employed full-time, more mature, and with many nonacademic responsibilities) represent a large and increasing percentage of our student bodies.

To serve the academy and the public, a national accountability register would publish current data on a predictable schedule, present easily understood information, and enable observers to appreciate institutional accomplishments and to make well informed but not invidious comparisons among institutions. Recommendations on the elements of this new accountability could include the following:

- an annotated listing of all regional accreditation decisions disclosing, institution by institution, examples of progress made and priorities for improvement

- a similar listing of specialized and professional accreditation decisions with regard to specific programs, disclosing instances of noncompliance but emphasizing the results of programmatic improvement initiatives
- institutional data similar to that now called for in the VSA, including measures of student attainment according to well-defined outcomes, but enhanced to provide information on the means institutions use to encourage and affirm educational attainment
- information regarding any changes made or contemplated with regard to the standards for assessing and reporting educational outcomes

As with the Bologna Process, U.S. higher education's readiness to embrace the summons to highly visible and informative accountability will suggest its resolve to engage in significant reform on other fronts. Given the range and depth of current efforts, we can find some reason to be optimistic. But there is much to be done—and the work should be undertaken with a sense of urgency.

Enable students to provide more informative documentation of their competences and accomplishments. In the Bologna Process, this commitment takes two forms. First, as we have seen, the mission of a registry established in the 1990s to facilitate the international transfer of credits has been expanded to include maintaining students' accumulation of such credits. Hence the European Credit Transfer and Accumulation System (ECTS) now offers a clearinghouse for academic credentials. Of course, for this to work well, such credentials must represent comparable levels of challenge and workload—an expectation more easily expressed than fulfilled. Second, European students have been assured of their right to a diploma supplement. Such a credential enables students to interpret their educational histories to employers and to graduate institutions within and beyond their borders.

But there is a clear opportunity for the United States to improve on both initiatives. The benefits of a national registry of academic qualifications should give further impetus to the development of standards required for such a resource, for as we define outcomes at the baccalaureate, programmatic, and course sequence levels, we lay the groundwork for a registry capable of reflecting the diversity of institutional missions in the United States and of attesting to shared values that transcend that diversity. As for the diploma supplement, while any additional interpretive information is better than none, we should follow Adelman's (2009) suggestion by adding important distinguishing information about student research and service experiences, about second language competency, and about academic honors the student may earned. Experiments in U.S. higher education with electronic portfolios, which report measurable attainments, incorporate recommendations from mentors, intimate particular abilities and potentials, and provide an archive of representative work, may offer a particularly promising means for translating specific credentials into readily understood terms. The challenge of Bologna should prompt agreement on a common standard for a descriptive and revealing baccalaureate portfolio and create the expectation that all institutions of higher education will make it available to all students.

Provide leadership in the development of a standard nomenclature. The Bologna Process has made a significant contribution to the intelligibility of higher education in Europe through the implementation of a three-cycle degree system closely comparable to that of the United States and through efforts to agree on a widely understood vocabulary, albeit one in many different languages. U.S. higher education should build on this precedent by leading an effort to create a shared multilingual vocabulary for higher education. Otherwise, as colleges and universities become more credible in ensuring the attainment of clear learning outcomes, the present welter of acronyms, jumble of degree titles, and variety of different descriptors for often closely comparable programs will continue to befuddle.

An immediate incentive for the United States to seek clearer terminology lies in its hope to remain competitive in the recruitment of international students. Agreement on the meaning of such terms as *credit, term, degree, outcome, competence,* and so on would enable the academy to speak to the world with a coherent and intelligible voice. Moreover, the development of a common vocabulary would enable U.S. higher education to clarify the distinct advantages it offers students in comparison with those being promoted by Europe. By moving beyond rhetorical and linguistic differences to expose real differences among otherwise comparable programs, we would make higher education more accessible to international students and more intelligible to our own.

Support mobility. Broad agreement on the ends of a liberal education and of majors within the baccalaureate should facilitate the acceptance of academic credit across state lines even by institutions pursuing different kinds of missions. And by making the expectations of American higher education more understandable for international students and international employers, greater consistency in defining intended educational outcomes should also support student recruitment abroad and the placement of U.S. students overseas. For large research universities, the advantage of heightened competitiveness would be considerable, but for small colleges, more effective recruitment of students from other countries and the placement of their students internationally could represent a critical survival strategy.

Whatever the scale, efforts to facilitate mobility must consider several fronts. A pragmatic interest in enabling students to accumulate credits toward a degree through enrollment at several institutions places a priority on expeditious and consistent review of academic credentials against a common standard. The more readily an institution, a state, or a nation can interpret and assign value to the educational credentials of another, the more welcoming its higher education portal, and the more competitive in recruiting students the institution, state, or nation becomes. In addition, a student interested in obtaining greater breadth and perspective through study in another state or through study abroad will place a high priority also on open borders, on the portability of student aid, and on helpful student services. For access to international experiences, language training and the ready availability of (or lack of necessity for) visas may also prove instrumental. Only a consideration of the many facets of mobility will ensure genuine progress and lead to a far closer realization for U.S. students of the Bologna goal of increased mobility.

But such reforms may accomplish little unless the United States looks critically within its own borders where mobility is often discouraged by academic and economic disincentives. One priority must be that of persuading community college students to proceed to the baccalaureate at a four-year institution. As we have noted more than once, Adelman (2009) effectively addresses this issue through proposing concurrent enrollments of associate's degree candidates at cooperating baccalaureate institutions. But if that approach should prove feasible only for limited numbers, a more modest but more easily implemented approach could offer community college students access to information, resources (libraries, cultural and athletic events), and services (pretransfer advising, financial counseling) at cooperating four-year institutions. Both approaches emphasize bonding the community college student to a four-year or graduate institution and providing an inviting bridge from one to the other.

And other approaches might be considered. Transfer 101, a program linking the University of Texas, Texas A&M University, and the Texas Association of Community Colleges relies on a Web-based information center offering community college students instructions on the choice of a four-year college, admissions standards, financial aid, and the transferability of credits. Other colleges are offering dedicated orientation programs for community college transfer students, sponsoring transfer student advisory councils, and linking new transfer student with peer advisers.

State-to-state mobility is in some ways almost as great a challenge in the United States as in Europe, but while Europe may be making progress in reducing barriers, the United States is for the most part raising them. Even if a broad consensus on outcomes should enable students seeking an out-of-state public education to anticipate and address academic barriers, economic and political ones may remain formidable. At the University of Virginia, for instance, 2009–10 tuition for out-of-state students is $31,872, compared to $9,872 for in-state students. But even such a formidable barrier may not satisfy xenophobic legislators. In Virginia and in several other states, efforts have been made to limit by fiat the proportion of out-of-state students admitted to their most highly competitive universities. Of course, in states such as California that cannot meet increasing demands from in-state students, lowering the tariff for out-of-state students may feel like a step in the wrong direction.

Yet there are some positive initiatives to consider. For fall 2009, Southern Illinois University offered far less-expensive in-state tuition rates ($6,975 vs. $17,437) to residents of neighboring states: Missouri, Indiana, and Kentucky. Others, such as Kent State University in Ohio and the University of Tennessee at Chattanooga, have begun to discount the in-state versus out-of-state difference for students from neighboring states. North Dakota is going even further by offering in-state tuition to some international applicants. And the National Student Exchange deserves mention. Mobility is its reason for being. Since its inception in 1968, more than 90,000 Canadian and American students have pursued the opportunity to study in another state or province for one year. But only 200 colleges and universities participate.

If expanded mobility within the borders of the United States represents a priority, there are strategies that could be applied in addressing it, but they would require the cooperation of higher education, private supporters, and public policy makers. Current efforts to support one-year student exchanges among the states could be expanded considerably. Aid programs to address current discrepancies between in-state and out-of-state tuitions would require increased funding. In the long run, such barriers could come down entirely if states would agree to a carefully calibrated national network of reciprocity arrangements. Many states already maintain such agreements with neighbors. Extrapolating from a network of such agreements to a national understanding would be a formidable but attainable goal.

Here, too, the challenge of Bologna can and should be met. By some appearances, mobility within Europe may not be the priority that it was at the beginning of the Bologna Process. The 4% of European students taking advantage of opportunities for study in countries other than their own may not increase significantly in the near term. But the United States cannot stand still. If the states should continue to discourage the crossing of state lines for educational purposes, we will limit the opportunities we offer students, hamper many of our most effective institutions from achieving their full potential, impede the mobility required for robust economic development, and further damage our credibility on the stage of global higher education.

Encourage progress through the degrees. Another kind of mobility appears in one of the most direct challenges posed by the Bologna Process: its commitment to encourage baccalaureate graduates to undertake master's-level study. Although Europe has a head start in this regard, given its pre-Bologna convention of a five-year academic program, U.S. higher education could begin with a coordinated effort that would provide students at early stages of the major a comprehensive overview of the requirements for graduate study and of the opportunities it offers. Too often, students who might benefit from pursuing a master's degree must sort through a confusing jumble of flyers, Web sites, and published guides with little guidance. A collaborative effort to provide qualified students with an appreciation for the broader educational continuum could cut through much that is confusing or discouraging and lead to significantly stronger enrollments at the master's level. But better information alone will not suffice. If increased enrollments at the master's and doctoral levels are recognized as national priorities in response to the challenge of Bologna, there will have to be increased support, public and private, to encourage students to undertake and continue graduate education. Perhaps the notion of concurrent enrollments might be extended to link undergraduates to graduate programs well in advance of their baccalaureate graduations.

Celebrate and demonstrate the value of diversity. Although the Bologna Process has expanded to include attention to its social dimension, that is, the accessibility of higher education to less-traditional constituencies, its documents make little reference to what American higher education regards as the educational values of cultural and ethnic diversity. As evidence continues to accumulate that students learn more effectively in a heterogeneous environment, insistence in the United States on diversity as a discrete value may be a further means of enhancing competitiveness and providing leadership.

But the value placed on diversity must be reflected in actions to ensure it. Because issues of access bear disproportionately on the less well advantaged, a commitment to expanded diversity in U.S. higher education must include a determination to address the barriers—financial, social, academic—that continue to grow.

Examine Everything

A genuine commitment to reform should begin with the assumption that no element of the academy is immune from examination and reconsideration. We should inquire into all conventions, protocols, and paradigms, including terms, hours, grades, degrees, courses, and departments, from the perspective of a single question: How might the academy become more effective in enabling students to learn? And our inquiry should reach within and beyond university walls to include appreciation for the substantive learning that takes place outside the classroom through employment, on-campus or off-campus living, cocurricular activities, and noncurricular activities.

Quite apart from what it has accomplished for Europeans, the impetus provided by the Bologna Process for undertaking a fresh view of higher education—its structures, protocols, and values—is well worth embracing. And expanding. For Bologna's limitations are as compelling as its vigor. For instance, the three-year baccalaureate represents a commendable willingness to examine the status quo, to consider which conventions still make sense and which may not, and to frame initiatives intended to explore more productive approaches. On the other hand, Bologna has not gone very far with its examination. The real issue is not the length of the baccalaureate, but how it is organized and what it is expected to accomplish. So long as the outcomes frameworks remain a brief listing of generalizations, participating nations may comply with the new cycles by simply rearranging current programs through the insertion of a partition between the first three and second two years. Some have done just that.

Higher education in the United States should approach this and the other issues raised by Bologna more creatively. For instance, there may be good reason to stand by the four-year baccalaureate. But the interests of part-time and nontraditional students should influence policy at least as much as those of students aged 18–22. Colleges and academic departments may still represent the most effective approach to organizing a university, but we cannot be confident this is so unless we are willing to consider alternatives. What is sacred about the semester? Why should three-week courses not be routinely available? What would be the result if senior professors were assigned introductory courses for first-year students while assistant professors fresh from graduate study were offered the opportunity to teach graduate students? Would a no-frills, no student activity tuition rate attract new students to higher education or weaken a sense of academic community? Should we continue to expect students to proceed directly from high school to college, or should we encourage an interval of community or military service? Should we regard the baccalaureate as an interim qualification for most students and make routine the advancement to study at the master's level? If we have difficulty creating coherent programs of general education at large institutions, should we create instead standards for coherence that would inform individual learning contracts for each student—one element in an electronic diploma supplement?

Another example lies in the Tuning Process as practiced in Europe and as conceived in pilot activities in the United States. While it may be a useful interim process to define more clearly the outcomes associated with the completion of existing degree levels in existing disciplines, defining venerable academic structures more definitively might be regarded as a provisional accomplishment. Just as the environment for learning, typified by the associative range of the Internet, can no longer be limited by the traditional structures of the university, the world that graduates enter (or in many instances already inhabit) should reward above all the capacity to think beyond categories, to synthesize disparate sources of information, and to create knowledge out of data determined to be reliable and pertinent. Like so many of the most compelling problems that college graduates will have to address—global warming, pandemics, cultural insularity and nationalism, agricultural exploitation—the conversations of the future will be not only cross-disciplinary but multidisciplinary. The reform of higher education must be as inclusive and wide ranging as knowledge itself. As we face the challenge of Bologna, we face also an unprecedented intellectual adventure—but one requiring a resolute focus on learning as opposed to the conventional structures and conventions that frame learning. And one requiring as well not a little courage.

In Sum

The Bologna Process offers U.S. higher education a compelling example and an immediate challenge. If we were simply to adopt the European process and all its priorities, to get on board as Adelman (2008) has urged, we would doubtless accomplish more than we have in the past. And to aspire to more than a modest refinement of Bologna may prove to be too ambitious within the near term. For there is a real question whether U.S. higher educators will understand the challenge being offered and accept the opportunity to take that challenge several steps further.

Thus it remains to be seen whether we can agree to a comprehensive program of reform as ambitious as that of our European colleagues while standing up for the singular strengths of U.S. higher education—our long-standing commitment to broad access, our embrace of diversity as an educational good, and, most notably, our distinctive commitment to providing tertiary-level students with a liberal education. As is so often the case, the answer may lie in the willingness of the academy to make the hard choices and the strategic investments required and in the vision of a society capable of securing again, in Jefferson's charming words, the "publick happiness" of securely funded educational opportunity.

Some of these choices have informed the higher education discussion for years, of course. But they have never been more urgent than they are now. And by impressing that urgency upon us through its challenge, Bologna can contribute significantly to the future of U.S. higher education. As Adelman (2009) observes, when you pay close attention to international colleagues working through different cultures and languages to a fresh perspective, "new ways of configuring your own solutions inevitably arise" (p. ix). One hopes.

But our review of the progress Bologna has made and the values that its efforts embody may prompt a few final caveats also.

First, the drive for objective evaluation, a critical element in the Bologna vision of improved accountability and in any credible approach to quality assurance, must not obscure the continuing importance to higher education of expert subjective judgment, carefully and thoughtfully expressed. Deny this, and we deny the value we assign to expertise itself. Even aviation, which employs extensive checklists and detailed measures, depends on comprehensive assessments of pilot performance by experienced professionals.

Second, notwithstanding the aspirations of the Bologna Process, higher education in Europe is still widely varied and idiosyncratic in its programs and structures and likely to remain so. And it continues to express a different vision of entitlement. Whether A-levels in England or the *baccalauréat* in France, make-or-break examinations will continue to regulate the access of Europeans to higher education. By contrast, in seeking to offer virtually universal access to higher education, the United States accepts deeply indigenous challenges and opportunities.

And, finally, the framing of qualifications frameworks and the creation of a bureaucracy to evaluate and enforce them may require a formidable investment on the part of institutions, private sources, and governments. As we undertake to achieve many of the benefits in responding to the challenge of Bologna, we should be candid about the support an effective response will require.

But we should be no less candid about the dividends an effective response to Bologna might offer. First, unlike the Bologna process, which began to articulate its social dimension only at midcourse, a coordinated U.S. reform can operate from the start under the aegis of a traditional commitment to the expansion of opportunity and the enrichment of diversity. Second, the U.S. effort can improve on Bologna by inviting faculty members and students to the conversation from the start and by vesting authority for reform in the academy rather than with bureaucrats. Third, attentive to findings about the importance of the vocabulary used in defining and explaining reform, leaders in higher education change can honor from the start a commitment to transparency. And we can learn a lesson also in terms of articulating a consistent focus as a common ground among the diverse initiatives required. That focus: sustaining the advancement of knowledge and ensuring student learning.

Joining the Club—or Creating One?

While joining the Bologna club is an option well worth considering, a better idea may be to strengthen the U.S. club, one whose members may draw on the strongest elements of the Bologna Process while maintaining values that continue to distinguish higher education in the United States. By taking up this responsibility, the United States has the opportunity to assert its leadership once again. But that leadership must arise from the example we set in making good at home on the Bologna issues of increased accountability; expanded access; heightened intentionality and effectiveness; enhanced mobility, domestic and international; and our much broader understanding and pursuit of the social dimension.

Writing in advance of a book announced for publication in fall 2009, Robert Zemsky (2009) considers whether U.S. higher education is capable of undertaking genuine reform. In the light of failed efforts in the past, he suggests that a "dislodging event" may be required—a massive congressional reform in student aid programs, a federal decision to tax the interest on endowments, or adoption of the three-year baccalaureate as a national standard. He may be right, but the challenge of Bologna, if taken seriously, could offer U.S. higher education no less powerful an incentive for change, and one considerably less disruptive. If U.S. higher education leaders were to provide the guidance the academy now sorely needs, we would be in a position to work with our European colleagues to create an alliance conferring benefits on both "clubs"—a kind of SkyTeam for higher education. With access to all that European and American colleges and universities have to offer, the world's college students could find themselves upgraded to first class.

LIST OF ACRONYMS

AAC&U	Association of American Colleges and Universities
AACC	American Association of Community Colleges
AASCU	American Association of State Colleges and Universities
AAU	Association of American Universities
ACT	American College Testing
AJCU	Association of Jesuit Colleges and Universities
APLU	Association of Public and Land-Grant Universities
AQIP	Academic Quality Improvement Program
ASPA	Association of Specialized and Professional Accreditors
AUCC	Association of Universities and Colleges of Canada
BFUG	Bologna Follow-Up Group
CAAP	Collegiate Assessment of Academic Proficiency
CAE	Council for Aid to Education
CEPES	European Center for Higher Education
CHEA	Council for Higher Education Accreditation
CLA	Collegiate Learning Assessment
COE	Council of Europe
COMETT	Community Program in Education and Training for Technology
CUMU	Coalition of Urban and Metropolitan Universities
EC	European Commission
ECTS	European Credit Transfer and Accumulation System
EHEA	European Higher Education Area
ENIC	European Network of Information Centres
ENQA	European Association for Quality Assurance in Higher Education
EQAR	European Quality Assurance Register for Higher Education
EQF	European Qualifications Framework
ERA	European Research Area
ERASMUS	European Region Action Scheme for the Mobility of University Students

ESIB	National Unions of Students in Europe (now the ESU)
ESU	European Students' Union (formerly the ESIB)
ETS	Educational Testing Service
EU	European Union
EUA	European University Association
EURASHE	European Association of Institutions in Higher Education
HEA	Higher Education Act
HEI	higher education institution
HLC	Higher Learning Commission
IB	International Baccalaureate
IBE	International Bureau of Education
IES	Institute of Education Sciences (U.S. Department of Education)
IPC	International People's College
MAAP	Measure of Academic Proficiency and Progress
NAICU	National Association of Independent Colleges and Universities
NARIC	National Academic Recognition Information Centers
NCATE	National Council for the Accreditation of Teacher Education
NCHEMS	National Center for Higher Education Management Systems
NQF	National Qualifications Framework
OECD	Organization for Economic Cooperation and Development
PETRA	Action Program for the Vocational Training of Young People
QAA	Quality Assurance Agency for Higher Education
QEP	Quality Enhancement Plan
SACS	Southern Association of Colleges and Schools
TEU	Treaty on European Union
UNESCO	United Nations Educational, Scientific, and Cultural Organization
WASC	Western Association of Schools and Colleges

REFERENCES

The most convenient and comprehensive platform for further reading in the significant documents of the Bologna Process may be found on the official Bologna Process Web site 2007–2010 at http://www.ond.vlaanderen.be/hog eronderwijs/Bologna/.

This site offers

- a calendar of events
- a current listing of participating countries and organizations
- an overview of the process as a whole
- summaries of performance relative to each of the action lines
- texts of the primary documents, including
  - the seven declarations and communiqués arising from the ministerial conferences
  - the general reports prepared prior to these conferences
  - the stocktaking reports commissioned by the ministers
  - the Trends reports developed by the European University Association (EUA)
  - the *Bologna With Student Eyes* reports prepared by the European Students' Union (ESU), and many others

References that may be accessed through this platform are designated by the symbol • Note also that all documents developed under the aegis of the National Unions of Students in Europe (ESIB) appear under the acronym of the organization's current name, the ESU.

AAC&U. (2008). *Our students' best work: A framework for accountability worthy of our mission.* Retrieved November 5, 2009, at http://www.aacu.org/publications/pdfs/StudentsBestReport.pdf

AAC&U Outcomes. (2007). *College learning for the new global century.* Washington, DC: AAC&U.

AAC&U Poll. (2009, May 15). New survey finds colleges moving away from pure "cafeteria-style" general education requirements. [Press release]. Washington, DC: AACU&U.

Access. (2001). *A report of the* Advisory Committee on Student Financial Assistance. Retrieved most recently March 3, 2009, from http://www.ed.gov/about/bds comm/list/acsfa/access_denied.pdf

Adelman, C. (2008). *The Bologna club: What U.S. higher education can learn from a decade of European reconstruction.* Washington, DC: Institute for Higher Education Policy.

Adelman, C. (2009). *The Bologna Process for U.S. eyes: Re-learning higher education in the age of convergence.* Washington, DC: Institute for Higher Education Policy. Retrieved most recently April 9, 2009, from http://www.ihep.org/assets/files/EYESFINAL.pdf

Alexander, L. (2009). *Alexander calls on universities to reduce tuition.* Retrieved most recently March 11, 2009, from http://alexander.senate.gov/public/index.cfm?-FuseAction = PressReleases.Detail&PressRelease_Id = e299713a-5e3a-4d15-badb-6846ae2b96f3

Altman, R. (2009). The great crash. *Foreign Affairs, 88*(1), 2–14.

Amaral, A., & Magalhaes, A. (2004). Epidemiology and the Bologna saga. *Higher Education, 48*(1), 79–100.

AQIP. (2009.) *Academic Quality Improvement Program.* Retrieved most recently February 7, 2009, from http://www.aqip.org/

Arum, R., Roksa, J., & Velez, M. (2008). *Learning to reason and communicate in college: Initial report of findings from the CLA longitudinal study.* Brooklyn, NY: Social Science Research Council.

ASPA Code. (1995). *Code of good practice.* Retrieved most recently October 1, 2009, from http://www.aspa-usa.org/codeofethics/code.html

AUCC. (2009). *The Bologna Process and implications for Canada's universities, January 26–27, 2009.* Retrieved most recently July 15, 2009, from http://www.aucc.ca/events/2009/int_mtgs/bologna_presentations_e.html

Australia. (2006). *The Bologna Process and Australia: Next steps.* Retrieved most recently January 20, 2009, from http://www.aei.gov.au/AEI/GovernmentActivities/BolognaProcess/AVC C_pdf.htm

Baccalaureate. (n.d.). *International baccalaureate.* Retrieved most recently September 8, 2008, from http://www.ibo.org/general/who.cfm

Bergan, S. (2007). *Qualifications: Introduction to a concept.* Strasbourg: COE.

• Bergan, S. (2009). *Introductory statement at the ministerial meeting of the Bologna Process, Leuven/Louvain-la-Neuve.* Available at http://www.ond.vlaanderen.be/hogeronderwijs/Bologna/

• Bergen Communiqué. (2005). *The European Higher Education Area: Achieving the goals.* Available at http://www.ond.vlaanderen.be/hogeronderwijs/Bologna/

• Berlin Communiqué. (2003). *Realising the European Higher Education Area: Communiqué of the Conference of Ministers responsible for higher education.* Available at http://www.ond.vlaanderen.be/hogeronderwijs/Bologna/

Berlin News. (2003). *A substantial document with concrete priorities for 2005.* Retrieved most recently October 25, 2009, from http://www.bologna-berlin2003.de/en/aktuell/haupt.htm

Bilefsky, D., & Castle, S. (2009, Nov. 4). Way is clear to centralize Europe's power. *New York Times,* p. A5.

Bologna. (1988). *The Magna Charta: Text of the Bologna Declaration.* Retrieved most recently September 19, 2008, from http://www.magna-charta.org/magna.html

• Bologna. (1999). *Joint declaration of the European ministers of education.* Available at http://www.ond.vlaanderen.be/hogeronderwijs/Bologna/

• Bologna. (2009). *Overarching framework of qualifications of the EHEA.* Retrieved most recently August 1, 2009, from http://www.ond.vlaanderen.be/hogeronder wijs/bologna/qf/overarching.asp

• Bologna 2020. (2008). *Bologna 2020: Unlocking Europe's potential—contributing to a better world. Summary of Participants' debate on the general rapporteur's tentative conclusions and recommendations.* Retrieved most recently June 1, 2009, from http://www.ond.vlaanderen.be / hogeronderwijs / bologna / BolognaSeminars / Ghent2008 .html and available also at http://www.ond.vlaanderen.be/hogeronderwijs/Bologna/

Bologna Explanation. (2000). *The Bologna Declaration on the European space for higher education: An explanation.* Retrieved most recently June 30, 2008, from http://ec.europa.eu/education/policies/educ/bologna/bologna.pdf

Caddick, S. (2008). Back to Bologna. *EMBO Reports, 9*(1), 18–21. Retrieved most recently May 4, 2009, from http://www.pubmedcentral.nih.gov/articlerender .fcgi?artid = 2246620

CAE. (2009). *CLA: Returning to learning.* Retrieved most recently March 13, 2009, from http://www.cae.org/content/pro_collegiate.htm

Castle, S. (2009, June 8). Disaffection dominates European Parliament voting. *New York Times,* p. A5.

CEPES. (2008). *European Centre for Higher Education: Brief history of the centre.* Retrieved most recently November 6, 2009, http://www.cepes.ro/cepes/mis sion.htm

CHEA Initiative. (2009). *Building the future of accreditation.* Retrieved most recently November 3, 2009, from http://www.chea.org/About/CI/index.asp

COE. (2008). *About the Council of Europe.* Retrieved most recently October 3, 2008, from http://www.coe.int/T/e/Com/about_coe/

Coleman, J. (2004). *Navigating the new landscape for languages.* Retrieved most recently October 30, 2008, from http://www.llas.ac.uk/navlang

Commission. (2006). *A test of leadership: Charting the future of U.S. higher education.* Washington, DC: U.S. Department of Education.

Commons. (2007). *Purposes and action lines of the Bologna Process: Comparability v. standardisation.* Retrieved most recently February 13, 2009, from http://www .publications.parliament.uk/pa/cm200607/cmselect/cmedus ki/205/20506.htm

Cohen-Tanugi, L. (2005). The end of Europe? *Foreign Affairs, 84,* 55–67.

Cultural Convention. (1954). *European Cultural Convention.* Retrieved most recently November 6, 2008, from http://conventions.coe.int/Treaty/EN/Treaties/Html/ 018.htm

Dillon, S. (2009, May 28). New push to end need for remedial classes before college. *New York Times,* p. A14.

Diploma. (2006). *The diploma supplement.* Retrieved most recently November 12, 2008, from http://ec.europa.eu/education/policies/rec_qual/recognition/diploma_en.html#1

Driver, C. (1971). *The exploding university.* London: Hodder & Stoughton.

Dublin Descriptors. (n.d.). *Dublin descriptors as used in the Framework for Qualifications of EHEA compared to the descriptors as used in the EU Commission staff working document "Towards a European Qualifications Framework for Lifelong Learning."* Retrieved most recently November 11, 2008, from http://www.smpf .lt/get.php?f.1201

EC. (2005). *Communication to the spring European council: Working together for growth and jobs. A new start for the Lisbon Strategy.* Retrieved most recently January 7, 2009, from http://ec.europa.eu/growthandjobs/pdf/COM2005_024_en.pdf

EC Education. (2009). *Erasmus Program.* Retrieved most recently October 5, 2009, from http://ec.europa.eu/education/lifelong-learning-programme/doc80_een.htm

ECTS. (2008). *European Credit Transfer and Accumulation System.* Retrieved most recently December 12, 2008, from http://ec.europa.eu/education/lifelong-learning-policy/doc48_en.htm

ECTS. (2009). *European Credit Transfer and Accumulation System.* Retrieved most recently April 18, 2009, from http://ec.europa.eu/education/lifelong-learning-policy/doc48_en.htm

ENQA. (2009). *Standards and guidelines for quality assurance in the European Higher Education Area.* Retrieved most recently June 15, 2009, from http://www.enqa .eu/files/ENQA%20Bergen%20Report.pdf

ENQA Past. (2009). *Current projects.* Retrieved most recently November 3, 2009, from http://www.enqa.eu/projects.lasso

EQAR. (2009). *EQAR now lists nine quality assurance agencies.* Retrieved most recently April 25, 2009, from http://www.eqar.eu/fileadmin/documents/eqar/press/PR_090415_EQAR_NewAgenciesIncluded.pdf

Erasmus. (2008). *The Erasmus Programme.* Retrieved most recently October 1, 2008, from http://ec.europa.eu/education/lifelong-learning-programme/doc80_en.htm

Erasmus Mundus. (2009). *Erasmus Mundus—Scholarships and Academic Cooperation: What does Erasmus Mundus offer?* Retrieved most recently May 1, 2009, from http://ec.europa.eu/education/external-relation-programmes/doc72_en.htm

Erasmus Overview. (n.d.). *Erasmus—higher education.* Retrieved most recently December 11, 2008, from http://eacea.ec.europa.eu/static/en/overview/erasmus_overview.htm

Erlanger, S., & Castle, S. (2009a, March 2). Dire economy threatens idea of one Europe. *New York Times,* p. A1.

Erlanger, S., & Castle, S. (2009b, May 14). Coming vote on assembly elicits shrugs in Europe. *New York Times,* p. A10.

ESU. (2003). *Bologna with student eyes 2003.* Retrieved most recently November 12, 2009, from http://www.esib.org/index.php/Publications/official-publications/571-bologna-with-student-eyes-2003

- ESU. (2005a). *Bologna with student eyes 2005.* Retrieved most recently October 25, 2009, from http://www.esib.org/index.php/Publications/official-publications and available at http://www.ond.vlaanderen.be/hogeronderwijs/Bologna/

ESU. (2005b). *Bologna black book.* Retrieved most recently October 25, 2009, from http://www.esib.org/index.php/issues/european-processes/79-bologn a-process

- ESU. (2007). *Bologna with student eyes.* Available at http://www.ond.vlaander en.be/hogeronderwijs/Bologna/

ESU. (2009a). *Prague students declaration towards the 2009 ministerial conference of the Bologna Process.* Retrieved most recently March 18, 2009, from http://www .esib.org/documents/declarations/090222_Prague_Student_Declaration-final .pdf

ESU. (2009b). *Bologna with student eyes.* Retrieved most recently June 1, 2009, from http://www.esib.org/index.php/Publications/official-publications

ESU Berlin. (2007). *Berlin Declaration.* Retrieved most recently November 4, 2009, from http://www.esib.org/documents/declarations/0703_berlin-declaration.pdf

ESU Policy. (2007). *Policy paper: Degree structures.* Retrieved most recently April 3, 2009, from http://www.esib.org/index.php/documents/policy-papers/292-pol icy-paper-qdegree-structuresq

EU. (2008). *Lisbon Strategy: Results of the meeting with the 27 national coordinators.* Retrieved most recently December 15, 2008, from http://www.eu2008.fr/ impressionPDF83b1.pdf?url = %2FPFUE%2Flang%2Fen%2Faccueil%2FPFUE-12_2008%2FPFUE-05.12.2008%2FStrategie_de_Lisbonne_Resultats_de_la_reun ion_des_27_coordonateurs_nationaux

EUA. (2003). *EUA press release after the Prague summit.* Retrieved most recently September 27, 2008, from http://www.bologna-berlin2003.de/pdf/EUA_position_ paper.pdf

EUA. (2008). *EUA at a glance.* Retrieved most recently December 1, 2008, from http://www.eua.be/about-eua/

EUA Prague. (2009). *Prague Declaration: European universities—looking forward with confidence.* Retrieved most recently May 5, 2009, from http://www.eua.be/ .../EUA_Prague_Declaration_European_Universities_-_Looking_forward_ with_confidence.pdf

- EUA Trends I. (1999). *Trends in learning structures in higher education.* Available at http://www.ond.vlaanderen.be/hogeronderwijs/Bologna/

- EUA Trends II. (2001). *Towards the European higher education area: Survey of main reforms from Bologna to Prague.* Available at http://www.ond.vlaanderen.be/hog eronderwijs/Bologna/

- EUA Trends III. (2003). *Progress towards the European Higher Education Area.* Available at http://www.ond.vlaanderen.be/hogeronderwijs/Bologna/

- EUA Trends IV. (2005) *European universities implementing Bologna.* Available at http://www.ond.vlaanderen.be/hogeronderwijs/Bologna/

- EUA Trends V. (2007). *Universities shaping the European Higher Education Area.* Available at http://www.ond.vlaanderen.be/hogeronderwijs/Bologna/

Eurydice. (2009). *Eurybase: Education systems in Europe.* Retrieved most recently November 3, 2009, from http://eacea.ec.europa.eu/education/eurydice/index_en.php

Excellence. (2008). *Excellence initiative: General information.* Retrieved most recently June 1, 2009, from http://www.dfg.de/en/research_funding/coordinated_pro grammes/excellence_initiative/general_information.html

Fircroft. (2009). *Welcome to Fircroft College of Adult Education.* Retrieved most recently October 26, 2009, from http://www.fircroft.ac.uk/

• Framework. (2005). *Overarching framework for qualifications of the EHEA.* Retrieved most recently December 15, 2008, from http://www.ond.vlaanderen .be/hogeronderwijs/bologna/qf/overarching.asp

Ganley, E. (2009, May 20). Months of strikes humble French university system. *Seattle Times.* Retrieved most recently October 27, 2009, from http://seattle times.nwsource.com/html/nationworld/2009241576_apeufranceuniversitieslost semester.html

Gardner, M. (2009, May 10). Germany: Different credits for Bologna. *University World News, 75.* Retrieved most recently May 30, 2009, from http://www.uni versityworldnews.com/article.php?story = 20090508120216730

Gateway. (2008). *Gateway to recognition of academic and professional qualifications.* Retrieved most recently December 16, 2008 from http://www.enic-naric.net/

Gelb, L. (2009). Necessity, choice, and common sense. *Foreign Affairs, 88*(2), 56–72.

Giannino-Racine, B. (2008). *Ensuring higher education access for all: A New Deal for equalizing opportunity and enabling hopes and dreams.* Retrieved most recently October 27, 2008, from http://www.compact.org/20th/read/ensuring_higher_ education_access_for_all

Gonzáles, J., & R. Wagenaar. (2008). *Introduction to the third cycle (doctoral) studies as part of the Tuning "Process".* Retrieved most recently December 11, 2008, from http://tuning.unideusto.org/tuningeu/images/stories/Third_cycle/INTRODUC TION_TO_THIRD_CYCLE.pdf

Guidelines. (2005). *UNESCO/OECD guidelines on "Quality provision in cross-border higher education."* Retrieved most recently December 3, 2008, from http:// www.oecd.org/document/11/0,2340,en_2649_201185_35793227_1_1_1_1,00.html

Gumport, P. J. (2000). Academic restructuring: Organizational change and institu tional imperatives. *Higher Education, 39*(1), 67–91.

Hart, P. (2007). *Learning and assessment: Trends in undergraduate education.* Retrieved November 5, 2009, from http://www.aacu.org/membership/docu ments/2009MemberSurvey_Part1.pdf

Hartwick. (2009). *Three-year bachelor's degree program.* Retrieved most recently March 3, 2009, from http://www.hartwick.edu/x26204.xml

HLC. (2006). *Task force: Professional doctorates.* Retrieved most recently October 21, 2009 from http://www.ncahlc.org/index.php?option = com_content&task = view&id = 92&Ite mid = 86

IBE. (2009). *History of IBE.* Retrieved most recently October 15, 2008, from http:// www.ibe.unesco.org/en/organization/about-the-ibe/history.html

IES. (2006). *Number of associate's degrees awarded by degree-granting institutions.* Retrieved most recently February 17, 2009, from http://ies.ed.gov/search/ ?output = xml_no_dtd&client = ies&site = ies&q = associate + degrees

IES. (2009). *College Navigator.* Retrieved most recently July 13, 2009, from http:// nces.ed.gov/COLLEGENAVIGATOR/

Illing, D. (2006, June 14). Calls for care on Bologna. *The Australian,* p. 31.

Immerwahr, J., Johnson, J, & Gasbarra, P. (2008). *The iron triangle: College presidents talk about costs, access, and quality.* Retrieved most recently April 2, 2009, from http://www.highereducation.org/reports/iron_triangle/IronTriangle.pdf

Jaschik, S. (2008, November 10). Assessing a hot assessment tool. *Inside Higher Ed.* Retrieved most recently November 18, 2008, from http://insidehighered.com/ news/2008/11/10/cla

Jefferson, T. (1984). A bill for the more general diffusion of knowledge. In *Writings/ Thomas Jefferson* (pp. 365–373). New York: Literary Classics of the U.S.

Keller, G. (2008). *Higher education and the new society.* Baltimore: Johns Hopkins University Press.

Kennedy, E. (2007, February 15). Grant access to higher education. *Boston Globe.* Retrieved most recently January 7, 2009, from http://www.boston.com/news/globe/ editorial_opinion/oped/articles/2007/02/15/grant_access_to_higher_education/

Kok, Wim. (2004). *Facing the challenge: The Lisbon Strategy for growth and employment.* Retrieved most recently October 24, 2009, from http://europa.eu.int/ comm/lisbon_strategy/index_en.html

Labi, A. (2009a, June 15). In Europe, skeptics of new 3-year degrees abound [Electronic version]. *Chronicle of Higher Education.* Retrieved most recently June 19, 2009, from http://chronicle.com/article/In-Europe-Skeptics-of-New/44467/

Labi, A. (2009b, July 28). France's professors vow to continue fight against reform efforts [Electronic version]. *Chronicle of Higher Education.* Retrieved most recently July 27, 2009, from http://chronicle.com/article/Frances-Professors-Vow-to/47447/?utm_source = at&utm_medium = en

Lederman, D. (2007, March 29). Explaining the accreditation debate. *Inside Higher Ed.* Retrieved most recently October 4, 2008, from http://insidehighered.com/ layout/set/print/news/2007/03/29/accred it

Lederman, D. (2008, April 15). Margaret Spellings, where are you? *Inside Higher Ed.* Retrieved most recently February 7, 2009, from http://www.insidehighered .com/news/2008/04/15/assess

Lederman, D. (2009, March 6). Back to normal (read: boring). *Inside Higher Ed.* Retrieved most recently from http://www.insidehighered.com/news/2009/03/ 06/accredit

• Leuven/Louvain-la-Neuve Communiqué. (2009). *The Bologna Process 2020: The European Higher Education Area in the new decade.* Retrieved most recently May 1, 2009, from http://www.ond.vlaanderen.be/hogeronderwijs/bologna/docu ments/declarations_communiques.htm

Lewin, T. (2008, December 3). Higher education may soon be unaffordable for most Americans, report says. *New York Times,* p. A17.

Lisbon. (2008). *Higher education in the Lisbon Strategy: Commission communication on modernizing Europe's universities.* Retrieved most recently November 3, 2008, from http://ec.europa.eu/education/policies/2010/lisbon_en.html

• Lisbon Convention. (1997). *Convention on the recognition of qualifications concerning higher education in the European region, November 4, 1997.* Available at http://www.ond.vlaanderen.be/hogeronderwijs/Bologna/

Lisbon Report. (1997). *Explanatory report to the convention on the recognition of qualifications concerning higher education in the European region.* Retrieved most recently March 3, 2009, from http://unesdoc.unesco.org/images/0011/001112/111236Mb.pdf

Lisbon Statement. (2000). *Lisbon Special European Council: Towards a Europe of innovation and knowledge.* Retrieved most recently November 5, 2009, from http: / / europa.eu/legislation_summaries/education_training_youth / general_framework/c10241_en.htm

• London Communiqué. (2007). *Towards the European Higher Education Area: Responding to challenges in a globalised world.* Retrieved most recently November 24, 2008, from http://www.ond.vlaanderen.be/hogeronderwijs/bologna/documents/dec larations_communiques.htm

Long, B. T., & Kurlaender, M. (2009). Do community colleges provide a viable pathway to a baccalaureate degree? *Educational Evaluation and Policy Analysis, 31*(1), 30–53.

Lorenz, C. F. G. (2006). Will the universities survive the European integration? Higher education policies in the EU and in the Netherlands before and after the Bologna Declaration. *Sociologia Internationalis, 44,* 23–151. Retrieved most recently May 7, 2009, from http://hdl.handle.net/1871/11005

Lourtie, P. (2001). *Furthering the Bologna Process: Report to the ministers of education of the signatory countries.* Retrieved most recently October 28, 2008, from http://www.bologna-berlin2003.de/pdf/Lourtie_report.pdf

Lourtie, P. (2003). From "Lisboa 1997" to the European area in 2001: Trends and developments in European Higher Education. In S. Bergan (Ed.), *Recognition issues in the Bologna Process* (pp. 43–46). Brussels: COE.

Mabut, P. (2009). *Protests continue against Sarkozy's university reforms.* Retrieved most recently March 16, 2009, from http://www.16beavergroup.org/mtarchive/archives/002833.php

Magna Charta. (1988). *Magna Charta Universitatum.* Retrieved most recently October 27, 2009, from http://www.magna-charta.org/pdf/mc_pdf/mc_english.pdf

Measuring. (2008). *Measuring up 2008.* Retrieved most recently April 5, 2009, from http://measuringup2008.highereducation.org/print/NCPPHEMUNationalRpt .pdf

Merisotis, J. P. (2008). *Complexity, complacency, and college success.* Retrieved most recently May 2, 2009, from http://www.luminafoundation.org/about_us/president/speeches/2008-07-30.html

Mission. (2008). *European Center for Higher Education: Mission.* Retrieved most recently November 9, 2008, from http://www.cepes.ro/cepes/mission.htm

Mullen, J. (2009, April 26). France: Universities exploding in anger. *University World News, 73*. Retrieved most recently May 6, 2009, from http://www.univer sityworldnews.com/article.php?story = 20090424120526792

Nokkola, T. (2007). The Bologna Process and the role of higher education: Discursive construction of the European Higher Education Area. In J. Enders & B. Jongbloed (Eds.), *Public-private dynamics in higher education* (pp. 221–245). New Brunswick, NJ: Transaction Publishers.

Obama, B. (2009a). *Remarks of President Barack Obama—as prepared for delivery— address to joint session of Congress, Tuesday, February 24th, 2009.* Retrieved most recently March 10, 2009, from http://www.whitehouse.gov/the_press_office/ remarks-of-president-barack-oba ma-address-to-joint-session-of-congress/

Obama, B. (2009b). *Remarks by the president on higher education.* Retrieved most recently May 7, 2009, from http://www.whitehouse.gov/the_press_office/ Remarks-by-the-President-on-Higher-Education/

Pope, J. (2009). *Some colleges offering degrees in 3 years.* Retrieved most recently November 4, 2009, from http://abcnews.go.com/US/wireStory?id = 6948382

Powell, S. (2008, November 12). Asian nations aim to harmonise systems. *The Australian*, p. 26.

• Prague Communiqué. (2001). *Towards the European Higher Education Area: Communiqué of the meeting of European ministers in charge of higher education.* Retrieved most recently July 27, 2008, from http://www.ond.vlaanderen.be/ hogeronderwijs/bologna/documents/dec larations_communiques.htm

QAA. (2009). *About us.* Retrieved most recently March 12, 2009, from http://www .qaa.ac.uk/aboutus/default.asp

Quality. (2005). *Standards and guidelines for quality assurance in the European Higher Education Area.* Retrieved most recently December 4, 2008, from http://www .enqa.eu/files/ENQA%20Bergen%20Report.pdf

• Rapp, J-M. (2009). *Statement to the Leuven/Louvain-la-Neuve ministerial meeting, 28/29 April 2009.* Retrieved most recently May 5, 2009, from http://www.ond .vlaanderen.be/hogeronderwijs/bologna/conference/documents.htm and available at http://www.ond.vlaanderen.be/hogeronderwijs/Bologna/

SACS. (2008). *The principles of accreditation: Foundations for quality enhancement.* Retrieved most recently February 2, 2009, from http://www.sacscoc.org/prin ciples.asphttp://www.sacscoc.org/pdf/2008PrinciplesofAccreditation.pdf

Sarkozy, N. (2009). *Discours à l'occasion du lancement de la réflexion pour une Stratégie Nationale de Recherche et d'Innovation.* Retrieved most recently February 4, 2009, from http://www.elysee.fr/documents/index.php?mode = cview& press_id; eq2259&cat_id = 7&lang = fr

Schuwey, G. M. (2000). Memorandum: Meeting of the Enlarged Group, Lisbon, June 30. Retrieved most recently October 29, 2008, from http://www.bologna .msmt.cz/PragueSummit/report%20Switzerland.doc

Schwinges, R. C. (2003). The accessibility of universities. In H. de Ridder-Symoens (Ed.), *A history of the university in Europe: Universities in the Middle Ages* (pp. 172–177). Cambridge, UK: Cambridge University Press.

Sorbonne. (1998). *Joint declaration on harmonisation of the architecture of the European higher education system*. Retrieved most recently September 27, 2008, from http://www.aic.lv/rec/Eng/new_d_en/bologna/sorbon.html

State Legislatures. (2006). *Transforming higher education: National imperative—state responsibility*. Washington, DC: National Conference of State Legislatures.

• Stocktaking. (2005). *Bologna Process stocktaking*. Available at http://www.ond.vlaanderen.be/hogeronderwijs/Bologna/

• Stocktaking. (2007). *Bologna Process stocktaking London 2007*. Retrieved most recently December 14, 2008, from http://www.ond.vlaanderen.be/hogeronder wijs/bologna/documents/ and available at http://www.ond.vlaanderen.be/hog eronderwijs/Bologna/

• Stocktaking. (2009). *Bologna Process stocktaking report 2009*. Retrieved most recently May 1, 2009, from http://www.ond.vlaanderen.be/hogeronderwijs/ bologna/conference/documents.html and available at http://www.ond.vlaanderen .be/hogeronderwijs/Bologna/

Strasbourg. (2004). *Strasbourg Statement on recognition issues in the European Higher Education Area: Contributions by the ENIC and NARIC networks to the Bologna Process*. Retrieved most recently February 7, 2009, from http://www.aic.lv/ace/ WP/DGIVEDUHE2004_17StrasStat-2.pdf

Terry, L. S. (2008). The Bologna Process and its impact in Europe: It's so much more than degree changes. *Vanderbilt Journal of Transnational Law, 41*, 107–228.

TEU. (1992). *Treaty on European Union*. Retrieved most recently October 15, 2009, from http://eur-lex.europa.eu/en/treaties/dat/11992M/htm/11992M.html

Treaties of Rome. (1957). *Treaty establishing the European Economic Community*. Retrieved most recently October 5, 2008, from http://eur-lex.europa.eu/en/trea ties/index.htm#founding

Treaty. (1992). *Treaty on European Union. Official Journal C 191, 29 July 1992*. Retrieved most recently August 4, 2008, from http://eur-lex.europa.eu/en/trea ties/dat/11992M/htm/11992M.html

Tuning. (2004). *Tuning educational structures in Europe: What is Tuning?* Retrieved most recently November 8, 2008, from http://tuning.unideusto.org/tuningeu/

Tuning. (2006). *Tuning educational structures in Europe*. Retrieved most recently July 6, 2009, from http://www.ihep.org/assets/files/gcfp-files/Tuning_Objectives .pdf

U-CAN. (2009). *U-CAN*. Retrieved most recently July 9, 2009, from http://www .ucan-network.org/

UNESCO. (2009). *The organization's history*. Retrieved most recently October 20, 2009, from http://portal.unesco.org/en/ev.php-URL_ID = 6207&URL_DO = DO_TOPIC&URL_SECTION = 201.html

U.S. Department of Education. (1999). *College for all? Is there too much emphasis on getting a 4 year college degree?* Retrieved most recently May 4, 2009, from http:// www.ed.gov/pubs/CollegeForAll/es.html

U.S. Department of Transportation. (2002). *Mobility and economic growth.* Retrieved most recently June 15, 2009, from http://www.dot.gov/perfacc2002/mobility.html

VSA. (2008). *About VSA.* Retrieved most recently December 19, 2008, from http://www.voluntarysystem.org/index.cfm?page = about_vsa

Warden, R. (2008, December 7). Spain: Protests against Bologna begin to spread. *University World News,* 56. Retrieved most recently February 19, 2009, from http://www.universityworldnews.com/article.php?story = 2008120509191347

Workers' Educational Association. (1908). *Oxford and working-class education: Being the report of a joint committee of university and working-class representatives on the relation of the university to the higher education of workpeople.* Oxford, UK: Clarendon Press.

Zemsky, R. (2009, August 3). Will higher education ever change as it should? [Electronic version]. *Chronicle of Higher Education.* Retrieved most recently August 3, 2009, from http://chronicle.com/article/Will-Higher-Education-Ever/47536/?utm_source = at&utm_medium = en

Zgaga, P. (2003). *Bologna Process between Prague and Berlin: Report to the ministers of education of the signatory countries.* Retrieved most recently October 19, 2008, from http://www.bologna-berlin2003.de/pdf/Zgaga.pdf

Also available from Stylus

For-Profit Colleges and Universities
Their Markets, Regulation, Performance, and Place in Higher Education
Edited by Guilbert C. Hentschke, Vicente M. Lechuga, and
William G. Tierney
Foreword by Marc Tucker

"For-profit higher education is exploding in the U.S. and across the globe. Th
has produced a torrent of rhetorical claims from advocates and opponent
little of which is based in evidence. At last, a fair minded and comprehensi
examination of this phenomenon by a team of top thinkers and researchers. Th
book is a jewel, must reading for policy makers, practitioners and scholars
higher education, whether in the for-profit or not-for-profit sectors."—*Arthur Levine*, President, Woodro
Wilson National Fellowship Foundation, and President Emeritus, Teachers College, Columbia University

Do for-profit colleges and universities (FPCUs) pose a threat to traditional providers of higher educatio
or do they play a vital role at a time when the capacity of public and private non-profits to meet deman
is constrained? With the United States no longer the leader in developing a college-educated workforce, ca
FPCUs help redress the competitive gap? What can be learned from the management practices and grow
of FPCUs—now numbering close to 3,000 institutions in the United States—whose increase in enrollmen
has out-paced that of traditional institutions, and who now grant around 8 percent of all degrees?

This book offers a clear-eyed and balanced analysis of for-profit colleges and universities, reviewing the
history, business strategies, and management practices; setting them in the context of marketplace cond
tions, the framework of public policy and government regulations; and viewing them in the light of tl
public good.

Taking Ownership of Accreditation
Assessment Processes That Promote Institutional Improvement and Faculty Engagement
Edited by Amy Driscoll and Diane Cordero De Noriega
Preface by Judith A. Ramaley

"*Taking Ownership of Accreditation* outlines a way to use the accreditation
process to develop a new, productive intentionality, aligning it with learning outcomes assessment and recursive qualitative and quantitative institutional research. Driscoll and Cordero demonstrate how California State University,
Monterey Bay, by aiming at issues of high priority and keen interest, clarified
and deepened its ability to educate students and serve its community. Of particular importance to community colleges is CSUMB's focus on engaging external constituents as both constituents and a prime audience for the self-study
reports. This is a comprehensive primer for those who care about creating productive institutional change at colleges and universities."—*Gail O. Mellow*,
President, LaGuardia Community College

22883 Quicksilver Drive
Sterling, VA 20166-2102

Subscribe to our e-mail alerts: www.Styluspub.co